MASSINGER: THE CRITICAL HERITAGE

THE CRITICAL HERITAGE SERIES

GENERAL EDITOR: B.C. SOUTHAM, M.A., B.LITT. (OXON.)
Formerly Department of English, Westfield College, University of London

For a list of books in the series see back of book

MASSINGER

THE CRITICAL HERITAGE

Edited by
MARTIN GARRETT

London and New York

TO COLIN GIBSON

First published 1991
by Routledge
2 Park Square, Milton Park, Abingdon, Oxfordshire OX14 4RN

Simultaneously published in the USA and Canada
by Routledge
711 Third Avenue, New York, NY 10017

First issued in paperback 2014

Routledge is an imprint of the Taylor and Francis Group, an informa business

Reprinted 2001

Transferred to Digital Printing 2007

© 1991 Martin Garrett
Set in 10/12pt Bembo by Columns of Reading

All rights reserved. No part of this book may be reprinted or
reproduced or utilized in any form or by any electronic,
mechanical, or other means, now known or hereafter invented,
including photocopying and recording, or in any information storage or
retrieval system, without permission in writing from the publishers.

British Library Cataloguing in Publication Data

Massinger: the critical heritage. – (The critical heritage series).
1. Drama in English. Massinger, Philip, 1583–1640
I. Garrett, Martin   II. Series
822.3

Library of Congress Cataloging in Publication Data

Massinger: the critical heritage/ edited by Martin Garrett.
p.   cm. — (The Critical heritage series)
Includes bibliographical references and index.
1. Massinger, Philip, 1583–1640—Criticism and interpretation.
I. Garrett, Martin   II. Series.
PR2707.M36 1991
822'.3—dc20   90–39724

ISBN 978-0-415-03340-4 (hbk)
ISBN 978-0-415-75523-8 (pbk)

Publisher's Note
The publisher has gone to great lengths to ensure the quality of this reprint
but points out that some imperfections in the original may be apparent

General Editor's Preface

The reception given to a writer by his contemporaries and near-contemporaries is evidence of considerable value to the student of literature. On one side we learn a great deal about the state of criticism at large and in particular about the development of critical attitudes towards a single writer; at the same time, through private comments in letters, journals or marginalia, we gain an insight upon the tastes and literary thought of individual readers of the period. Evidence of this kind helps us to understand the writer's historical situation, the nature of his immediate reading-public, and his response to these pressures.

The separate volumes in the *Critical Heritage Series* present a record of this early criticism. Clearly, for many of the highly productive and lengthily reviewed nineteenth- and twentieth-century writers, there exists an enormous body of material; and in these cases the volume editors have made a selection of the most important views, significant for their intrinsic critical worth or for their representative quality – perhaps even registering incomprehension!

For early writers, notably pre-eighteenth century, the materials are much scarcer and the historical period has been extended, sometimes far beyond the writer's lifetime, in order to show the inception and growth of critical views which were initially slow to appear.

In each volume the documents are headed by an Introduction, discussing the material assembled and relating the early stages of the author's reception to what we have come to identify as the critical tradition. The volumes will make available much material which would otherwise be difficult of access and it is hoped that the modern reader will be thereby helped towards an informed understanding of the ways in which literature has been read and judged.

B.C.S.

Contents

ABBREVIATIONS	xi
PREFACE AND ACKNOWLEDGEMENTS	xiii
INTRODUCTION	1
NOTE ON THE TEXT	51
TEXTS	53
1 NATHAN FIELD, ROBERT DABORNE, and PHILIP MASSINGER, letter to Philip Henslowe, c. 1613	53
2 JOHN TAYLOR, from *The Praise of Hemp-Seed*, 1620	54
3 SIR THOMAS JAY	55
(a) Poem published with *The Roman Actor*, 1629	55
(b) Poem published with *The Picture*, 1630	56
(c) Poem published with *A New Way to Pay Old Debts*, 1633	57
4 THOMAS MAY, poem published with *The Roman Actor*, 1629	58
5 PHILIP MASSINGER, Prologue to *The Maid of Honour*, 1630	59
6 WILLIAM DAVENANT(?), 'To my honored ffriend Mr Thomas Carew', 1630	61
7 PHILIP MASSINGER, 'A Charme for a Libeller', 1630	63
8 SIR HENRY HERBERT	68
(a) Records of the Master of the Revels, 1631	69
(b) Records of the Master of the Revels, 1638	69
9 WILLIAM HEMINGE, elegy on Thomas Randolph's finger, 1631–2	70
10 SIR ASTON COKAINE	71
(a) Poem published with *The Emperor of the East*, 1632	71
(b) Epitaph on John Fletcher and Philip Massinger, 1640–58	72
(c) '*To Mr.* Humphrey Mosley *and Mr.* Humphrey Robinson', 1647–58	72
(d) From '*To my Cousin Mr.* Charles Cotton', 1647–58	73

CONTENTS

11	WIT'S RECREATIONS, 'To Mr. Philip Massinger', 1640	74
12	ABRAHAM WRIGHT, 'Excerpta quaedam per A.W. Adolescentem', c. 1640	74
13	PHILIP KYNDER, from The Surfeit to ABC, 1656	76
14	SAMUEL PEPYS, Diary	77
	(a) The Bondman, 1661–6	78
	(b) The Virgin Martyr, 1661–8	79
15	GERARD LANGBAINE, from An Account of the English Dramatick Poets, 1691	80
16	ANTHONY WOOD, from Athenae Oxonienses, 1691	81
17	NICHOLAS ROWE, from The Fair Penitent, 1703	82
18	OLIVER GOLDSMITH, review of Thomas Coxeter (ed.), The Dramatic Works of Philip Massinger, The Critical Review, July 1759	89
19	GEORGE COLMAN, Critical Reflections on the Old English Dramatick Writers, 1761	90
20	THOMAS DAVIES, Some Account of the Life of Philip Massinger, 1779	94
21	Unsigned reviews of The Bondman, 1779	99
	(a) The Westminster Magazine, 1779	100
	(b) The Town and Country Magazine, 1779	100
22	HENRY BATE, Advertisement to The Magic Picture, 1783	101
23	Unsigned reviews of The Magic Picture, 1783	102
	(a) The Town and Country Magazine, 1783	103
	(b) The English Review, 1783	103
24	RICHARD CUMBERLAND, from The Observer, 1786	104
25	CHARLES LAMB	113
	(a) Letter to Samuel Taylor Coleridge, June 1796	114
	(b) Letter to Samuel Taylor Coleridge, June 1796	114
	(c) Letter to Robert Lloyd, June 1801	114
	(d) Letter to William Wordsworth, October 1804	115
	(e) From Specimens of English Dramatic Poets, 1808	116
26	WILLIAM GIFFORD, from Introduction to The Plays of Philip Massinger, 1805	117
27	Unsigned review of Gifford's edition, The Edinburgh Review, April–July 1808	120
28	WILLIAM GIFFORD, from Introduction to The Plays of Philip Massinger, 1813	122
29	SAMUEL TAYLOR COLERIDGE	123
	(a) Note on Barclay's Argenis, c. July–December 1809	123

CONTENTS

	(b) Marginalia from *The Dramatic Works of Ben Jonson and Beaumont and Fletcher* (1811), *c*. 1817–19	123
	(c) Notes for lecture 'On Ben Jonson, Beaumont and Fletcher, and Massinger' given in February 1818	124
	(d) Notes from a copy of Massinger's works, date uncertain	127
	(e) *Table Talk*, February and April 1833, March 1834	128
30	SIR JAMES BLAND BURGES, from *Riches; or the Wife and Brother*, 1810	129
31	SIR WALTER SCOTT	133
	(a) Letter to Joanna Baillie, March 1813	133
	(b) From 'Essay on the Drama', 1819	134
32	Unsigned review of *A New Way to Pay Old Debts*, *The Times*, January 1816	134
33	WILLIAM HAZLITT	136
	(a) Review of *A New Way to Pay Old Debts*, *The Examiner*, January 1816	137
	(b) Review of *The Duke of Milan*, *The Examiner*, March 1816	138
	(c) Prefatory Remarks to *A New Way to Pay Old Debts*, 1818	140
	(d) From *Lectures Chiefly on the Dramatic Literature of the Age of Elizabeth*, 1820	143
34	JOHN HAMILTON REYNOLDS	145
	(a) From 'On the Early Dramatic Poets, I', *The Champion*, January 1816	145
	(b) Review of *A New Way to Pay Old Debts*, *The Champion*, January 1816	146
35	Unsigned Advertisement to *Beauties of Massinger*, 1817	148
36	JOHN KEATS	149
	(a) Letter to Fanny Brawne, July 1819	150
	(b) Letter to Charles Wentworth Dilke, September 1819	150
37	GEORGE GORDON, LORD BYRON, letter to John Murray, August 1819	150
38	THOMAS CAMPBELL, from *Essay on English Poetry*, 1819	151
39	THOMAS LOVELL BEDDOES	154
	(a) Letter to Thomas Forbes Kelsall, November 1824	154
	(b) Letter to Thomas Forbes Kelsall, January 1825	154

CONTENTS

	(c) Letter to Thomas Forbes Kelsall, February 1829	155
	(d) Letter to Thomas Forbes Kelsall, July 1830	155
40	RICHARD LALOR SHEIL(?), from *The Fatal Dowry*, 1825	155
41	HENRY NEELE, from *Lectures on English Poetry*, 1827	159
42	HENRY HALLAM, from *An Introduction to the Literature of Europe*, 1839	161
43	HARTLEY COLERIDGE, from Introduction to *The Dramatic Works of Massinger and Ford*, 1840	165
44	From *The City Madam*, 1844	171
45	EDWIN P. WHIPPLE, from lectures on Beaumont and Fletcher, Ford and Massinger, 1859	175
46	SIR ADOLPHUS WILLIAM WARD, from *A History of English Dramatic Literature to the Death of Queen Anne*, 1875	178
47	SIR LESLIE STEPHEN, 'Massinger', 1877	187
48	FRANCES ANN KEMBLE, from *Record of a Girlhood*, 1878	201
49	ALGERNON CHARLES SWINBURNE	203
	(a) 'Philip Massinger', 1882	204
	(b) 'Prologue to *A Very Woman*', 1904	204
	(c) 'Philip Massinger', 1889	205
50	JAMES RUSSELL LOWELL, from *The Old English Dramatists*, 1887	216
51	ARTHUR SYMONS, Introduction to *Philip Massinger*, 1887	220
52	EDMUND GOSSE, from *The Jacobean Poets*, 1894	233
SELECT BIBLIOGRAPHY		240
INDEX		242

Abbreviations

Ball — Robert Hamilton Ball, *The Amazing Career of Sir Giles Overreach*, Princeton, 1939.

Bentley, *JCS* — Gerald Eades Bentley (ed.), *The Jacobean and Caroline Stage*, 7 vols, Oxford, 1941–68.

EG — Philip Edwards and Colin Gibson (eds), *The Plays and Poems of Philip Massinger*, 5 vols, Oxford, 1976.

Preface and Acknowledgements

When [Charles James] Fox was a young man, a copy of Massinger accidentally fell into his hands: he read it, and, for some time after, could talk of nothing but Massinger.
(*Recollections of the Table-Talk of Samuel Rogers*, London, 1856, p.90)

It is very natural, especially for a young reader, to fling Massinger to the other end of the room, and to refuse him all attention.
(Edmund Gosse, 1894, No. 52 below)

Swinburne opened his essay on Massinger of 1889 with the declaration that 'The fame of no English poet can ever have passed through more alternate variations of notice and neglect'. The distribution of entries in this volume reflects these vagaries of taste: for instance there are sixteen between 1613 and 1670 but ten for 1670–1786; comments from no fewer than nine authors date from 1816–19 while I have chosen only four pieces to represent the years 1840–75.

Amidst such shifts there has been a broad consensus that Massinger is an eloquent, rarely obscure, politically aware playwright rather than an impassioned or lyrical poet. Yet for much of the twentieth century it was an unusually extreme version of this verdict which was accepted and repeated: Massinger the cold and mechanical rhetorician (prefigured at times in the writing of Lamb and Hazlitt) appeared in various guises in essays by A.W. Ward, Leslie Stephen, Arthur Symons, and T.S. Eliot. New departures in Massinger criticism were long inhibited by the prestige of these figures and the sheer impressive bulk of their writing for respectable journals and works of instruction (by contrast with the usually briefer and more various remarks of their immediate predecessors in essays, 'table talk', letters, diaries, theatre reviews). A tradition – unavailable for instance to John Webster, who was taken seriously by few but Lamb in Massinger's late eighteenth- and early nineteenth-century heyday – was established. Only recently (see Introduction, pp.41–2, and Select Bibliography) has the tradition begun to founder. The Critical Heritage seeks to contribute to this opening of newer approaches to Massinger by drawing on our increasingly detailed understanding of the politico-theatrical context in which Massinger originally scripted his plays; by presenting the eighteenth- and early nineteenth-century reception – including some theatre reviews and extracts from adaptations – more completely than has hitherto been possible; and by presenting the Victorian material fairly fully in order to show how Gosse's dull Massinger was constructed.

I should like to thank Lord Downshire and the Berkshire County Archivist, Dr P. Durrant, for permission to include extracts from Trumbull Add. MS 51 in Nos 5–7, and Professor Andrew Gurr, Editor of *The Yearbook of English Studies*, for permission to use these extracts as edited by Peter Beal (see headnote to No. 5).

I should like to thank A.& C. Black Ltd for permission to reprint most of Arthur Symons's introduction to his Mermaid *Philip Massinger* (No. 51).

Mr Michael Foster kindly obtained for me a copy of the 1820 version of the Massinger portrait (see p.49, n.125). My wife, Helen, gave invaluably of her patience, time, and understanding. To Professor Colin Gibson of the University of Otago, Dunedin, to whom this volume is dedicated, I owe an inestimable scholarly and personal debt. Over a period of several years I have been fortunate to have the benefit of his generosity and encouragement and the example of his tireless pursuit of knowledge. My debt throughout to Philip Edwards' and Colin Gibson's 1976 Clarendon Press *Massinger* (a debt shared by all those working in this field) will be apparent.

Introduction

1. CONTEMPORARY RESPONSES

Massinger was one of the best-known playwrights of the 1620s and 1630s. For fifteen years (1625–40), in succession to Shakespeare and John Fletcher, he remained principal dramatist for the King's Men. At the end of his life at least twelve plays of his sole authorship remained in repertory, together with eleven plays of which he was co-author or reviser.[1] The (far from complete) records for court performances during Massinger's career again include a reasonable number of works wholly or partly by him.[2] Other 'circumstantial evidence of popular favour' cited by Colin Gibson includes frequent title-page claims (unlikely to be fabricated) that the plays have met with 'good allowance' in the theatre, and the fact that 'the leading actor Joseph Taylor publicly associated himself with the publication of *The Roman Actor*'.[3]

But we also have considerable evidence of unpopularity in some quarters, especially in the early 1630s, and many questions remain about the exact nature of Massinger's contemporary reception. What we do, increasingly, know, allows a glimpse into a theatrical world of faction, topicality, and contingent reactions far removed from the chiefly aesthetic and moral responses of later generations.

One of the areas we know least about, however, is the reputation of the twenty-odd collaborative plays in which he had a share before 1625 (or, as reviser, later). A number of plays he wrote with John Fletcher were still in demand both in the theatre and at court after 1625, and later made their way into the popular collected works of Beaumont and Fletcher. But the evidence that Massinger so much as had any share in these famous productions is, while generally accepted, almost entirely internal.[4] We have no idea how Massinger's role was regarded, how widely it was known, whether he was seen as Fletcher's drudge or as his worthy foil and Beaumont's apt successor. Massinger's own testimony on the subject is inconclusive. His disclaimers in the prologue and epilogue to his revision of *The Lovers' Progress* (1634) – 'What's good was Fletchers, and what ill his own' – may or may not be disingenuous. His apparently contrasting claim that the revised *A Very Woman* '*is much better'd now*' (Prologue, 1634) has been convincingly explained as referring only to parts of the play which he himself had originally written.[5] Presumably Massinger is talking about collaborations when he refers to 'those toyes I would not father' in his verse letter to the Earl of Pembroke, 'The Copy of a Letter', but the remark may again be disingenuous or, since the poem could date from as early as 1615, could pre-date the bulk of the joint work with Fletcher. Collaboration, as G.E. Bentley showed, was a usual practice, a 'common expedient in such a cooperative enterprise as the production of a play';[6] few can have shared the purism of Jonson when, in publishing *Sejanus*, he replaced his collaborator's lines with his own in order not 'to defraud so happy a *Genius* of his right, by my lothed vsurpation'.[7]

All that can be concluded is that although Massinger clearly cared less about recognition for collaborative work than for the unaided plays he later gathered and corrected,[9] the collaborations probably won him more prestige than we have evidence for; John Taylor's listing of Massinger with the best-known playwrights of the day in *The Praise of Hemp-Seed* (No. 2) suggests that by 1620 – before any known non-collaborative work – he was already well known in literary circles. A positive response was not, however, projected to later readers, most obviously because of this lack of evidence, the omission of his name from the much-used 'Beaumont and Fletcher' folios of 1647 and 1679 (to which I shall return presently), and the chance of survival of the 'tripartite letter' from prison (No. 1) which dates from Massinger's early period as one of Philip Henslowe's team of writers and which became the 'melancholy' or 'pitiful' document of nineteenth-century tradition.

Rather more is known of the reception of the plays Massinger scripted alone. Commendatory verses and a few other scattered remarks reveal an emphasis on qualities which may be loosely grouped as constructive strength and skill, and purity, dignity, and theatrical appropriateness of language.[9]

In 1632 Aston Cokaine (No. 10(a)) hails '*thy neat-limnd peeces, skilfull* Massinger', and craftsmanship and finish (of language as well as of plotting) are also celebrated later (1650) in an unpublished poem on *The Picture* by Richard Washington, for whom Massinger was 'that great Architect of Poetry',[10] and by Sir Thomas Jay (No. 3(c)) commending *A New Way* in 1632:

> *The craftie* Mazes *of the cunning plot;*
> *The polish'd phrase, the sweet expressions; got*
> *Neither by theft, nor violence; the conceipt*
> *Fresh, and unsullied.*

At about the same time William Heminge, in his 'Eligie' on Randolph's finger (No. 9), refers to 'Messenger that knowes / the strength to wright or plott In verse or prose'.

Most of the remaining favourable response of any importance (including many of the remarks about Massinger's language) is to be found in the poems published with *The Roman Actor*, which the author, according to the dedication, '*ever held . . . the most perfit birth of my* Minerua', in 1629. There is much on the play's appropriate classical dignity: Robert Harvey, probably one of a group of young ex-Oxford Massinger enthusiasts,[11] declares that 'Each line speakes [Domitian] an Emperour', and Massinger's usually more grudging friend Jay agrees (No. 3(a)) that this 'loftie straine' restores Caesar to life and power, that Paris's defence of actors has every suitable grace and excellence of argument 'for that subject . . . / Contracted in a sweete Epitome', and that the women's speech is proper too. Similar Roman aptness is observed by the more established literary figures Thomas May (No. 4) and John Ford, for whom Massinger has actually 'out-done the Roman story', making the participants speak and act again 'In such a height, that Heere to know their Deeds / Hee may become an Actor that but Reades'. The playwright Thomas Goffe pays tribute in his Latin poem to the play's stageworthiness as well as its readability (as do Ford and May and as Ford does again in his piece on *The Great Duke of Florence* in 1636).

There were those who disagreed, however. Some, if we are to credit William Bagnall's poem on *The Bondman* (1624) and Massinger's dedication to *The Roman Actor* (1629), preferred 'Gipsie Iigges . . . Drumming stuffe, / Dances, *or other* Trumpery' or '*Iigges and ribaldrie*' to Massinger's grave or worthy story. Clearly Massinger was not alone in finding it difficult to please those who sat 'on the Stage at *Black-Friers*, or the *Cock-pit*, to arraigne Playes dailie'.[12] And even without external evidence we might suppose that some members of the Caroline audience, with

3

their love of 'self-regarding witty artifice',[13] found little to delight them in the sheer earnestness of *The Roman Actor* and its commenders, or George Donne's emphasis on Massinger's hard work in *The Great Duke* – '*thy later labour (heire / Vnto a former industrie*') – or the respectful tone of the poem to Massinger in the 1640 miscellany *Wit's Recreations* (No. 11). We would, however, only be able to speculate about the causes of the unpopularity referred to in the front-matter of Massinger's plays, especially those of the early 1630s, were it not for quite recent discoveries about his involvement in the 'Untun'd Kennell' theatre quarrel of this period.[14] Where the remarks about audience dissatisfaction once spoke eloquently of persecuted, modest, melancholy Massinger, they now help to put Massinger's contemporary reception in an altogether more precise historical context.

The 'gallants' whose disapproval is referred to in a manuscript poem to Massinger by Henry Parker[15] and the '*tribe, who in their Wisedomes* dare accuse, / this ofspring of thy *Muse*' (James Shirley's poem printed with *The Renegado* in 1630) certainly included Thomas Carew and William Davenant, and they or their supporters were probably the detractors – those who '*delight / To misapplie what euer hee shall write*', unleashing on it '*the rage, / And enuie of some Catos of the stage*' ('Prologue at the Blackfriers' and 'Prologue at Court') – partly responsible for making *The Emperor of the East* a fiasco at the Blackfriars in 1632. The quarrel, no doubt already simmering, boiled over in the 'Untun'd Kennell' affair in 1630.

Early in 1630 supporters of Davenant, whose *The Just Italian* had been poorly received at the Blackfriars in October 1629, launched an attack on James Shirley's popular success of that November, *The Grateful Servant*, and the theatre which had staged it, the Phoenix or Cockpit. Seizing on the Queen's Men's use also of the traditionally unrefined Red Bull, Davenant's commender Carew claims that 'men in crowded heapes . . . throng'

> To that adulterate stage, where not a tong
> Of th' untun'd Kennell, can a line repeat
> Of serious sence: but like lips, meet like meat

while the true actors at Blackfriars, interpreters of Beaumont and Jonson, 'Behold their Benches bare'.[16] In the 1630 quarto of Shirley's play his supporters replied in kind. They included

Massinger, who contrasted Shirley's composition 'all so well / Exprest and orderd', with Davenant's 'forc'd expressions', 'rack'd phraze', and 'Babell compositions to amaze / The tortur'd reader'. The emphasis on order and on appropriateness of language is a familiar one from Massinger's own commenders; and here again these qualities are claimed as moral as much as aesthetic, since it is also implied that Davenant is guilty of authoring both a 'beleeu'd defence / To strengthen the bold atheists insolence' and syllables obscene enough to make a chaste maid blush.[17]

The sheer vitriol of the quarrel became apparent only in 1980 with Peter Beal's publication of three further documents of the second stage of the dispute. Massinger's prologue for a revival of his Phoenix play *The Maid of Honour* (No. 5) reflects adversely on those resolved to dislike any play put on there and on Carew and his Italianate 'Chamber Madrigalls or loose raptures'. A reply (No. 6), almost certainly by William Davenant, defends Carew, his 'ditties fit only for the eares of Kings', and all 'Ingenious Gentlemen' and attacks both Massinger and the actors – as a professional playwright he is the mere 'hirelinge' of these 'knaues' whom the likes of Carew and Davenant 'feed . . . / ffor our owne sporte & pastime'. In Massinger's furious counter-defence, 'A Charme for a Libeller' (No. 7), the libeller is condemned for hiding behind the alleged 'Poets Tribune' Carew and as one of the so-called 'wiser few' whose works are dedicated to slander and immorality. Massinger upholds writing plays for money on classical precedent, and maintains that 'witlesse malice' cannot overthrow 'The buildinge of that Meritt whiche I owe / To knoweinge mens opinions'.

The argument is not so much between two companies or theatres as between the established playwrights Massinger, Shirley and Heywood and their newer courtly rivals (Massinger is defending the Phoenix actors while continuing as staple dramatist at the Blackfriars). Forced into a defensive position by their fashionable rivals' easy exclusiveness, the professional and his adherents are compelled to redefine his virtues.

Davenant asserts that in daring to challenge Carew's authority Massinger is like the 'rude Carpenter or Mason' who lays 'his axe or trowell in the ballance . . . / With Euclides learned pen', and it is probably in reply to this and similar remarks, it is now possible to appreciate, that Jay (No. 3(c)) hails Massinger's 'craftie' and 'cunning' composition: it is not 'rude' workmanship but skilled or knowing ('cunning') craftsmanship.[18] Cokaine's Massinger, similarly, is a skilled 'limner' (No. 10(a)). Both encomiasts are in effect agreeing with Massinger that 'Mechanique playwright' is 'a non=sence name'. It is conceivable that Heminge (No. 9) may, punning on 'write' and 'wright', either be giving the carpenter more of his due as a skilled worker than Davenant does or – the tone of the 'Eligie' is often irreverent – rubbing an old sore for the amusement of readers who had followed the quarrel.[19] When Jay (No. 3(b)) forthrightly tells Massinger that he is only one amongst other good dramatists and is rightly modest, he is not engaging in faint praise but conducting another attack, by implication, on the perception of Carew as the 'Poets Tribune', criticism of whom is 'high treason to Apollo' ('A Charme for a Libeller'): '*Apollo*'s guifts are not confind alone / To your dispose, He hath more heires then one'. Jay's assurance to Massinger in the same piece that 'your Muse alreadie's knowne so well' and Parker's reference to his 'soe ponderous a masse of Fame' emphasize Massinger's established position – as against, no doubt, Carew's fame in the ears of kings and Davenant's newness on the scene and sycophancy.

So too the terms in which *The Roman Actor* is commended may have been dictated by an earlier or related fracas, or just possibly in immediate response to *The Just Italian* and *The Gratefull Servant*. (We do not know exactly when in 1629 Massinger's play was printed; it is tempting to see Joseph Taylor's encomium as a declaration of solidarity between the professional actors and professional playwrights about to be cast as knaves and hirelings; could Taylor's 'some sowre Censurer' conceivably be Carew and his courtly sycophant be Davenant, 'borrowing from His flattering flatter'd friend / What to dispraise, or wherefore to commend'?) Moral exempla, grave language suited to speaker and setting, earnestness about the purposes of drama, have continued to be found in Massinger, but they were perhaps first found, influencing this later reception, in antithesis to alleged immorality, loose and bombastic language, and undervaluing of the established professional drama.

Less flattering images were also distilled in, or prompted by, the 'Untun'd Kennell' affair. Davenant says that Massinger's work consists of 'flat / dull dialogues fraught with insipit chatt', 'lines forc[d], ruffe, / Botch'd & vnshap'd in fashion, Course in stuffe', and such criticisms, Beal points out, anticipate by around ten years Abraham Wright's verdict on *A New Way to Pay Old Debts* ('onely plaine downright relating ye matter; without any new dress either of language or fancy' (No. 12). They have contributed to the tradition which has made 'Massinger's relatively unmetaphorical language . . . the chief subject of complaint in modern criticism of this dramatist from Charles Lamb to T.S. Eliot'.[20] And there are other ways in which the quarrel may have conditioned Massinger's later reception. It is arguable, for instance, that his continuing difficulties with parts of his audience in 1631-2 humbled him before the likes of Carew. This may account for the hesitant, 'still doubting' prologues and epilogues of *The Guardian* (1633), *A Very Woman* (1634), and *The Bashful Lover* (1636), which in turn provided yet further material for the modest, downtrodden Massinger myth. Yet in these years (perhaps partly as a result of some adaptation to the 'Cavalier' manner)[21] Massinger's career seems to have been thriving again: *The Guardian* was 'well likte' at court in January 1634, and that May Massinger's *Cleander* received a performance before the Queen at the Blackfriars.[22] No doubt the reception remained mixed, shifting play by play in the small and volatile world of the Caroline theatre, where the quarrel, however seriously or otherwise most people may have taken it, must have been good for trade at both theatres.

Early audiences and readers, then, came to the plays with expectations rather different from those of the critics of later centuries: some must thoughtfully have judged the aesthetic merits of the play, but many must have been more interested in seeing how Carew took the prologue to *The Maid of Honour* (with *sang-froid*, according to Massinger himself in 'A Charme') and congratulated themselves on their sagacity or their up-to-dateness in picking up the catch-phrases and witty passing blows. They watched or read the plays too, to an extent increasingly apparent, to catch political allusions ranging from oblique suggestion to the outright caricature of Middleton's *A Game at Chesse*. While Coleridge's 'Democrat' (No. 29(b)) and Sir Paul Harvey's supporter of 'the popular party' (in the old *Oxford Companion to English Literature*) have long been discredited, it remains likely that Massinger was particularly known for his treatment of contemporary issues. There are three items of external evidence for this: *Sir John van Olden Barnavelt*, a play about recent Dutch history by Massinger and Fletcher, was censored by the Master of the Revels and banned by the Bishop of London (temporarily) in 1619,[23] and we have Sir Henry Herbert's reasons (No. 8) for not allowing *Believe As You List* in 1631 and the now lost *The King and the Subject* in 1638, the first because at a time of Anglo-Spanish peace 'itt did contain dangerous matter, as the deposing of Sebastian king of Portugal, by Philip the [Second]', the second because, when consulted, Charles I himself found 'too insolent, and to bee changed' a passage obviously aimed against forced loans.

The plays' detailed political engagement has been argued by several recent writers, notably Annabel Patterson, who have made more plausible the general drift, if not always the details, of the early political readings by Thomas Davies (No. 20) in 1779 and S.R. Gardiner in 1876. Engagement, Patterson shows, does not equal the production of simple propaganda; censorship is one of the factors which make for a more flexible obliqueness of comment and suggestion, so that much can be said as long as it does not contravene codes of expression implicitly agreed by censor and writer. For instance *The Bondman*, while in its opening scenes supporting 'the new anti-Spanish militancy of Charles and Buckingham', also sounded a warning note through the slaves' rebellion and Pisander's lecture on its cause ('the descent from a benevolent patriarchy to governmental tyranny'). Delivery of this mixed message (to the Prince of Wales himself, in the private performance of 27 December 1623) was facilitated by the tragicomic structure, allowing a workable compromise. The apparently minimal alterations which obtained allowance for *Believe* and the other censored plays 'were the signs of [Massinger's] submission to the conventions of political drama, his willingness to encode, up to a point'.[24]

We do not possess extensive evidence as to how members of audiences reacted to political allusions, exactly who most often applauded, were offended by, or missed them. But it is likely that Massinger was esteemed not as a notorious harrier of abuses and wrong policies but as an alert and subtle commentator, if far from the only one, on current events; that many hearers rejoiced in the disingenuousness of the prologue of *Believe* which blames the apparent similarity of ancient things to 'a late, & sad example' on the author's ignorance of '*Cosmographie*', or were keenly aware of the political as much as aesthetic reasons for the 'liberall suffrage' which made Massinger dedicate *The Bondman* to the Earl of Montgomery. In the political context as in the context of the 1630 theatre war, reinterpretation of some commendatory verses may be necessary. For example, in the setting of 1629, when parliamentary freedom of debate was in danger, the 'sowre Censurer' of Joseph Taylor's poem on *The Roman Actor* 'may be either critic or censor' and Jay's poem on *The Roman Actor* (No. 3(a)) invokes 'both the drama's responsibility to inform the monarch of his faults, and the penalty the dramatist risks thereby', providing a daring account 'of how the theater can "revive" the past to meet the needs of the present and to circumvent the censors'.[25] The emphasis on the play's Roman tone and faithfulness to Roman history may in itself be intended to alert readers to the play's political colouring.[26]

Massinger's plays and their reception were formed contingently. Generalizations about 'the audience' or 'the readers' are made suspect by what we know about conflicts over Massinger's reputation during his lifetime. Some people expected from him forceful, sometimes topical, basically serious, perhaps sententious,[27] clearly understandable dramatic writing. Others were ready for dullness, crude moralizing (Davenant's 'rude / Modells of vice and virtue vnpursued' in No. 6), insolent political reflections, unimaginative dialogue. Both groups (loose and fluctuating, overlapping and inconsistent groups no doubt) must to an extent have been conditioned by the opinions and sectional interests of alleged 'knoweinge men' of one sort or another from Joseph Taylor or John Ford to Thomas Carew and the Earl of Montgomery. To an even greater extent, of course, reactions to plays depend on how they are acted: most of Massinger's plays benefited from, and must have been shaped by the views and styles of, Burbage and Field's successors Taylor and Lowin, while *The Emperor of the East* suffered, according to its epilogue, from an emperor whose '*burden was too heauie for his youth / To vndergoe*'. Both acting styles and politics were crucial to reception in ways ignored or unknown to later observers, who would see more simply and steadily, arranging the theatrical profession into separate units, promoting character and poetry over politics and theatre, turning shifting alliances into political parties. Certain messages were selected, certain dialectics set up.

2. 1640–1703

Massinger died in 1640 at the height of his fame. Yet seven years after his death the many commenders of Beaumont and Fletcher in the folio of 1647 failed to mention his substantial share in the plays. In so doing they altered the entire course of his critical heritage, for they separated him from the Restoration triumph of the folio plays and saved him for the late eighteenth century to rediscover. There are many possible explanations for the omission. Massinger's political reputation was less amenable than his colleagues' to the strongly Royalist vein running through the verses[28] and his aesthetic reputation was not primarily, as we have seen, for the witty artifice so emphasized in the verses and in Shirley's address to the reader. It was more poetically appropriate – and more likely to sell the book – to say with Sir John Berkenhead that Beaumont's soul had entered Fletcher than that a new contract had been drawn up for Massinger. Such was Fletcher's established popularity (less prosaically recent than Massinger, he and Beaumont had '*Lived a* Miracle' according to Shirley) that even when Aston Cokaine (No. 10(c)–(d)) writes to protest about the omission of Massinger's name it is less on Massinger's behalf than on Fletcher's.

Having thus been separated from the Restoration triumph of the folios of 1647 and 1679, and having failed to publish any edition of his own collected works, Massinger was increasingly neglected in the late seventeenth and early eighteenth centuries. Dryden, for whom Beaumont and Fletcher were indispensable, simply did not mention Massinger. Nevertheless, the decline in reputation was not immediate, to judge by the number of surviving allusions to and extracts from Massinger plays during the closure of the theatres. The popular miscellany *The Academy of Complements* included the song 'The blushing rose', from *The Picture*, in its nine editions between 1646 and 1663 and the songs from *The Fatal Dowry* up to 1684.[29] Like most of his fellow dramatists Massinger is well represented in Cotgrave's *English*

Treasury (1655). *A New Way to Pay Old Debts* was still apparently well known in 1656 (Philip Kynder, No. 13). *The Guardian, A Very Woman,* and *The Bashful Lover* first became available to readers in 1655 and *The City Madam* in 1658. Finally, Interregnum and Restoration lists of notable poets include Massinger considerably more often than the likes of Webster, Marston, Ford, Dekker, Middleton, and Heywood. With the 'Untun'd Kennell' doubtless long forgotten he was grouped with Davenant, Suckling, and Cartwright as well as Shirley and the canonical 'Triumvirate of Wit' (Shakespeare, Jonson, and Beaumont/Fletcher).[30] There seem to have been just enough of these mentions to prepare the way for Massinger to re-emerge in the mid eighteenth century long before his contemporaries other than the triumvirate.

At the Restoration some of Massinger's plays – along with other pre-war successes – remained popular on stage. There were productions of *The Bondman* (1661–4), *The Virgin Martyr* (1661, 1668), probably of Massinger's revision of Fletcher's *A Very Woman* (Oxford, 1661), *The Renegado* (1662), and *A New Way to Pay Old Debts* (1662; Norwich, 1663). Betterton probably played Paris in *The Roman Actor* in about 1682–92.[31] A number of the collaborations with Fletcher also continued to be staged, again particularly during the 1660s but sometimes, as in the case of *The Spanish Curate,* in the 1670s and 1680s too.[32]

From such fragmentary evidence it is difficult to generalize about Restoration preferences. But *The Bondman* – although the Duke's Company started performing it only because it was one of the few plays it legally owned in 1660 – seems to have been a particularly successful vehicle for Betterton, whose Pisander was so praised by Pepys (No. 14(a)). The play was popular in the early 1660s for various reasons. J.G. McManaway suggested that Pisander appealed because he has many of the qualities 'of the lover of heroic drama. His love for Cleora is as extravagant and his submission to her will as complete as in the later plays'; he is 'a perfectly chaste, perfectly self-controlled, almost Platonic lover'.[33] Similar conclusions might be reached about Cleora, robust to the Senate in Act One and her family in Act Five, but called upon to exercise considerable delicacy, to combine romantic feeling and great self-control, during her silent courtship with Pisander.[34] This sort of combination is rare in Massinger. But a rather less speculative explanation for the play's appeal in the 1660s is surely its relevance to the events of the preceding twenty years: slaves overthrow their masters and are then overthrown by them in a bloodless coup; there is mercy as for all but a few in 1660. The parallels are suggestively loose, evoking the times without taking sides: the noble Pisander associates with the rebels only temporarily and for noble, non-revolutionary purposes, but also, as do Cleora and Timoleon, castigates the faulty pre-rebellion rulers of Syracuse. Censorship and widely differing opinions are thus provided for as in the original political circumstances of the 1620s. Conceivably Massinger's or the play's political reputation had remained strong since pre-war days; certainly *The Bondman* would be used for political purposes as late as the Napoleonic wars.[35]

More immediately, Pepys responded to the virtuoso acting, dancing, and musicianship of this for him 'nothing more taking in the world' play (though he also read it several times). Where *The Virgin Martyr* was concerned (No. 14(b)) he laid even greater stress on production: in February 1668 the play is not 'worth much' but the 'wind-musique when the Angell comes down' is so sweet that it ravishes him, and Beck Marshall acts Dorothea finely. This play is more obviously suited to Restoration spectacular staging than *The Bondman*. And it has again been seen as proto-Heroic, a baroque mingling of sacred and profane whose 'combination of fleshly longing and spiritual sublimation, of divinely exalted idealism and vulgarity, points ahead to the startling blend of sensual exuberance and moral restraint in a play like Dryden's *Tyrannic Love*'.[36]

Early Restoration attention was insufficient to build Massinger a strong reputation for the remainder of the century. There were no new editions of any of the plays between 1658 and the 1715 version of *The Virgin Martyr*, and Betterton, Beck Marshall, and the musicians were no doubt remembered for their performances long after the names Massinger or Dekker. Naturally, as new plays were written and new tastes established, there was a sharp decline in the number of performances of pre-1642 drama other than the work of the triumvirate. Comedies like *A New Way to Pay Old Debts* (a 'highly edifying story' full of 'definite characters and strong passions expressed in blunt language')[37] were little to the taste of Etherege's audience, and the tragedies or graver tragicomedies were not as evenly Heroic in tone as those of Dryden. In this climate much of Beaumont and Fletcher and

Shakespeare was subject to adaptation and alteration, Jonson was cut down to a basic repertory of four or five comedies, and their contemporaries increasingly dropped.

Later in the Restoration period Massinger still merited the attention of Aubrey, Langbaine (No. 15), and Wood (No. 16).[38] But such writers cast their net wider than did the reading or theatre-going public. Langbaine, for instance, writes about earlier drama not least in order to expose 'our modern *Plagiaries*, by detecting *Part* of their Thefts', so vindicating plays which in many cases are beginning to be forgotten: for it is easy to steal from '*Authors not so generally known* [as Shakespeare and Fletcher], *as* Murston [*sic*], Middleton, Massenger, &c.'.[39] Langbaine spots the borrowing of comic incidents from *The Guardian, A Very Woman,* and *The Bashful Lover* (published together in 1655 as *Three New Playes*) for the droll *Love Lost in the Dark* (1680) and from *The Guardian* for Aphra Behn's *The City Heiress* (1682) but died before Ravenscroft's *The Canterbury Guests* (1695), where Justice Greedy of *A New Way*, his name and nature unchanged, becomes one of the main characters, for ever complaining of 'wamblings in my stomach'.[40] In 1694 James Wright (an unusually widely read theatre historian, son of Abraham Wright) has to argue the case for the decreasingly popular drama of Massinger and his best known contemporaries:

Julio, in a long Discourse, produced out of *Ben. Johnson, Shakspear, Beaumont* and *Fletcher, Messenger, Shirley*, and Sir *William Davenant*, before the Wars, and some Comedies of Mr. *Drydens*, since the Restauration, many Characters of Gentlemen, of a quite different Strain from those in the Modern Plays. Whose Conversation was truly Witty, but not Lewd, Brave and not Abusive; Ladies full of Spirit and yet Nicely Virtuous; with abundance of Passages discovering an admirable Invention, and quickness of thought, and yet decently facetious.[41]

For much of the eighteenth century Nicholas Rowe's *The Fair Penitent* (No. 17, 1703), whose unacknowledged original was *The Fatal Dowry* (by Massinger and Nathan Field), was more popular than any work by Massinger. It seems clear that few in 1703 would have regarded Rowe's version as plagiarism, but the failure to mention Massinger's name suggests how far his fame had declined, and the nature of the adaptation suggests some of the reasons for this. Rowe introduces a neo-classical 'regularity', cutting the cast of *The Fatal Dowry* by about two thirds, substituting retrospective narrative for the original first two acts, and introducing throughout a 'single continuous action'. These changes, together with the promotion of Calista (Beaumelle in the old play) rather than Altamont (Charalois) to the central role, enable an 'unashamed insistence upon domestic bliss and perfect connubial frankness as a desirable thing'.[42] In this influential first in Rowe's series of what the epilogue to *Jane Shore* (1714) calls his 'She Tragedies', Rowe works sentimental variations on 'The Sorrows that attend unlawful [and unhappy] Love' (V.p.61) where Massinger (who wrote most of *The Fatal Dowry* other than Act Two) is more interested in the ethical dilemmas which face Charalois and Rochfort. Whereas much of *The Fatal Dowry* happens either in or as if in a law-court, the new play becomes '*A melancholy Tale of private Woes*' (Prologue) and decorum is satisfied.

3. THE EIGHTEENTH CENTURY

Samuel Johnson's esteem for *The Fair Penitent* suggests some of the reasons for the low ebb of interest in Massinger between Rowe's day and Johnson's: 'The story is domestick, and therefore easily received by the imagination, and assimilated to common life; the diction is exquisitely harmonious, and soft or spritely as occasion requires'.[43] By comparison the public debates and more rough-hewn language of the Renaissance dramatists seemed crude and heavy. Such writers, when they were referred to at all (Johnson, like Dryden, nowhere mentions Massinger), found little favour. In 1730 Pope listed Massinger with Webster, Marston, Goffe, and Kyd as 'tolerable writers of tragedy in Ben Jonson's time' but in 1736 said that 'Chapman, Massinger, and all the tragic writers of those days' shared Shakespeare's fault of stiffening 'his style with high words and metaphors for the speeches of his kings and great men'.[44] Goldsmith (No. 18) unequivocally snubbed the first collected edition of Massinger in 1759: neither as sublime nor as 'incorrigibly absurd' as Shakespeare, he will please only those readers who will 'lay his antiquity against his faults, and pardon the one for the sake of the other'.

But the very appearance of the Coxeter edition suggests that by

1759 the tide was beginning to turn; already the compilers who did so much to save the plays' 'neglected and expiring merit', William Oldys in his collection of excerpts *The British Muse* (1738; published as the work of Thomas Hayward) and Robert Dodsley in his *Select Collection* of the plays themselves (1744), had combined a thoroughly Augustan aim of showing 'the Progress and Improvement of our Taste and Language'[45] with a more modern faith in the intrinsic value of earlier literature. Oldys feels, for example, that it is 'but an indifferent compliment to the *readers of our age*' to suppose that most of them '*have no ear for*' the language of Shakespeare's day.[46] Dodsley's choice of only one tragedy (*The Unnatural Combat*) as against four comedies (*A New Way, The City Madam, The Guardian,* and *The Picture*) reflects both a characteristically Augustan preoccupation with manners and a declared historical aim of illustrating the 'Humour, Fashion, and Genius' of the past.[47]

Naturally attitudes remained mixed: Brian Vickers notes 'the extraordinary contradictions between [Garrick's] professed admiration for Shakespeare, and his actual theatrical practice' and how often in mid-eighteenth-century Shakespeare criticism 'Older ideas and methods carry on side by side with those designed to replace them; new ideas are developed using older methods . . . It is far too early to speak of the demise of Neo-classicism'.[48] Old concerns lingered: in his essay attached to the 1761 reissue of Coxeter (No. 19), George Colman, generally enthusiastic about Shakespeare's and Massinger's rule-breaking, finds it politic or reassuring to report that some of the plays he is lauding (Jonson's, *The Merry Wives of Windsor, A New Way, The City Madam*) do in fact observe the Unities; as late as 1783 Henry Bate, adapting *The Picture* (No. 22), finds it necessary to explain that he could not keep to the Unities because Massinger totally disregarded them; reviewers of this adaptation and of *The Bondman* in 1779 (Nos 23, 21) are still calling insistently for probability and propriety. Nevertheless, confidence about the value of Renaissance drama increases steadily from Oldys and Dodsley onwards. In particular their historical interest is developed by their successors. Colman argues for the pleasures of seeing 'the Manners of a former Age pass in Review before us' and 'the Actors drest in their antique Habits'.[49] In the 1779 edition of Massinger Thomas Davies (No. 20) expresses disapproval of the plays' 'grossness' but excuses it as the vice of the times, and conducts a pioneering enquiry into Massinger's politics. And there is a noticeable change in attitudes to the revision of old plays for the modern stage between Aaron Hill's comments on his adaptation of an earlier alteration of *The Fatal Dowry* in 1746 and Henry Bate's on his *The Magic Picture* in 1783: Hill can still boast that 'from one end to the other' he has reformed the plot, conduct, and diction, 'chang'd the sentiments, and heighten'd and preserv'd the characters' and finds it 'impossible to use a single thought, or word' of the original Act Five,[50] but Bate is more apologetic and historical as he compares *The Picture* to an 'antique structure' whose 'Alterer set about its reparation with the utmost diffidence, fearing, like an unskilful architect, he might destroy those venerable features he could not improve!' Between Hill and Bate historicism and primitivism had gone from strength to strength in the work of Hurd, Gray, the Wartons, and Percy and the general post-1750 'refusal to validate the contemporary social world' and search for purity which 'often took the form of a journey into the remote'.[51]

A more immediate influence on the rise of Massinger's fortunes was the preceding and concurrent upsurge of enthusiasm for Shakespeare. From the late 1730s there was a Shakespeare 'boom' in the theatre, where the Theatrical Licensing Act of 1737 caused such a 'great spurt in performances of Shakespeare' as safe, low-risk vehicles for the actors that in 1740–1 25 per cent of all performances were of Shakespeare.[52] Oldys and Dodsley were published no doubt in the expectation that where Shakespeare led (in Theobald's historically aware 1733 edition[53] as well as in the theatre) his contemporaries might follow – or for ever be elbowed aside by him.

Association with the national poet was evidently desirable; but there was even greater hope for a Renaissance playwright to re-establish himself if he could become associated with David Garrick, whose name from the early 1740s became so indelibly linked with Shakespeare's that he was credited with being personally responsible for the boom.[54] In 1748 Garrick had put on *A New Way* at Drury Lane, 'possibly because of the existence of Dodsley',[55] but had not taken a part himself. In 1761, however, Colman's essay took the bull by the horns, claiming that Garrick is so dazzled by Shakespeare that Beaumont, Fletcher, and Jonson are neglected and Massinger languishes in obscurity; if the much talked-of Truth to Nature will defend the improbable and fantastic elements in Shakespeare, it will defend them in others too: in *The Picture*

Nothing can be more fantastick, or more in the extravagant Strain of the *Italian* Novels, than this Fiction: And yet the play, raised on it, is extremely beautiful, and abounds with affecting Situations, true Character, and a faithful Representation of Nature.

Colman's essay, 'thrown together' at Garrick's own instigation 'to serve his old subject Davies',[56] resulted in no immediate flurry of Massinger productions, but amidst all the puffing he does lay an important emphasis on the theatrical viability of the plays (particularly *The Picture* and *The Duke of Milan*), and their opportunities for 'the most masterly Actor'. Whatever Garrick's views on the stageworthiness of Massinger, the association had been publicly made (by Colman, himself a well-known playwright) and this still meant quite enough for the piece to be reprinted in the Monck Mason edition published by Davies in 1779, the year of Garrick's death.

The growing mid-century interest in Massinger which followed Oldys, Dodsley, and Coxeter is perhaps most tellingly demonstrated by the fact that while *The Beauties of the English Stage* (1756) contains no Massinger quotations, its revised version *The Beauties of English Drama* (1777) has sixteen.[57] The 1779 edition (whatever the deficiencies of Monck Mason as an editor) either prompted or coincided with a marked increase in interest in Massinger. Davies's *Life*, included in the edition, was followed by essays by Dr John Ferriar and Richard Cumberland (No. 24) in 1786. Hester Thrale refers enthusiastically to *The Fatal Dowry* in 1780:

[Johnson] should have been more sparing of Praise to the Fair Penitent I think, because the Characters are from Massinger – I care not how much good is said of the Language; but Old Phil: has the Merit of that Contrast, more happy perhaps than any on our Stage, of the Gay Rake, and the virtuous dependent Gentleman. – I used to say I would be buried by old Massinger when I lived in S[t] Saviour's Southwark.[58]

James Boswell, in his *Life of Samuel Johnson* (1791) under 10 October 1779 refers to the 'refined sentiments' of *The Picture* on the infidelity of husbands, which 'must hurt a delicate attachment, in which a mutual constancy is implied'.

There was a remarkable increase, too, in theatrical activity: Cumberland's adaptation of *The Duke of Milan* with John Henderson as Sforza played in 1779, and his *The Bondman* (rather better received) between 1779 and 1781; in Bath the Cleora was Sarah Siddons, and in 1781 Henderson became 'the first to turn' Sir Giles Overreach 'into a role which a recognized star must essay'.[59] Henderson had probably read both Davies and Colman. He owned a Coxeter and a separate copy of Davies's *Life* (in addition to most of the Massinger quartos).[60] The rise of esteem for the theatre which had accompanied Garrick's career is suggested by the amount of contact between an edition at least ostensibly scholarly and these men of the theatre (Henderson, who was the leading actor in Colman's company at the Haymarket in 1777, the playwrights Colman and Cumberland, Davies the ex-actor leading his campaign for a Massinger whose works would fill both his bookshop and the stage). The cross-fertilization was to help Massinger in both spheres, vouchsafing him an establishment aura now lacked by the over-familiar entertainers Beaumont and Fletcher, but sparing him the dead classical reputation which was increasingly Jonson's fate at this time.[61]

The essays by Davies and Cumberland are more confident and ambitious than earlier writing about Massinger. Certainly Davies (No. 20), like Colman before him, wants to sell his author and edition, but, dedicating the piece to his old patron Johnson, he also wants to write a thorough Life of the Poet. In the process he addresses himself with gusto to the then known biographical details, to the probable financial reasons for the 'querulous' manner of his dedications, the testimony of friends to Massinger's 'Modesty, Candour, Affability, and other amiable Qualities of the Mind', the fact that he collaborated with Fletcher,[62] and, more unusually, to a detailed enquiry into Massinger's political alignments and their projection through individual plays. On this occasion at least, antiquarianism gave way to an awareness of the way plays may have functioned in their own day – what they did for seventeenth-century people rather than what they can do solely for the suitably enlightened modern.

Cumberland (No. 24), in 'the first real critical analysis of a Massinger play',[63] skilfully combines close argument and comparison with appeals to sentiment and 'nature'. (This blend of passion and intellectual rigour is much what he found in *The Fatal Dowry* itself.) Above the declining rules ('there are . . . certain things in all dramas, which must not be too rigidly insisted upon . . . provided no extraordinary violence is done to reason and common sense') and the mere probability demanded by contemporary reviewers, he values what seems most dramatically and psychologically convincing: he studies motives and reactions and is aware of the dramatic effect of Charalois' opening silence, comparing it to Hamlet's. Massinger is repeatedly 'natural', his characters passionate for good reason and to good effect where Rowe aims for more superficial 'stage effect' and produces in at least one place 'mere ravings in fine numbers without any determinate idea'. A vigorous, psychologically acute, morally certain Massinger subordinates a vaguer, smoother, often more confused Rowe. Although *The Fair Penitent* rather than *The Fatal Dowry* continued to hold the stage, Cumberland (whose essay was later included in Gifford's editions) had done much to consolidate Massinger's reputation as a serious dramatist.

The continued rise of Massinger in the late eighteenth century is explicable partly in terms of his editors' and proselytizers' efforts to link his name with Shakespeare's amidst renewed enthusiasm for and developments in Shakespeare studies (Garrick's much publicized Stratford festival had taken place in 1769 and there were three major editions between 1765 and 1773), and a general educated interest in the antique and the primitive. But one is still left asking 'Why Massinger in particular?' Other than the triumvirate, after all, his were the only complete works of an English Renaissance dramatist to be published (three times) before 1800. (Ford, Marlowe, Webster, Greene, Shirley, and Middleton followed between 1811 and 1840, Heywood, Marston, and Lyly between then and 1858, Davenant, Chapman, and Tourneur not until the 1870s.) As so often with trends in Massinger's popularity, his language seems to hold the key. Colman (No. 19) admires his 'flowing, various, elegant, and manly' diction. For Monck Mason in the preface to his edition it is 'the easy Flow of natural yet elevated Diction' and for Ferriar his 'majesty, elegance, and sweetness of diction'; according to Charles Dibdin in 1800 'the writing' of *The Guardian*

is of that fluent and easy kind that, nevertheless, has strength and force, and that gives to manliness, and greatness of mind, the unaffected expression of nature; but this is the peculiar beauty of MASSINGER; who, let his subjects be ever so common, never descends.[64]

Massinger came to embody one version of the 'clean reduction to essentials' often sought in the second half of the century, 'the manly simplicity' of 'our elder poets' which was the fashion amongst Coleridge and his schoolfellows in the 1780s.[65] At this stage Massinger provided a half-way house between Augustan elegance and dignity and the more difficult, sensuous, unpredictable language of Shakespearean drama. For Davies (No. 20), the contrast with Shakespeare is emphatic:

> the Current of his Style is never interrupted by harsh, and obscure Phraseology, or overloaded with figurative Expression. Nor does he indulge in the wanton and licentious Use of mixed Modes in Speech; he is never at a Loss for proper Words to cloath his Ideas. And it must be said of him with Truth, that if he does not always rise to *Shakespeare*'s Vigour of Sentiment, or Ardor of Expression, neither does he sink like him into mean Quibble, and low Conceit.

Monck Mason says that Massinger, Beaumont, and Fletcher were 'more correct and grammatical' than Shakespeare, and had a better knowledge of foreign languages, 'which gave them a more accurate Idea of their own'.[66] In this context we can see how Coxeter can rank Massinger beneath Shakespeare only and Monck Mason can say that he excels him in the general 'Harmony of his Numbers' and diction[67] or how Dibdin, while devoting some pages to Massinger, can include only two uninformative paragraphs on Webster. So the manly simplicity was pleasingly modern without being too revolutionary, and the 'naturalness' of the scenes of passion and violence (and the political views discussed by Davies) were kept within non-subversive bounds by the elegantly flowing language. Also acceptable where Webster could not yet be were the plays' clear morality as emphasized by Davies and Cumberland, strength of characterization (stressed by Colman, Ferriar, Dibdin, and others), and theatricality based, for Colman, Cumberland, and the actor Dibdin, on this characterization and on scenes 'wrought up very masterly' (Dibdin on the big scene between Sforza and Francisco also praised by Colman)[68] rather than composed necessarily with poetic effects in mind.

Massinger ends the eighteenth century poised for further triumphs, but not without hints of the recurrent problem. In its eloquence the style is, according to Dibdin, 'warm and fervid' but also 'pure and decorous', beyond its time for polish and refinement. Or as Ferriar puts it, 'The prevailing beauties of his productions are dignity and eloquence; their predominant fault is want of passion'; in tragedy 'Massinger is rather eloquent than pathetick . . . he is as powerful a ruler of the understanding, as Shakespeare is of the passions'.[69]

4. 1800–30

In the early nineteenth century Massinger became an institution, with all the privileges and penalties involved in that, as a result mainly of 'the admirable manner in which he has been edited by Mr Gifford and . . . the circumstance of some of his Plays having been illustrated on the Stage by the talents of a popular Actor', Edmund Kean (Henry Neele, No. 41). The edition and the acting each took Massinger to his apogee while at the same time contributing, directly or by reaction, to his subsequent decline.

Gifford's editions of 1805 and 1813 did much for the text and the fame of Massinger. No other contemporary of Shakespeare had so far been accorded the tribute of such thorough editing. Introducing the second edition (No. 28) Gifford was able to announce, in the teeth of his critics, that 'Massinger has taken his place on our shelves', a place indicated in the first edition as beneath Shakespeare only. (Some impression of the scarcity of editions of old plays before Gifford is given in Lamb's letter to Wordsworth (No. 25(d)) of October 1804.) But the bulk and belligerence of the front-matter – the continual sniping at predecessors pilloried by *The Edinburgh Review* and Hazlitt – laid Massinger open to a degree of guilt by association. An even more vulnerable institutionality was conferred by the inclusion of what the *Edinburgh* (No. 27) dubbed the 'dull and pious dissertations' of Dr John Ireland, Latin tags and all. Such conclusions as 'Let us use the blessings of life with modesty and thankfulness. He who aims at intemperate gratifications, disturbs the order of Providence' (on *The Duke of Milan*) culminate in the Mr Collins-like assurance to the reader that while Ireland's act of friendship to the editor has been performed, 'the higher and more important duties have not suffered'.[70] And Gifford too aligns Massinger firmly with the establishment. He is hard-working, well connected, moderate and modest: he is a gentleman, and his dedications express not Davies's 'servility' but gratitude and humility to patrons who 'All . . . appear to be persons of worth and eminence'; his poverty was deplorable in 'the life of a man who is charged with no want of industry, suspected of no extravagance'.[71] He combines 'the warmest loyalty . . . with just and rational ideas of political freedom'. The style befits the man: 'simplicity, purity, sweetness and strength' (or, for *The Edinburgh Review*, 'flowing, stately periods' which 'are perhaps too lofty for the stage, and contribute to render his plays heavy and wearisome to the reader').

A very different spirit was soon to be abroad in the work of Hazlitt (No. 33) – Gifford's personal and political opponent – and Lamb (No. 25). Hazlitt's strong views on Massinger as harsh, crabbed, and unpoetic (which did not stop him from finding these qualities sublime when personified in Kean's Sir Giles) were perhaps influenced by his perception of Gifford's editing as concerned only with dry bibliographical minutiae while 'the spirit of the writer or the beauties of his style were left to shift for themselves'.[72] Probably he has Charles Lamb in mind as a contrastingly model editor, or at least inspired compiler and fragmentary interpreter. The Massinger of Lamb's *Specimens* of 1808 (No. 25(e)) is as old-fashioned, conservative, and unadventurous as Hazlitt's Gifford: inferior in 'the higher requisites of art' to 'Ford, Webster, Tourneur, Heywood, and others', 'He never shakes or disturbs the mind with grief. He is read with composure and placid delight'; in *The Virgin Martyr* he lacks the 'poetical enthusiasm' of Dekker. It is these other playwrights (especially Webster, Tourneur, and Ford) who carry with them the excitement of a new discovery, decontextualized by Lamb's impressionistic brevity to become in effect his and his successors' passionately poetic contemporaries. Massinger is already established, an old favourite who can now safely be excluded from Scott's 1810 updating of Dodsley 'on account of the excellent edition of Mr. GIFFORD'.[73] He is decreasingly challenging: four of the plays were felt fit to appear in an expurgated edition (*The Mirror of Taste and Dramatic Censor*) as early as 1810, the tone is positively reverential in the extensive and morally aware selection *Beauties of Massinger* of 1817 (No. 35), and *The Duke of Milan* stands first in Miss Macauley's 1822 collection of tales from the drama which have the intention, says the publisher, of inculcating morality and rendering 'the real beauties of the British stage more familiar, and better known to the younger class of readers, and even of extending that knowledge to family circles where the drama itself is forbidden'.[74] One of Lamb's (No. 25(e)) aims is

to bring together the most admired scenes in Fletcher and Massinger, in the estimation of the world the only dramatic poets of that age who are entitled to be considered after Shakspeare, and to exhibit them in the same volume with the more impressive scenes of old Marlowe, Heywood, Tourneur, Webster, Ford, and others. To shew what we have slighted, while beyond all proportion we have cried up one or two favourite names.

Lamb does not expect sublimity from the over-familiar Massinger; not surprisingly, his intense responses to Webster became, in the long run, much better known than the faint praise and unfavourable comparison he bestows on Massinger.

Most of Lamb's contemporaries, however, were not yet ready for Webster. In many places the 'favourite names' continued to be 'cried up' - for instance at Cambridge University from 1816 there was a Porson Prize 'for the best translation into Greek of a passage to be selected from Shakespeare, Jonson, Massinger, or Beaumont and Fletcher'.[75] Webster continues to receive brief and sometimes hostile coverage in lectures and dramatic histories which afford Massinger far more space. Coleridge gave to Massinger's verse a lifetime of 'intent and affectionate study',[76] but nowhere mentions Webster unless in the *Annual Review* assessment of Lamb of which he may be the author, where the horrors of *The Duchess of Malfi* are absurd and the play 'contains nothing half so fine as the praise which [Lamb] has misbestowed upon it'.[77] Thomas Campbell in 1819 has several pages on Massinger in his *Essay on English Poetry*, room to develop and illustrate the insight that 'He delighted to show heroic virtue stripped of all adventitious circumstances, and tried, like a gem, by its shining through darkness' (No. 38), but space only to acknowledge somewhat grudgingly that Webster's nightmarish 'gloomy force of imagination' is 'not unmixed with the beautiful and pathetic' and that 'Middleton, Marston, Thos. Heywood, Decker, and Chapman, also present subordinate claims to remembrance in that fertile period of the drama'.[78] Like many of his predecessors Campbell continued to value consistency of character and unity of tone and found these conspicuously in Massinger, feeling these to outweigh 'the forcible utterance of the heart and . . . the warm colouring of passion'. Such emphases could easily be reconciled with a respect for clarity and strength of the sort that we find in Gifford and even, in passing, in Lamb ('equability of all the passions . . . made his English style the purest and most free from violent metaphors and harsh constructions, of any of the dramatists who were his contemporaries') or with the organic unity sought by the first generation of Romantics, the 'continuous under-current of feeling . . . everywhere present, but seldom anywhere as a separate excitement' of *Biographia Literaria*, chapter 1.[79] Coleridge admired Massinger's style and his ingenious binding together of two or three well-chosen tales. For him as for Lamb the language is pure, 'equally free from bookishness and from vulgarism' (No. 29(d)); more positively, the verse is 'the nearest approach to the language of real life at all compatible with a fixed metre' (No. 29(c)) and 'in Massinger the style is differenced, but differenced in the smallest degree possible, from animated conversation, by the vein of poetry' (No. 29(e)). 'He excells in narration' (No. 29(c)) and 'his plays have the interest of novels' (No. 29(e)).

Lamb's emphases rather than Coleridge's won the day, however. Coleridge's Massinger of conversational narrative skill is, besides (No. 29(c)), 'not a poet of high imagination; he is like a Flemish painter, in whose delineations objects appear as they do in nature, have the same force and truth, and produce the same effect upon the spectator'. For searchers out of the sublime this is scant praise; and Coleridge at once goes on to contrast Shakespeare who 'always by metaphors and figures involves in the thing considered a universe of past and possible experiences'. Many of Coleridge's more critical remarks on Massinger, especially in his lecture of 1818 (No. 29(c)), are governed by such contrasts with Shakespeare. They are sometimes stated to apply to 'most of his contemporaries, except Shakespeare', but the other dramatists apart from Jonson and Beaumont and Fletcher are not even mentioned by name and it is Massinger who can easily seem to stand for everything that Shakespeare is not. Lamb provides some very definite alternatives to Massinger, does so in an energetic, spasmodic vein itself more congenial ('with such kindred power', as the *Annual Review* piece puts it) to Webster and *The Revenger's*

Tragedy than to Massinger, and is interested in moving touches, poetic moments, rather than the deep structure and metrical technicalities (No. 29(b)) explored by Coleridge. He also had a much wider influence through his much published *Specimens* than Coleridge with his scattered spoken or manuscript ruminations on Massinger. In the second decade of the century Hazlitt (No. 33(c)–(d)) moulds Lamb's doubts about Massinger into a more incisive attack and follows him in praise of Webster's inspired 'occasional strokes of passion' and listing of ten Renaissance dramatists who are 'next, or equal, or sometimes superior . . . in power' to the Jonson, Massinger, and Beaumont and Fletcher whose works 'still keep regular possession of the stage'.[80]

After Lamb, Massinger continues to be mentioned enthusiastically by Keats (No. 36), Byron (No. 37), Shelley, who wrote to Leigh Hunt on 26 May 1820 that in *The Cenci* 'my scenes are as delicate & free from offence as' those of 'Sophocles, Massinger, Voltaire & Alfieri', Peacock, who was reading Gifford's Massinger by 1810 and declared that *The Cenci* 'would have been a great work in the days of Massinger', and Landor, who in 1833 talked to Emerson 'of Wordsworth, Byron, Messenger, Beaumont, and Fletcher'.[81] But increasingly his name is one in a group. The invocation of Massinger's name in discussion of *The Cenci* seems less significant when we note that Thomas Medwin remembers that Shelley 'was a great admirer of *The Duchess of Malfy*' and 'indeed he was continually reading the Old Dramatists – Middleton, and Webster, Ford and Massinger, and Beaumont and Fletcher, were the mines from which he drew the pure and vigorous style that so highly distinguishes *The Cenci*', and Godwin had written to Shelley in 1812 praising 'Ben Jonson, Beaumont and Fletcher, Webster, Ford, Dekker, Heywood, and Massinger'.[82]

The realization, promoted by Lamb, that Massinger indeed was one of a number of dramatists (several of whom are more obviously close to Romantic interests in the plight of the individual) was furthered by the spate of new editions including the Fords of Weber (1811) and Gifford (1827), the Marlowe editions of 1818–20 and 1826, Dyce's Webster (1830) and Greene (1831) and the Gifford/Dyce Shirley of 1833. Amidst so much newly revived competition, the hierarchy is changing, with Massinger guaranteed a considerable position by tradition and the size of his corpus, but now accorded pre-eminence only of a rather routine nature: Henry Neele finds Massinger unsurpassed in sweetness and purity of style and clear descriptive powers, but lacking in the feeling and nature of other tragic dramatists; according to *The Gentleman's Magazine* in 1833 Webster is 'far below *Massinger* in the conduct of his plot and the consistency of his characters', but he 'far, very far, surpasses' him and all the others 'in the depth of his pathos, his tragic powers, and his command over the sublime, the terrible, and the affecting'.[83] Massinger's late eighteenth-century fame played its part in the rediscovery of Renaissance drama, but in so doing exposed his priority of eminence to scrutiny. His perceived lack of imagination or sublimity was mentioned in graver tones, not shrugged off so often as concomitant with his eloquence or robustness: Thomas Lovell Beddoes, while he admires *The Fatal Dowry* and feels Massinger to be 'a very effective "stage-poet"' (No. 39(a)), is in no doubt that *The Second Maiden's Tragedy*, attributed to Massinger by Ludwig Tieck, is simply 'too imaginative for old Philip' (No. 39(d)).

The currency of the idea of literature as self-expression by the author encouraged in many quarters a 'personal' rather than political approach to the plays of Massinger and his contemporaries. Coleridge declares that Massinger was a Democrat (No. 29(b)) and notes his continual flings at kings and courtiers (No. 29(c)), but does not engage in detailed political analysis. Lamb briefly alleges that he caters for 'the females of the Herbert family' in *The City Madam*. The evident political interests of *The Bondman* and *The Maid of Honour* were made little of during this period.[84] Perhaps partly for this reason Lamb does not excerpt these plays and, with Coleridge and Keats, likes the innocuous wooing of Almira by Don John Antonio disguised as a slave (*A Very Woman*) in preference to the similar situation of Cleora and Pisander/Marullo in the politically more challenging *Bondman*. And more generally Massinger's most popular plays in the early nineteenth century apart from *A New Way* and *The City Madam* are the love-tragedies *The Duke of Milan*, *The Fatal Dowry*, and *The Unnatural Combat*, more personal than the historical tragedies and less dangerously open-ended than the tragicomedies. Even incest in *The Unnatural Combat*, though seen as distasteful, has the advantage of keeping the play's focus highly personal and passionate. Thomas Campbell's statement (No. 38) that Malefort 'strikes us as no object of moral warning, but as a man under the influence of insanity' partly explains some writers' ambivalent fascination with the play. Henry Neele (No. 41) admires 'the tremendous tone of the whole picture' and feels that Massinger's genius is perhaps 'more conspicuous in this Play, with all its faults, than in any other'. In 1807 Sir James Mackintosh is moved to feelings both of horror and disgust at and of admiration for this 'noble' and, but for decency, stageworthy drama, and indeed Kean reportedly 'longed' to stage it, 'yet dared not'.[85]

Another feature of the growth of the importance of the personal in late eighteenth- and early nineteenth-century literary criticism was an interest in the author's 'sentimental biography'.[86] Rather more was known or surmisable about Massinger than most of his contemporaries, especially as a result of the publication of the 'tripartite letter' (No. 1) by Malone in 1790. Commentators made the most of this, with Gifford lamenting that Massinger's 'life was all one wintry day', although he bore his poverty with patience; Reynolds (in a note omitted from No. 34(a)) sorrowfully quotes Gifford's remark and reflects that 'He led a life of dependence and penury — and it is therefore a wonder that he preserved his elegance of mind, and suavity of temper', and Campbell again describes the 'distressful document' in his life of Massinger[87] and suggests in his *Essay on English Poetry* (No. 38) that Massinger, 'Poor himself, and struggling under the rich man's contumely', solaced his 'neglected existence' by depicting 'worth and magnanimity breaking through external disadvantages'. Massinger's virtues arise despite, or through noble struggle with, unpropitious circumstances; these always have to be mentioned, and act as something of a damper.

In the theatre, the time-scale of Massinger's rise and fall was very different. In the early years of the century *A New Way* was establishing itself in the repertory in the hands of Cooke and Kemble (see No. 31(a) for Scott's contrast between the two) but it was from 1816 that Kean's Sir Giles came so to dominate theatrical and social life that it allegedly superseded 'the Englishman's darling theme of the weather'.[88] The gap between stage adulation and incipient critical disenchantment mirrors the nineteenth-century divide between theatre and 'literature'.

A New Way found the right actor at the right time. Kean's

technique was perceived as in harmony with Sir Giles and Richard III: according to George Vandenhoff, a later Sir Giles, 'His style was impulsive, fitful, flashing, abounding in quick transitions; scarcely giving you time to think, but ravishing your wonder, and carrying you along with his impetuous rush and change of expression.'[89] Frequently character and actor fuse in the enthusiastic reviews and comments of 1816 and later. The famous last scene is spoken of in terms which suggest at once natural passion and the artifice which achieves its impression: Sir Giles's rage 'is wrought up to a wonderful height' (Henry Crabb Robinson);[90] the whole scene is 'worked up to a pitch of passion that I could not have imagined' (Mary Shelley);[91] 'The variety, and at the same time the intensity of passion, which burned within him throughout this high-wrought scene, has never been surpassed by any actor' (*The Times*, No. 32). Everywhere tribute is paid to the 'breadth, force, and grandeur' (Hazlitt, No. 33(b)) of both Kean and Sir Giles; both are triumphantly energetic and – for most of the play – successful (in his biography of Kean, Bryan Waller Proctor comments consecutively on Kean's 'surprising energy of . . . acting', stamina in performing the role seventeen times before 9 March 1816, and success in bringing 'a prodigious sum of money into the Drury Lane treasury').[92] Celebrating the actor's passion (and sometimes, too, appreciating the calmer moments that set it off), audiences were not so much aghast at the criminality as participants in an amoral sublimity like that experienced by witnesses of Kean's *Richard III*. According to *The Times* the character 'belongs to tragedy; it is a vivid picture of terrific and untameable passions, leading to the commission of the most odious crimes'; the final phrase is perhaps the least important (Hazlitt (No. 33(c)) says that 'We hate him very heartily, and yet not enough; for he has strong, robust points about him that repel the impertinence of censure'). There is a continual emphasis on the passion, sublimity, and originality of the play's close: 'the conclusion was as terrific as anything that has been seen upon the stage' (Proctor),[93] Byron (No. 37) was seized by 'convulsions . . . the agony of reluctant tears', Reynolds (No. 34(b)) described Kean as becoming 'all energy' until, gazing fixedly at Margaret with 'hatred, fierceness, and hopelessness', 'all his vital powers were withered up, and he sunk lifeless into the arms of his servants'. More generally Mary Shelley 'never was more powerfully affected by any representation than by his Sir Giles Overreach' in 1824–5, and from an older generation Hester Lynch Piozzi (Mrs Thrale), a Massinger enthusiast back in the less heady atmosphere of the 1780s (see p.17), was favourably surprised by the fineness of Kean's Sir Giles at Bath in 1817.[94]

Audiences, then, seem to have been deeply affected, almost stupefied, by Sir Giles's outrageous boldness, ambition, energy, and sudden and total overthrow, and Kean's suitably spasmodic and passionate style.[95] Such preferences are in line with the contemporary vogue for the villain–hero, whether in *Richard III* or the melodrama,[96] and were the product in part of the 'Sympathetic' philosophy and criticism which has been studied in detail by Joseph W. Donohue. This emphasized moments of reaction rather than action, and character and motive rather than morality (seeing, for instance, the Macbeths of Kemble and Siddons as 'two essentially virtuous persons, victimized by exterior forces and interior passions against which their natural goodness has no defense').[97]

The available adaptations catered to Kean's and his contemporaries' emphasis on motive and on moments of reaction like Sir Giles's much-chronicled collapse. For example, the alteration of *A New Way* (attributed to Kemble) made the play more consistently serious and emotional than the original, aspiring 'as much as possible to harrow the feelings of . . . audiences that they might leave the theatre with awe as well as relief'. In particular, Sir Giles's last two entries were compressed into one, allowing the actor 'to build up to a romantic *crescendo* of emotion uninterrupted by less important motifs', whence the remarkable concentration of reviewers, audiences, and theatrical painters, on this last scene.[98] A similar tendency is apparent in the version of *The City Madam*, Burges's *Riches* (No. 30), in which Kean played from 1814: Luke remains a villain, but in his final towering defiance in defeat (where in *The City Madam* he remains largely silent) demands the lion's share of our emotional engagement. And in the 1825 *Fatal Dowry* (No. 40) Charalois becomes noble and pathetic, dying not for taking the law into his own hands but because there is nothing left to live for. In all three adaptations the focus shifts, broadly speaking, from Renaissance estrangement and ethical concerns to Romantic involvement (according to *The Theatrical Inquisitor and Monthly Mirror* for January 1816, 'Mr. Kean appears to have thrown his whole soul, as it were, into the part of Sir Giles')[99] and tracing of motives. The British Library copy of the 1816 *Duke of Milan* adaptation 'Correctly marked according to the directions of Mr Kean' ends not with Pescara's moralizing but at Sforza's death when, the manuscript direction indicates, the '*Curtain falls to slow Music*'.[100]

The dominance of the central character also fitted *A New Way* to the star system and to the setting in which only a star could shine, namely the vast Drury Lane stage where large gestures and rugged passions communicated in a way that more delicate and enigmatic effects could not (Kean was generally more esteemed for his Richard III than for his Othello or Macbeth).[101]

For a number of reasons, however, the success of Kean and his contemporaries and immediate successors as Sir Giles was a mixed blessing for Massinger's reputation. Obviously there was a risk that other, less-established plays by Massinger would disappoint audiences; Kean's Sforza in *The Duke of Milan*, for instance, struck Hazlitt (No. 33(b)) as entirely lacking the grandeur of his Sir Giles. There were, besides, relatively few opportunities to judge Massinger's other plays, partly as a result of the restrictions of a small repertory in whose repeated roles audiences delighted to compare different actors. The theatrical event was oriented 'towards the actor in character . . . Massinger was of no particular interest in himself, but London audiences flocked to see Kean's Sir Giles Overreach all the same'.[102]

Immense theatrical success, moreover, was no passport to literary respectability at a time when poets and men of letters were leaving the theatre, writing 'dramatic poems', or expressing discontent with the theatrical medium itself, when 'Readers like Lamb, Coleridge, and, to a lesser degree, Hazlitt found themselves put off by what less perspicacious playgoers took as the lucid, straightforward simplicity of action on the stage'.[103] Critics responded to the extremism of a Sir Giles with appropriately tremendous language, but in moments of cooler reflection sometimes missed complex motive of the sort the poets were writing into their closet-dramas. Neele (No. 41) looks in Massinger for 'all the delicate tints of the back ground' but finds only 'bold, prominent features', and Hazlitt (No. 33(d)) finds 'motives unaccountable and weak' in Massinger's villains including the Sir Giles whom he celebrates in the theatre. The play's perceived theatricality obscures the quieter dramatic potential implicitly observed by Coleridge in his analyses of Massinger's language, metrics, and plotting, and reinforces the familiar unpoetic image. For *The Critical Review*, for instance, Massinger suits Kean better than Shakespeare because the character of Sir Giles is 'divested of the sublimities of Shakspeare'; the author is 'bold in conception, and daring in delineation; but he is unskilled in that exquisite refinement by which Shakspeare pervades the labyrinths of the heart'.[104] According to *The Annual Review* Massinger constructed plays better than, and with less violent and monstrous action than, the playwrights whose neglect Lamb had remedied, 'and for this reason it is that Massinger, the feeblest poet of them all, is perused with the most pleasure'.[105] Hazlitt's two 1816 reviews of *A New Way*, recording emphatic passions, eye-rollings, and hysterics, are separated by his experience of the conversion of 'a delightful poem [*A Midsummer-Night's Dream*] . . . into a dull pantomime' by panoply and noise; but the delightful poem continued to please Hazlitt in the study while his later verdicts on Massinger's general 'hardness and repulsiveness of manner' and 'convulsive efforts of the will' (No. 33(d), (c)) were surely influenced by his encounter with the non-poetic qualities which *A New Way* required to succeed on the Drury Lane stage.

5. 1830–1920

A New Way went on from success to success until the 1860s, with reviewers continuing to find the various Sir Gileses (notably Charles Kean, Samuel Phelps, and, in America, Junius Brutus Booth) 'fearfully impressive', 'terrifically grand' or characterized by passion, convulsions, and flashes of genius.[106] But the reviewers and commentators were not, for the most part, influential in non-theatrical circles. Sir Giles and the theatre were both, on the whole, too crude for latterday Hazlitts and Scotts. Theatrical success no longer qualified or diversified critical strictures. Elizabeth Barrett Browning alone among the prominent earlier Victorian poets mentions that she has read Massinger, but remains unconvinced, after reading hard at him and his fellows in Dodsley's collection, that the theatre can be 'a means of great moral good'.[107] From the theatre itself William Charles Macready, who prided himself on being one of the more thoughtful actors of his day, found *Riches* (No. 30), for all his success in it, psychologically unsophisticated: 'though possessing a considerable share of truth and much originality, [it] is still little more than a sketch . . . there are no struggles of the heart, no gradual revolutions of man's nature – it is a brief dramatic tale'.[108] The later version of *The City Madam* in which Samuel Phelps played a finally repentant Luke between 1844 and 1862 (No. 44) sentimentalizes the play still further away from the complexity missed by Macready. So too more interest was taken in Massinger by Macready's friend Dickens than by less theatrical, more consciously sophisticated novelists. Dickens owned a copy of Hartley Coleridge's edition of Massinger and Ford and and was familiar enough with *A New Way* to be afraid that Charles Kean's Overreach 'might upset me' in March 1839.[109] (Henry Woudhuysen has drawn attention to parallels with *Nicholas Nickleby*, in serial publication at the time, which possibly suggest one reason for Dickens's 'tenderness about going to see Massinger's play').[110]

By the time Leslie Stephen, A.C. Swinburne, and Arthur Symons wrote the most important Victorian essays on Massinger in the 1870s and 1880s, he was no longer popular even in the theatre. Only one English production of *A New Way* is recorded between 1861 and 1871; the change came most of all as a result of 'a tendency in the direction of realism' soon to be manifested in the taste for the plays of Tom Robertson, and for a more natural acting style.[111] But a diverse and often favourable readership remains in evidence throughout the nineteenth century. Among those reading or referring to Massinger after 1830 were John Wilson ('Christopher North', who said that Massinger drew female characters especially well), Macaulay, and John Addington Symonds (who in 1864 rated *The Virgin Martyr*, *The City Madam*, *The Roman Actor*, and *A New Way* amongst twenty-six 'masterpieces' of the old drama).[112] Thackeray, like Dickens, at least owned a copy of the 1840 Massinger and Ford; Edward Fitzgerald owned 'Massenger's Plays'.[113] And to the end of the century Massinger fares better than Marlowe or Webster in the dictionaries of quotations.[114] Indeed he became more widely available to readers from 1840 in a cheap one-volume Gifford and in Hartley Coleridge's edition of Massinger and Ford, and from

1868 in Cunningham's portable version of Gifford (with the addition of *Believe As You List*, found and first printed in the 1840s). But there was no comparable broadening in the range of critical responses.

Five main areas of enquiry are common to most accounts: morality (and especially 'decency' or the lack of it), coherence of structure and character, humour or the lack of it, Massinger's rhetorical eloquence (increasingly subject to Mill's distinction between eloquence as heard and poetry as overheard),[115] and his social background and alleged character and opinions as explanation of these other elements. These are familiar enough themes in pre-Victorian criticism, but they are now more relentlessly pursued. Conclusions may differ about how much Massinger's indecency matters or whether he was a Roman Catholic, but the counters of the argument are generally the same. Almost every account acknowledges that there are indecent elements (one acute defence is Macaulay's of 1841, that marital infidelity is treated either as a serious crime or as a matter for laughter turned against gallants),[116] that the 'melancholy document' tells us much about Massinger's melancholy nature, that he does not excel in 'flashes' of poetry. Unequivocally positive accounts of Massinger like that of James Russell Lowell in 1887 (No. 50) therefore sound old-fashioned. New perspectives, on the other hand, were restricted by the unusual weight of earlier criticism that writers had to take on board. Again and again due reference is made to Gifford, Coleridge, Hazlitt, Hallam, and, after 1877, Stephen. Also restricting, perhaps, was the comparative tradition which had grown up around Massinger – the compulsory comparisons of Massinger with Fletcher, *The Fatal Dowry* with *The Fair Penitent*, *The Duke of Milan* with *Othello*, the silver age of drama with the golden.

The oft-repeated but more spontaneous-sounding strictures of the past have now become more systematized. It was decreasingly acceptable (as the practice of Coleridge or Hazlitt or Carlyle percolated to more workaday critics) to judge a book simply by 'balancing a list of virtues and vices as if they were separate entities lying side by side in a box, instead of different aspects of a vital force'.[117] In 1839 Henry Hallam (No. 42) can judge Massinger's genius 'not eminently pathetic, nor energetic enough to display the utmost intensity of emotion', and at the same time maintain that it is perfectly commendable, abounding 'in sweetness and dignity, apt to delineate the loveliness of virtue, and to delight in its recompense after trial'. But to younger and less neo-classical critics these latter qualities would demonstrate rather than qualify the former. In keeping with a desire to see authors' works as whole, natural, organic growths, what had been qualifications of general praise from Gifford, Campbell, or Hallam now became the main substance of the argument: any faults, almost, make the organism seem imperfect. For Charles Kingsley you cannot dismiss the ribaldry of *The Virgin Martyr* by claiming it as exceptional in Massinger or blaming Dekker for it: in the scenes in question

even if they be Dekker's – of which there is no proof – Massinger was forced, in order to the success of his play, to pander to the public taste, by allowing Dekker to interpolate these villanies . . . No one denies that there are nobler words than any that we have quoted, in Jonson, in Fletcher, or in Massinger: but there is hardly a play (perhaps none) of theirs in which the immoralities of which we complain do not exist, – few of which they do not form an integral part.[118]

Even for those who did feel Massinger's moral earnestness outweighed his bawdiness, morality was often insufficient when unaccompanied by poetry and imagination: A.W. Ward (No. 46) prefers to the inadmissible immoralities of *The Unnatural Combat* and *The Guardian* the nobility or 'elevation of sentiment' of *The Bashful Lover*, but even there the reader is left rather cold because 'the rhetorical genius of Massinger could not even with such a subject as this pass beyond its bounds; there is too much argument, too much unction, and too much protesting in the dialogue'. For Elizabeth Barrett Browning 'Massinger writes all like a giant – a dry-eyed giant'.[119]

Language perceived as elegant or rhetorical rests uneasily with the notion of the true poet who speaks forth, as Carlyle puts it, 'because his heart is too full to be silent'.[120] For Edwin Whipple in 1859 (No. 45) Massinger's 'thoughts are not born in music, but mechanically set to a tune'. William Minto in 1874 says that 'The common remark that his diction is singularly free from archaisms shows us one aspect of the soundness of his taste, and bears testimony, at the same time, to his want of eccentricity and original force'.[121] George Craik in 1845 finds Massinger eloquent, but lacking in high imagination, pathos, wit, and comic power: he achieves 'all that can be reached by mere talent and warmth of susceptibility ... but his province was to appropriate and decorate rather than to create'.[122] Structure, too, may be an unnatural growth: according to Ward the ending of *The Fatal Dowry* is brought about 'inorganically', and Leslie Stephen studies the natural or unnatural growth of plot and character in a number of the plays.

One evident context for the organicist approach is evolutionary theory. Stephen's long essay of 1877 (No. 47), which further systematized the Massinger criticism of his age, sees Massinger as an organic growth on the way from the force of the Elizabethans to the corruption or affectation of the Restoration; his morality is the sort of plant 'which flourishes in an exhausted soil' – it creates weak and self-indulgent heroes or exalts passive virtues. Arthur Symons (No. 51) follows Stephen in saying that 'Massinger is the late twilight of the long and splendid day of which Marlowe was the dawn' and Swinburne (No.49(c)), while generally more favourable to Massinger, agrees that the tide has begun steadily to ebb and that the golden age of drama has given way to the silver. Saintsbury in his *History of Elizabethan Literature* (1887) feels Massinger has been underrated recently, but treats him in his logical position in the 'Fourth Dramatic Period'. Such methods go some way to explain the general lack of enthusiasm for Shirley's work, placed inexorably at the end of pre-1640 drama. By the time of Maurice Chelli the idea of 'la décadence dramatique' has been long established, even if Massinger is its 'figure la plus honorable'.[123]

Also in line with these systematizing tendencies is the increased interest in the author's biography as coherent explanation of his work. Gifford had made much of Massinger's poverty, but Hartley Coleridge and his successors see it as informing rather more fully what he writes and the way he writes it. The 'melancholy document' or tripartite letter so often referred to becomes the key to the melancholy, pallid, or unpoetic plays: together with 'the almost desperate mendicancy of his dedications' it feeds William Minto's sense of 'a certain sad didactic running through all Massinger's work' and belief that the 'serious motive' underlying his humour 'connects itself with the earnestness of his distressed life'.[124] In the 1880s Arthur Symons (like Swinburne in his poem of 1882, No.49(a)) brings in the posthumous 'portrait' of Massinger as a further external confirmation of literary conclusions (No. 51) since

> The whole man is seen in the portrait by which we know him: in the contrast and contradiction of that singular face which attracts, yet always at the last look fails to satisfy us, with its melancholy and thoughtful grace, tempered always and marred by the weakness and the want which we can scarcely analyse, nor by any means overlook.[125]

The letter lends authority to Hartley Coleridge's conclusion (No. 43) that 'Massinger seems to have been of a shy, reserved, and melancholy nature. Nothing in his writings betokens the exuberant life and dancing blood of Shakespeare and Fletcher'; it also gave rise to his more practical awareness of the number of debtors in the plays (*A New Way to Pay Old Debts* 'by its very title, indicates an embarrassed author'). Whipple and Symons echo him. Where Coleridge has no melancholy documents to illuminate the work, the work itself will do to illuminate the life:

> In all probability he never married; and if he loved, he has left not a stanza nor a hint of his success or rejection. Sometimes I have imagined that, like Tasso, he fixed his affections too high for hope, as his fortunes were certainly too low for marriage. I ground this fancy, – for it is but a fancy, – on the 'Bondman', the 'Very Woman', and the 'Bashful Lover', in all of which high-born ladies become enamoured, as they suppose, of men of low degree . . . Methinks, he soothed his despondency with a visionary unsphering of those stellar beauties.

The relentlessness of such biographical pursuit makes it easy to demote politics to the level of a facet of personality. Coleridge speculatively provides Massinger with a Wilton childhood (complete with Sir Philip Sidney as godfather) partly because he wants to argue, against his 'revered father', that Massinger's sympathies are, as befits a retainer's son, aristocratic. (Symons and Gosse later make similar use of the Wilton motif.) His falsetto remarks against kings and courtiers are personal rather than political: it is not that Shakespeare was loyal and Massinger a captious Whig, as Samuel Taylor Coleridge imagined, but that 'Shakspeare was a prosperous man, of a joyous poetic temperament, while Massinger's native melancholy was exacerbated by sorrow and disappointment' after Wilton. Thirty-seven years later

Leslie Stephen (No. 47) only nods in the direction of the historian S.R. Gardiner's detailed conclusions on Massinger's adherence to the politics of the Pembrokes.[126] He still wants a more personal explanation:

The difference between Fletcher and Massinger . . . was probably due to difference of temperament as much as to the character of Massinger's family connection. Massinger's melancholy is as marked as the buoyant gaiety of his friend and ally. He naturally represents the misgivings which must have beset the more thoughtful members of his party, as Fletcher represented the careless vivacity of the Cavalier spirit.

The times were enough to make a moralist, 'But he is also a moraliser by temperament'.

Most critics aligned Massinger roughly with Stephen's moderate royalist: he subscribes variously to moderate liberalism (Ward, No. 46), 'a kind of oligarchic liberalism' (Gosse, No. 52), or large and humane sympathies (Lowell, No. 50). Swinburne's Massinger (No. 49(c)), rather more concretely, foresees 'the inevitable result of lawless extortion and transgression on the part of the rulers of England'; but in so doing – the transgressions were 'lawless' – he is a true patriot, 'at once truly conservative and thoroughly liberal'. The aim of such (often vague and anachronistic) diagnoses was to reassure readers that Massinger was safe and non-radical. He was retained within the broad and liberal bounds of the establishment. For Minto, Massinger's zestful punishment of 'high-fed madams' in *The Bondman* and ridicule of 'the pretensions of upstart wealth' in *The City Madam*

are as consistent with a benevolent paternal Toryism as with Whiggery, and are to be looked upon as indications simply of the dramatist's range of sympathies, and not of any discontent on his part with the established framework of government or society.[127]

Margot Heinemann may be right that Symons's Mermaid selection includes *The Guardian* but not *The Bondman* in accordance with nineteenth-century editors' preference for private human interest and sexual or sentimental themes over politics.[128] *Believe As You List* is included, but is valued chiefly for the quiet endurance of Antiochus. Perhaps for similar reasons, Ward has a special fondness for *The Bashful Lover* and Swinburne for *A Very Woman*, where, the prologue he wrote for it claims (No. 49(b)),

Massinger took a rest from reproving kings. The widespread characterization of these plays and *The Great Duke of Florence* as elevated, melancholy, delicate, not only defused any threat of political engagement but excused Massinger from fervid poetry.

Nevertheless Massinger's politics were discussed, however vaguely, more often than those of most other contemporary playwrights. As the day of the touchstones arrived and the day of the text on the page loomed, treatment of Massinger's political (and religious) interests contributed to the perception of his coldness, his 'claims to honour . . . rather moral and intellectual . . . than imaginative and creative' (Swinburne, No. 49(c)), his interest in ideas and oratory rather than poetry. Massinger's politics and personality together override literary considerations: *Chambers's Cyclopaedia of English Literature* talks of 'Camiola's frank impeachment, controversial rather than poetic', of the divine right of kings,[129] and Whipple (No. 45) says that Massinger 'frequently violates the keeping of character in order to intrude his own manly political sentiments and ideas'. Discussions of his politics also emphasized his 'late', just pre-Civil War date, confirming his clear placing in a time of decadence or at least decay.

Leslie Stephen's urbane, authoritative unfolding of Massinger's pervasive 'want of vital force' (No. 47) set the seal on his nineteenth-century decline. Stephen says much that had been said before (particularly, as he acknowledges, by Ward) but he says it less apologetically. His own appearance of irrefragable logical consistency contrasts with what he sees as Massinger's lack of it. What Swinburne called his 'battery of adverse or depreciatory remarks' is unremitting: for Stephen, Massinger is

> a sentimentalist and a rhetorician. He is not, like the greatest men, dominated by thoughts and emotions which force him to give them external embodiment in life-like symbols. He is rather a man of much real feeling and extraordinary facility of utterance who finds in his stories convenient occasions for indulging in elaborate didactic utterances upon moral topics.

He cannot identify with his villains, not even, vital though for once he is, with Sir Giles. No amount of eloquence and 'sympathy for virtuous motive' can blind us to Massinger's lack of force, capacity to stimulate and fascinate, and intensity; accordingly, 'A single touch in Shakespeare, or even in Webster or Ford, often reveals more depth of feeling than a whole scene of Massinger's facile and often deliberately forensic eloquence'.

Stephen's artillery breached the outworks of Massinger's reputation. Symons's influential Mermaid introduction of 1887 (No. 51) follows Stephen on many points and in the insistent repetition of the words 'vital' and 'facile', and he too must find a central characteristic failure: 'Where Massinger most conclusively fails is in a right understanding and a right representation of human nature; in the power to conceive passion and bring its speech and action vividly and accurately before us'. He is facile both in verse and in 'the plot and conduct of the plays'. Above all, in Massinger 'there are scarcely a dozen lines of such intrinsic and unmistakeable beauty that we are forced to pause and brood on them with the true epicure's relish' (again the contrast with Webster, as well as Shakespeare, is made).

Swinburne (No. 49(c)), two years after Symons, is more independent and wide-ranging. Coleridge can only call Malefort a lunatic as a result of 'presumptuous ignorance as to the darker elements of human character'. Swinburne analyses an unprecedented number of single scenes outside the most famous two or three from *A New Way* and *The Duke of Milan*. *Barnavelt* is examined in a detail never before, and rarely since, bestowed on a Massinger/Fletcher collaboration. But Swinburne's familiar-sounding conclusion is that Massinger's style is already fixed here in the 'purity and lucidity of dignified eloquence' by contrast with Fletcher's more poetic contribution; in general he says little that violently contradicts Stephen's verdict.

In the late nineteenth and early twentieth centuries authors of literary history continued to discuss Massinger, but usually had nothing new or heterodox to say about him. There is much repetition and plagiarism: Symons (1887), Edmund Gosse in *The Jacobean Poets* (No. 52, 1894), and W.J. Courthope in *A History of English Poetry* (1903)[130] all use, if to slightly different effect, the image of puppetry when diagnosing Massinger's attitude to characterization; the 'facility' or easiness of the verse is commented on by J.H.B. Masterman in *The Age of Milton* (1897)[131] as well as by Stephen and Symons. Everywhere the lack of memorable lines, of Websterian 'flashes' is mourned: Saintsbury's 1887 protest that Massinger deserves a high rank 'Unless we are to count by mere flashes' failed to stem the tide, and he himself extolled those 'flashes of sheer poetry which . . . lighten the work of the Elizabethan and Jacobean dramatists proper [and sometimes Ford] with extraordinary and lavish brilliance';[132] there is none of Webster's and the Elizabethans' 'sudden sheet-lightning of poetry illuminating for an instant dark places of the soul', no 'jewels ten words long' (Gosse); 'scarcely a dozen lines [as Symons had already put it!] . . . that have power to arrest our attention or linger in our memory' (Masterman).[133] All too familiarly, Massinger's style 'is pure, correct, and dignified, but rhetorical, and verging towards eloquent and rhythmic prose' (Herbert Grierson in 1906) and Paris's speeches in *The Roman Actor* 'move as it were on a lofty though peakless table-land of stately rhetoric' (Oliver Elton in 1933).[134] Massinger's melancholy temperament continues to interest writers including A.H. Cruickshank, who tells us in 1920 that Massinger is as melancholy as Vitelli and Charalois and that Jonson would have regarded him as a 'pale-featured, gentle hack';[135] in 1923 the programme for a production of *The Duke of Milan* at Merton College, Oxford is still quoting Hartley Coleridge (as Whipple had) on Massinger's sad, lonely death and burial as a 'stranger', a term which, as Coleridge acknowledged in his second edition, refers only to his not having been born in the parish. His political interests, while often documented, are usually treated as a subsidiary area of enquiry. The indecency issue rumbles on without conclusion.

A number of writers register the plays' theatrical potential; Massinger's best qualities for Oliver Elton in 1912 are 'dignity, constructive power, and theatrical instinct'[136] (Symons had said that he 'thoroughly understood the art of the playwright'). Writers of this period set great store by the 'well-made play', Elton's 'skilled cog-work', A.H. Cruickshank's 'constructive skill', Chelli's 'bien-charpenté' plays. But the praise is often two-edged: ability to write good stage-plays is part of Massinger's all-important unpoeticality. Gosse's 'admirable artificer of plays' who 'composes . . . not for the study so much as for the stage' is still no poet. 'Perhaps the least poetical of all the early dramatists . . . as a dramatist he stands amongst the first', declared Richard Ferrar Patterson (like the *Annual Review* of 1808) in 1933.[137] Parrott and Ball believe that Massinger must be judged fairly as a playwright, but also say, as late as 1943 (as T.A. Dunn would lengthily agree in his book of 1957), that he is 'rather the master-craftsman of drama than the dramatic poet'.[138] This was not likely to fire readers of the age of Eliot.

Massinger sounded boringly simple and unadventurous to the first half of the twentieth century, a Georgian to Webster's Eliot (at least in terms of language, the true yardstick in most Massinger criticism, particularly where social or political content is undervalued). Where he was still admired, it was sometimes in terms which made him a sitting target, a form of Eminent Victorian, for anyone with fresh ideas. Cruickshank pronounced

In an age like the present, when many of our poets, like our musicians, whatever else they are, either will not or cannot be simple, it is refreshing to turn to an author who is always lucid, and who is content to tell a story to the best of his ability

and Eliot retorted with his famous devastation of Massinger's easy, bland, dissociated manner.[139]

On the whole Massinger's reputation did not recover from Eliot's prestigious *coup de grâce* for nearly half a century; Eliot completed the formidable line of Massinger's doubters – Lamb, Hazlitt, Stephen. After 1920 there were some interesting individual essays on Massinger, probably the best known of which remains L.C. Knights' on the 'city comedies' in their social and economic setting in *Drama and Society in the Age of Jonson* of 1937. Individual editions advanced the study of the text, and Massinger's biography was investigated with a new objectiveness. There were still, occasionally, successful stage productions. But there was really no new impetus to critical development until Edwards' and Gibson's opening up of the whole text and context of Massinger, and, more broadly, the modern shift from a chiefly poetic interest in Renaissance drama to one involving an awareness of genre, politics, and the implications of 'symbolic' staging. Since the publication of the complete works in 1976 there have been major professional productions of *The Roman Actor* and *A New Way*, there has been a distinct increase in the number of articles on Massinger, including the pieces in Douglas Howard's *Philip Massinger: a Critical Reassessment* (1985), and he has featured conspicuously in three of the most important 1980s treatments of seventeenth-century drama, Margot Heinemann's, Martin Butler's, and Annabel Patterson's (see below, Select Bibliography, section 4). Massinger is undergoing one of his periodical revaluations, and in the process may be able to repossess at least something of his immense importance to literary culture from the late eighteenth to the late nineteenth century.

NOTES

1 Seven plays wholly by Massinger (*The Bashful Lover, The Guardian, The City Madam* and four late lost plays) and eleven collaborations were protected from publication by the Lord Chamberlain for the King's Men in August 1641. In August 1639 five of his published plays (*The Bondman, The Maid of Honour, The Renegado, A New Way to Pay Old Debts,* and *The Great Duke of Florence*) were still popular enough to be similarly protected for the King and Queen's Young Company (Bentley, *JCS*, vol.1, pp.65–6, 330–1).
2 The lost *The Woman's Plot* in 1621, *The Bondman* in 1623, *The Guardian* in 1634; of the six collaborations recorded at court (which included *The Fatal Dowry* in 1631) the most popular was *The Spanish Curate* (1622, 1638, 1639), by Massinger and Fletcher. See Bentley, *JCS* vol.1, pp.94–100, 194.
3 Colin Gibson, 'Massinger's Theatrical Language', in Douglas Howard (ed.), *Philip Massinger: a Critical Reassessment*, Cambridge, 1985, pp.11–12. See also *EG*, vol.1, pp.xlvii–xlviii.
4 See Cyrus Hoy, 'The Shares of Fletcher and his Collaborators in the Beaumont and Fletcher Canon', *Studies in Bibliography*, vols 8–9 and 11–15, 1956–62.
5 *EG*, vol.4, p.202.
6 G.E. Bentley, *The Profession of Dramatist in Shakespeare's Time 1590–1642*, Princeton, 1971, pp.197–8, 197–234 *passim*.
7 C.H. Herford, Percy Simpson and Evelyn Simpson (eds), *Ben Jonson*, 11 vols, Oxford, 1925–52, vol.4, p.351.
8 *EG*, vol.1, pp.xxxii–xxxiii.
9 Cp. Gibson, op. cit., pp.14–15.
10 *EG*, vol.1, p.xlvi.
11 ibid., p.xxxviii.
12 John Heming(es) and Henry Condell, '*To the great Variety of Readers*', *Mr William Shakespeares Comedies, Histories, & Tragedies*, London, 1623, A3. This and many other examples of the 'critical connoisseurship' of the demanding late Jacobean and Caroline audience are cited by Michael Neill, '"Wits most accomplished Senate": the Audience of the Caroline Private Theaters', *Studies in English Literature, 1500–1900*, vol.18, 1978, pp.341–60.
13 ibid., p.341.

14 See Georges Bas, 'James Shirley et "Th' Untun'd Kennell": une petite guerre des théâtres vers 1630', *Études anglaises*, vol.16, 1963, pp.11–22; Peter Beal, 'Massinger at Bay: Unpublished Verses in a War of the Theatres', *The Yearbook of English Studies*, vol.10, 1980, pp.190–203; below, Select Bibliography, section 3.
15 See T.A. Dunn, *Philip Massinger: the Man and the Playwright*, Edinburgh, 1957, p.33.
16 Thomas Carew '*To my worthy Friend, M. D'AVENANT, Vpon his Excellent Play, the Iust Italian*', in Rhodes Dunlap (ed.), *The Poems of Thomas Carew*, Oxford, 1949, p.96.
17 *EG*, vol.4, p.416.
18 See *OED*, 'crafty' a.2 and 'cunning' a.1, 2, and 4.
19 *OED* records 'wright' in the sense 'to pursue the occupation of a wright' only as Scottish, 1886 (v.3), but earlier uses of 'wright' as a verb in other senses did occur (v.1–2).
20 Beal, op. cit., p.203.
21 See Martin Garrett, '*A diamond, though set in horn*': *Philip Massinger's Attitude to Spectacle*, Salzburg, 1984, pp.248–63.
22 Joseph Quincy Adams (ed.), *The Dramatic Records of Sir Henry Herbert*, New Haven, 1917, pp.54, 65, and n.2. *Cleander* was a revision of Fletcher's *The Lovers' Progress*.
23 See Bentley, *JCS*, vol.3, pp.415–17.
24 Annabel Patterson, *Censorship and Interpretation: the Conditions of Writing and Reading in Early Modern England*, Madison, Wisc., 1984, pp.85–6.
25 ibid., p.89.
26 See Martin Butler, 'Romans in Britain: *The Roman Actor* and the Early Stuart Classical Play', in Howard (ed.), op. cit., pp.139–70. The play's commenders included Thomas May (No. 4), classicist and future republican.
27 See *EG*, vol.1, p.xlvi.
28 Martin Butler, *Theatre and Crisis 1632–1642*, Cambridge, 1984, pp.9–10.
29 See Colin Gibson, 'Massinger at the Academy of Complements', forthcoming in *The Library*. A number of copies of the songs and of the poem 'The Virgins Character' are also extant in mid-seventeenth-century manuscript miscellanies, and there are manuscript extracts from *The Bondman*, *The Great Duke of Florence*, and *The Maid of Honour*. See Peter Beal (ed.), *Index of English Literary Manuscripts*, 2 vols, London, 1980, vol.1, Part 2, pp.337–40, 631.
30 See especially [George Wither (?)], *The Great Assises Holden in Parnassus*, London, 1645, A2, pp.9, 31, and Sir Richard Baker, *A Chronicle of the Kings of England*, London, 1660, p.503. Further

listings are cited in *EG*, vol.1, p.xlvi, n.1.
31 *EG*, vol.1, p.xlvii, point out the lack of evidence for J.G. McManaway's belief that considerably more of the plays may have been performed ('Philip Massinger and the Restoration Drama', *ELH: a Journal of English Literary History*, vol.1, 1934, pp.276–304).
32 See Bentley, *JCS*, vol.3, pp.314–15, 330, 333, 357, 395–6, 402–4, 412–13, 418–20.
33 McManaway, op. cit., pp.280, 287.
34 The situation also, no doubt, had an erotic appeal. In John Johnson's *Academy of Love* (1641) Massinger's work had figured in the Library of Love studied by 'our courtly dames' (*EG*, vol.1, p.xliii). The 1719 version of *The Bondman* was said to contain 'some Morality, and a World of Love'.
35 *EG*, vol.1, pp.309–10.
36 Cyrus Hoy, *Introductions, Notes, and Commentaries to Texts in 'The Dramatic Works of Thomas Dekker' Edited by Fredson Bowers*, 4 vols, Cambridge, 1980, vol.3, p.194. The subject of *Tyrannic Love* (1669) may have been suggested by the 1667–8 revival of *The Virgin Martyr* (Charles E. Ward, 'Massinger and Dryden', *ELH: a Journal of English Literary History*, vol.2, 1935, pp.263–6).
37 *Ball*, p.33.
38 Aubrey mentions Massinger or his widow as a pensioner of the 4th Earl of Pembroke in J. Britton (ed.), *The Natural History of Wiltshire*, London, 1847, p.91 and Andrew Clark (ed.), *Brief Lives*, Oxford, 2 vols, 1898, vol.2, pp.54–5. Wood and Langbaine were preceded by the brief references in Edward Phillips, *Theatrum Poetarum Anglicanorum*, London, 1675, p.151 and William Winstanley, *The Lives of the Most Famous English Poets*, London, 1687, p.139.
39 Gerard Langbaine, *Momus Triumphans: Or, the Plagiaries of the English Stage*, London, 1688, Preface, a3.
40 See McManaway, op. cit., on possible borrowings in several other plays c.1670–1700.
41 James Wright, *Country Conversations*, London, 1694, p.16.
42 J.R. Sutherland (ed.), *Three Plays by Nicholas Rowe*, London, 1929, pp.25–6; Donald B. Clark, 'An Eighteenth Century Adaptation of Massinger', *Modern Language Quarterly*, vol.13, 1952, pp.239–40; Sutherland, ed. cit., p.28.
43 George Birkbeck Hill (ed.), *Lives of the English Poets*, 3 vols, Oxford, 1935, vol.2, p.67.
44 James M. Osborn (ed.), Joseph Spence, *Observations, Anecdotes, and Characters of Books and Men*, 2 vols, Oxford, 1966, vol.1, pp.185, 183; Horace Walpole, in 1777, still dislikes 'metaphoric diction' in the tragedies of Shakespeare, Beaumont and Fletcher, and Massinger

(W.S. Lewis and others (eds), *The Yale Edition of Horace Walpole's Correspondence*, 48 vols, Oxford and New Haven, 1937–84, vol.41, p.372).
45. Robert Dodsley (ed.), *A Select Collection of Old Plays*, 12 vols, 1744, vol.1, p.xxxvi; cp. Thomas Hayward [William Oldys] (ed.), *The British Muse*, 3 vols, London, 1738, vol.1, title-page.
46. Hayward, op. cit., vol.1, p.xvi.
47. Dodsley, op. cit., vol.1, p.xxxvi. *The British Muse* did not sell well, but was used by Dodsley, Lamb, and Scott. Dodsley's collection did sell well, and clearly did much to stimulate growth of interest in 'the old drama' (Marie June Harley, 'The Eighteenth-Century Interest in English Drama Before 1640 Outside Shakespeare', MA thesis, Birmingham, 1962, pp.289–90, 292).
48. Brian Vickers (ed.), *Shakespeare: the Critical Heritage 1623–1801*, 6 vols, London and Boston, 1974–81, vol.5, pp.12, 43.
49. Thomas Coxeter (ed.), *The Dramatic Works of Philip Massinger*, 4 vols, London, 1761, vol.1, p.18.
50. Aaron Hill, *Works*, 4 vols, London, 1753, vol.2, pp.315, 319.
51. Marilyn Butler, *Romantics, Rebels and Reactionaries: English Literature and its Background 1760–1830*, Oxford, 1981, p.16.
52. Vickers, op. cit., vol.3, pp.12–13.
53. ibid., vol.2, pp.16–17.
54. ibid., vol.4, p.26.
55. *EG*, vol.1, p.1.
56. George Colman, *Prose on Several Occasions*, 3 vols, London, 1787, vol.1, p.x.
57. Harley, op. cit., p.240. The degree of general ignorance about most Renaissance dramatists before the 1770s is suggested by Capell's listing of Fletcher, Shirley, Middleton, Massinger, Brome, 'and others' as the props of Jonson's throne at a time when Shakespeare 'was held in disesteem' (*Mr William Shakspeare his Comedies, Histories, and Tragedies*, 10 vols, London, 1768, vol.1, p.14).
58. Katherine C. Balderston (ed.), *Thraliana: the Diary of Mrs. Hester Lynch Thrale (Later Mrs Piozzi) 1776–1809*, 2 vols, Oxford, 1942, vol.1, p.448.
59. Ball, p.43. In addition there were performances of Kemble's two-act *Roman Actor* (1781–2, 1796) and his version of *The Maid of Honour* with Sarah Siddons as Camiola (1785), another production of the same play at Chester (1785), a revival of *The City Madam* alteration possibly first played in 1771 (1783), Bate's the *Magic Picture* (1783–4), and an alteration of *The Bashful Lover* (1798). See the Stage History sections on each play in *EG*, and Donald J. Rulfs, 'Reception of the Elizabethan Playwrights on the London Stage 1776–1833', *Studies in*

Philology, vol.46, 1949, pp.58–63.
60 Ball, pp.40–1.
61 Harley, op. cit., pp.113, 171, 183.
62 Thomas Davies, *The Life of Philip Massinger*, in John Monck Mason (ed.), *The Dramatick Works of Philip Massinger*, 4 vols, London, 1779, vol.1, pp.lviii, lxv, lxvii.
63 *EG*, vol.1, p.xlviii.
64 Monck Mason, ed. cit., vol.1, p.vi; John Ferriar, 'Essay on the Dramatick Writings of Massinger' (1786), in William Gifford (ed.), *The Plays of Philip Massinger*, 4 vols, London, 1805, vol.1, p.cx; Charles Dibdin, *A Complete History of the English Stage*, 5 vols, London, [1797–1800], vol.3, p.240.
65 Marilyn Butler, op. cit., pp.18, 35.
66 Monck Mason, op. cit., p.iv.
67 Coxeter, op. cit., vol.2, p.341; Monck Mason, op. cit., p.vi.
68 Dibdin, op. cit., vol.3, p.233.
69 ibid., vol.3, p.232; Ferriar, op. cit., pp.cxxiv, cxxvii.
70 Gifford, ed. cit., vol.1, p.343; vol.4, p.583.
71 ibid., vol.1, pp.xlii, xliii.
72 P.P. Howe (ed.), *The Complete Works of William Hazlitt*, 21 vols, London, 1930–34, vol.11, pp.114–15.
73 [Walter Scott (ed.)], *The Ancient British Drama*, 3 vols, London, 1810–14, vol.1, p.vi; Ford, more surprisingly, is also omitted because of the edition being prepared by Weber (p.vii). *The Fatal Dowry*, *The Bondman*, and *A New Way to Pay Old Debts* were in fact included in Scott's *The Modern English Drama*, 5 vols, London, 1811.
74 Miss [E.W.] Macauley, *Tales of the Drama*, London, 1822, pp.vii, vi.
75 Joyce Hemlow and others (eds), *Letters and Journals of Fanny Burney*, 12 vols, Oxford, 1972–84, vol.9 (Warren Derry, ed.), p.48, n.7.
76 *EG*, vol.1, p.lvi.
77 *The Annual Review*, vol.7 1808, p.568. Lamb wrote to Coleridge on 7 June 1809, 'I am . . . obliged to you I believe for a Review in the Annual, am I not?' (Edwin Marrs, Jr (ed.), *The Letters of Charles and Mary Anne Lamb*, Ithaca and London, 3 vols, 1975–8, vol.3, p.12.)
78 Thomas Campbell, *Specimens of the British Poets*, 7 vols, London, 1819, vol.1, pp.224–5.
79 George Watson (ed.), *Biographia Literaria*, London, 1965, p.12. No comments on Massinger by Wordsworth are recorded, but he did buy copies of his work (see No. 25(d)). Southey included numerous quotations from him, many of them illustrative of historical customs, in John Wood Warter (ed.), *Southey's Common-Place Book*, series 4, London, 1849–51.
80 Howe, ed. cit., vol.6, pp.245, 193.
81 Frederick L. Jones (ed.), *The Letters of Percy Bysshe Shelley*, 2 vols,

Oxford, 1964, vol.2, p.200; H.F.B. Brett-Smith and C.E. Jones (eds), *The Works of Thomas Love Peacock*, 10 vols, London, 1924–34, vol.8, pp.183, 119; Emerson, *English Traits*, London, [1856], p.3.
82 Thomas Medwin, *The Life of Percy Bysshe Shelley*, ed. H. Buxton Forman, Oxford, 1913, p.256; William Godwin, letter to Shelley, 10 December 1812, in Jones, ed. cit., vol.1, p.341.
83 *The Gentleman's Magazine*, May 1833, p.416.
84 Exceptions include the 1803 broadsheet of *The Bondman*, I.iii.213– 368, published 'at the time an invasion by Napoleon was feared', *EG*, vol.1, p.309. For the use of Paris's defence of drama in *The Roman Actor* to protest against censorship and repression in 1822 see Patterson, op. cit., pp.87–8.
85 Robert James Mackintosh (ed.), *Memoirs of the Life of Sir James Mackintosh*, 2 vols, London, 1835, vol.1, p.363; *EG*, vol.2, p.193, n.2. The play was generally well received when an alteration substituting guardian and ward for father and daughter was eventually performed in 1834.
86 See Vickers, op. cit., vol.6, p.5.
87 Campbell, op. cit., vol.3, p.250.
88 *The Critical Review*, series 5, vol.3, 1816, p.190.
89 George Vandenhoff, *Leaves from an Actor's Note-Book*, New York, 1860, p.22.
90 Thomas Sadler (ed.), *Diary, Reminiscences, and Correspondence of Henry Crabb Robinson*, 2 vols, London, 3rd edn, 1872, vol.1, p.268 (12 February 1816).
91 Betty T. Bennett (ed.), *The Letters of Mary Wollstonecraft Shelley*, Baltimore and London, 3 vols, 1980–8, vol.1, p.416 (22 March(?) 1824); see also pp.449–50, 489, 493.
92 [Bryan Waller Proctor], *The Life of Edmund Kean*, 2 vols in 1, London, 1835, vol.2, p.141.
93 ibid., p.141.
94 Bennett, ed. cit., vol.1, p.416 (22 March(?) 1824); A. Hayward (ed.), *Autobiography, Letters and Literary Remains of Mrs. Piozzi (Thrale)*, 2 vols, London, 1861, vol.2, pp.183, 186 (27 December 1816 and 4 January 1817).
95 See further Joseph Donohue, *Theatre in the Age of Kean*, Oxford, 1975, pp.59–61.
96 See Joseph W. Donohue, Jr, *Dramatic Character in the English Romantic Age*, Princeton, 1970, pp.88–9, 229. The villain–hero shaded into 'the Byronic man of melancholy grandeur' (p.276).
97 ibid., p. 258.
98 *Ball*, pp.405–6; for reproductions of some of the paintings and engravings see ibid., facing pp.52, 136, 186, 200, 284.
99 ibid., p.67.

100 *The Duke of Milan* . . . *With Alterations and Additions*, London, 1816, p.67.
101 On the size of the theatres and the effect of this, see further Donohue, *Theatre in the Age of Kean*, p.164 and Vickers, op. cit., vol.6, p.63.
102 Donohue, *Theatre in the Age of Kean*, pp.62–3.
103 ibid., p.164.
104 *The Critical Review*, series 5, vol.3, 1816, p.190. Cp. Proctor, op. cit., vol.2, pp.138–9.
105 *The Annual Review*, vol.7, 1808, p.563.
106 *The Morning Advertiser*, 25 May 1852, and *Reynolds' Newspaper*, 30 May 1852 (quoted by Ball, p.149) on the American actor Buchanan in London; see especially the accounts of J.B. Booth in *Ball*, pp.195–231. His son, Edwin Booth, went on in the role until 1887 and the play remained generally more popular in America than in Britain into the early twentieth century.
107 Philip Kelley and Ronald Hudson (eds), *The Brownings' Correspondence*, 7 vols so far, London, 1984–9, vol.3, p.208; vol.5, p.280.
108 William Toynbee (ed.), *The Diaries of William Charles Macready 1833–1851*, 2 vols, London, 1912, vol.1, p.109.
109 Madeline House and others (eds), *The Letters of Charles Dickens*, 6 vols so far, Oxford, 1965–88, vol.4, p.717; vol.1, pp.520, 523; see also vol.6, p.273. Dickens played Eustace to Forster's Charles in *The Elder Brother* in 1846 (vol.4, pp.448–9).
110 Henry Woudhuysen, *The Times Literary Supplement*, 8 July 1983, p.726. There are earlier comparisons between Dickens and Massinger in George Saintsbury, *A History of Elizabethan Literature*, London, 1887, p.399 (shared plot improbabilities) and Herbert J.C. Grierson, *The First Half of the Seventeenth Century*, London and Edinburgh, 1906, p.129 (characters who impress without intelligibility).
111 Ball, pp.157–9.
112 R. Shelton Mackenzie (ed.), *Noctes Ambrosianae*, 5 vols, New York, 1865–6, p.179 (originally November 1832); *The Complete Works of Lord Macaulay*, 12 vols, London, 1898, vol.7, p.62, vol.8, p.205, vol.9, p.341; Herbert M. Schueller and Robert L. Peters (eds), *The Letters of John Addington Symonds*, 3 vols, Detroit, 1967–9, vol.1, pp.487–8 (6 July 1864), and vol.3, p.198 (9 January 1887).
113 J.H. Stonehouse (ed.), *Catalogue of the Library of Charles Dickens . . . Catalogue of the Library of W.M. Thackeray*, London, 1935, p.147; A.N.L. Munby (general editor), *Sale Catalogues of Libraries of Eminent Persons*, 12 vols, London, 1971–5, vol.1, p.352.
114 See, for example, S. Austin Allibone (ed.), *Poetical Quotations from Chaucer to Tennyson*, Philadelphia, 1875; Philip Hugh Dalbiac, *Dictionary of Quotations (English)*, London and New York, 1896.

115 J.S. Mill, 'Thoughts on Poetry and its Varieties' (1833), in John M. Robson and Jack Stillinger (eds), *Autobiography and Literary Essays*, Toronto, 1981, p.348.
116 Macaulay's *Works*, ed. cit., vol.9, p.341. Among the plays instanced are *The Elder Brother*, *The Picture*, and *The Fatal Dowry*.
117 Leslie Stephen, *Hours in a Library*, 3 vols, London, 1892, vol.2, p.142 (originally in *The Cornhill Magazine*, 1877).
118 Charles Kingsley, *Plays and Puritans*, London, 1873, pp.47–8.
119 Elizabeth Barrett Browning, 'The Book of the Poets', *Poetical Works*, Oxford, 1920, p.643 (originally in *The Athenaeum*, 1842).
120 Thomas Carlyle, review of W.G. Lockhart's *Life of Robert Burns* (1828), *Works*, 30 vols, London, 1896–9, vol.26, pp.267–8.
121 William Minto, *Characteristics of English Poets from Chaucer to Shirley*, Edinburgh and London, 1874, p.474.
122 George L. Craik, *Sketches of the History of Literature and Learning in England*, 6 vols, London, 1844–5, vol.3, p.205. He goes on (p.206) to assert the primacy of poetry in a contrast with Ford: 'Ford's blank verse is not so imposing as Massinger's; but it has often a delicate beauty, sometimes a warbling wildness and richness, beyond anything in Massinger's fuller swell'.
123 Maurice Chelli, *Le Drame de Massinger*, Lyon, 1923, p.343.
124 Minto, op. cit., pp.475, 477.
125 The engraving by R. Bocourt which is Symons's frontispiece makes Massinger look more melancholy and uncertain than the Grignion engraving used in the eighteenth-century editions, the version by Lascelles Hoppner in Gifford's edition, and the common original of all Massinger portraits, the Thomas Cross engraving in *Three New Playes*, 1655. (A quite different impression is given by the 1820 engraving by W.H. Worthington of John Thurston's version of the Cross picture: this presents a much more vigorous, earnest, and more nineteenth-century Massinger, the admired author of 1820 rather than the increasingly discredited figure of 1887.
126 Stephen, op. cit., pp.145–6; S.R. Gardiner, 'The Political Element in Massinger', *The Contemporary Review*, vol.28, 1876, pp.495–507.
127 Minto, op. cit., p.476.
128 Margot Heinemann, *Puritanism and Theatre: Thomas Middleton and Opposition Drama Under the Early Stuarts*, Cambridge, 1980, p.201.
129 David Patrick (ed.), *Chambers's Cyclopaedia of English Literature*, 3 vols, London and Edinburgh, 1902–3, vol.1, p.465.
130 W.J. Courthope, *A History of English Poetry*, 6 vols, London, 1895–1910, vol.4, p.357.
131 J.H.B. Masterman, *The Age of Milton*, London, 1897, p.78.
132 George Saintsbury, *A History of Elizabethan Literature*, London, 1887, pp.401, 394.

133 Masterman, op. cit., p.78.
134 Herbert J.C. Grierson, *The First Half of the Seventeenth Century*, Edinburgh, 1906, p.128; Oliver Elton, *The English Muse*, London, 1933, p.193. Cp. Felix E. Schelling, *Elizabethan Drama 1558–1642*, 2 vols, Boston and New York, 1908, vol.2, p.43.
135 A.H. Cruickshank, *Philip Massinger*, Oxford, 1920, pp.74, 119, 113.
136 Oliver Elton, *A Survey of English Literature 1780–1830*, 2 vols, 1912, p.374.
137 Richard Ferrar Patterson, *Six Centuries of English Literature*, 6 vols, London and Glasgow, 1933, vol.2, p.316.
138 Thomas Marc Parrott and Robert Hamilton Ball, *A Short View of Elizabethan Drama*, New York, 1943, p.268.
139 Cruickshank, op. cit., p.34; T.S. Eliot, 'Philip Massinger', *The Sacred Wood*, London, 1920, pp.123–43 (a reprint of Eliot's reviews of Cruickshank in *The Times Literary Supplement* of 27 May 1920 and *The Athenaeum* of 11 June 1920).

Note on the Text

The materials printed in this volume follow the original texts unless otherwise stated. Quotations from Massinger in the text are given in the form used by the authors, but to facilitate reference I have supplied act, scene, and line numbers from *EG* or, for *The Virgin Martyr*, from Fredson T. Bowers (ed.), *The Dramatic Works of Thomas Dekker*, 4 vols, Cambridge, 1953–61, vol.3. Original footnotes are, unless of particular significance, silently omitted. (Other omissions are indicated in the text.) My own notes and references are, wherever possible, included parenthetically; where length makes footnotes necessary, they are indicated by asterisks.

TEXTS

1. Nathan Field, Robert Daborne, and Philip Massinger

*c.*1613

The 'tripartite letter' which the three playwrights sent their employer Philip Henslowe was first published by Edmond Malone in 1790. It tells us little or nothing about contemporary responses to Massinger's work, but is included here because of its currency in the nineteenth century as a romantically 'melancholy' document (see Introduction, pp.27, 35–6).

Field (1587–1619/20) was one of the leading actors of his day as well as author of two unaided comedies, a number of collaborations with Fletcher and Massinger, and *The Fatal Dowry* (*c.*1617–19) with Massinger. Less is known of Daborne (?–1628?), only two of whose plays survive.

EG, vol.1, p.xvii.

Mr Hinchlow

You understand o^r vnfortunate extremitie, and I doe not thincke you so void of christianitie, but that you would throw so much money into the Thames as wee request now of you; rather then endanger so many innocent liues; you know there is x^1 more at least to be receaued of you for the play, wee desire you to lend vs v^1. of that, w^{c}h shall be allowed to you w^{t}hout w^{c}h wee cannot bee bayled, nor I play any more till this bee dispatch'd, it will loose you xx^1. ere the end of the next weeke, beside the hinderance of the next new play, pray Sr Consider our Cases wth humanitie, and now giue vs cause to acknowledge you our true freind in time of neede; wee haue entreated Mr Dauison to deliuer this note, as well to wittnesse yor loue as o^r promises, and

allwayes acknowledgment to be euer
  yor most thanckfull; and louing freinds,
                    Nat: Field

The mony shall be abated out of the mony remayns for the play of m^r Fletcher & owrs
                    Rob: Daborne

I have ever founde yow a true lovinge freind to mee & in soe small a suite it beeinge honest I hope yow will not faile vs.
                    Philip Massinger

To our most loving friend, Mr Philip Hinchlow, esquire, These.

2. John Taylor
1620

In *The Praise of Hemp-Seed* (1620) John Taylor (1578–1653), Thames boatman and 'water-poet', celebrates paper's preservation of authors old and new. The reference to Massinger suggests that he was well known earlier than might otherwise be expected (his first known non-collaborative plays probably date from 1621 at earliest); it seems that his work with Fletcher is, unusually, receiving acknowledgement. *All the Workes of Iohn Taylor the Water Poet*, London, 1630, p.72.

And many there are liuing at this day
Which doe in paper their true worth display:
As *Dauis*, *Drayton*, and the learned *Dun*,
Johnson, and *Chapman*, *Marston*, *Middleton*,
With *Rowley*, *Fletcher*, *Withers*, *Massinger*,

Heywood, and all the rest where e're they are,
Must say their lines but for the paper sheete
Had scarcely ground, whereon to set their feete.

3. Sir Thomas Jay
1629, 1630, 1633

Jay (?1598–1646) was M.P. for Netheravon in Wiltshire and Keeper of the King's Armouries (see further Donald Lawless, 'Sir Thomas Jay (Jeay)', *Notes and Queries*, vol.205, 1960, p.30). He was one of the three 'much Honoured, and most true Friends' to whom Massinger dedicated *The Roman Actor* in 1629.

See Introduction, pp.5–6, for the context of Jay's verses in the 'Untun'd Kennell' quarrel.

EG, vol.3, pp.16, 196–7, and vol.2, p.296.

(a) *The Roman Actor* (1629).

To his deare Friend the Author.
[Signed '*T.I.*'].

I AM no great admirer of the Playes,
Poets, or Actors, that are now adayes:
Yet in this Worke of thine me thinkes I see
Sufficient reason for Idolatrie.
Each line thou hast taught CEASAR is, as high
As Hee could speake, when groueling Flatterie,
And His own pride (forgetting Heavens rod)
By his Edicts stil'd himselfe great Lord and God.
By thee againe the Lawrell crownes His Head;
And thus reviu'd, who can affirme him dead?

Such power lyes in this loftie straine as can
Giue Swords, and legions to DOMITIAN.
And when thy PARIS pleades in the defence
Of Actors, every grace, and excellence
Of Argument for that subject, are by Thee
Contracted in a sweete Epitome.
Nor doe thy Women the tyr'd Hearers vexe,
With language no way proper to their sexe.
Iust like a cunning Painter thou lets fall
Copies more faire then the Originall.
I'll adde but this. From all the moderne Playes
The Stage hath lately borne, this winnes the Bayes.
And if it come to tryall boldly looke
To carrie it cleere, Thy witnesse being thy Booke.

(b)   *The Picture* (1630)

To his worthy friend M^r. *Philip Massinger*, vpon his *Tragæcomædie* stiled, *The Picture*.

Me thinkes I heere some busy Criticke say
Who's this that singly vshers on this Play?
'Tis boldnes I confesse, and yet perchance
It may be constur'd love, not arrogance.
I do not heere vpon this leafe intrude
By praysing one, to wrong a multitude.
Nor do I thinke that all are tyed to be
(Forc'd by my vote) in the same creed with me.
Each man hath liberty to iudge; free will,
 At his owne pleasure to speake good, or ill.
But yet your Muse alreadie's knowne so well
Her worth will hardly find an infidell.
Heere she hath drawne a picture, which shall lye
Safe for all future times to practisse by.
What ere shall follow are but Coppies, some
Preceding workes were types of this to come.
'Tis your owne liuely image, and setts forth
When we are dust the beauty of your worth.

He that shall dully read and not aduance
Ought that is heere betrayes his ignorance.
Yet whosoeuer beyond desert commends
Errs more by much then he that reprehends,
For prayse misplac'd, and honor set vpon
A worthlesse subiect is detraction.
I cannot sin so heere, vnlesse I went
About, to stile you only excellent.
Apollo's guifts are not confind alone
To your dispose, He hath more heires then one,
And such as do deriue from his blest hand
A large inheritance in the Poets land
As well as you, nor are you I assure
My selfe so enuious, but you can endure
To heere their praise, whose worth long since was knowne
And iustly to, prefer'd before your owne.
I know you would take it for an iniury,
(And 'tis a well becomming modesty)
To be paraleld with *Beaumont*, or to heare
Your name by some to partiall friend writt neere
Vnequal'd *Ionson*: being men whose fire
At distance, and with reuerence you admire.
Do so and you shall finde your gaine will bee
Much more by yeelding them prioritie
Then with a certainety of losse to hould
A foolish competition; Tis to bould
A tasque, and to be shunde, nor shall my prayse
With to much waight ruine, what it would rayse.

(c) *A New Way to Pay Old Debts* (1633)

To his friend the Author.

*You may remember how you chid me when
I ranckt you equall with those glorious men;
Beaumont, and Fletcher; if you loue not praise
You must forbeare the publishing of playes.
The craftie Mazes of the cunning plot;*

The polish'd phrase; the sweet expressions; got
Neither by theft, nor violence; the conceipt
Fresh, and unsullied; All is of weight,
Able to make the captiue Reader know
I did but iustice when I plac't you so.
A shamefast Blushing would become the brow
Of some weake Virgin writer; we allow
To you a kind of pride; and there where most
Should blush at commendations, you should boast.
If any thinke I flatter, let him looke
Of from my idle trifles on thy Booke.

4. Thomas May
1629

May (1595–1650) was best known in the seventeenth century as the translator and continuer of Lucan's *Pharsalia*, and as a parliamentary apologist (his history of the Long Parliament appeared in 1647). His plays include the classical tragedies *Cleopatra* (1626) and *Julia Agrippina* (1628); like *The Roman Actor*, which the poem below commends, these plays made close use of Roman sources under the inspiration of Jonson's *Sejanus* and *Catiline*. For the political implications of classicism in the 1620s and 1630s see Martin Butler, 'Romans in Britain: the Roman Actor and the Early Stuart Classical Play', in Douglas Howard (ed.), *Philip Massinger: a Critical Reassessment*, Cambridge, 1985, pp. 139–70.

EG, vol. 3, p. 18.

To his deseruing Friend Mr. Philip Massinger, *vpon his Tragœdie, the Roman Actor.*

PARIS, the best of Actors in his age
Acts yet, and speakes vpon our Roman Stage
Such lines by thee, as doe not derogate

From *Romes* proud heights, and Her then learned State.
Nor great *Domitians* favour; not th'embraces
Of a faire Empresse, nor those often graces
Which from th'applauding Theaters were pay'd
To his braue Action, nor His ashes layd
In the *Flaminian* way, where people strow'd
His Graue with flowers, and *Martialls* wit bestow'd
A lasting Epitaph, not all these same
Doe adde so much renowne to *Paris* name,
As this that thou present'st his Historie
So well to vs. For which in thankes would Hee
(If that His soule, as thought *Pithagoras*
Could into any of our Actors passe)
Life to these Lines by action gladly giue
Whose Pen so well has made His storie liue.

5. Philip Massinger
1630

This and the two items which follow are exchanges in the 'Untun'd Kennell' war of the theatres (see Introduction, pp.4–7). Massinger, Shirley, Heywood, and others were ranged against a courtly group led by Thomas Carew and his supporter William Davenant. Carew sparked off the quarrel by exalting Davenant's *The Just Italian* (a failure at the Blackfriars), at the expense of the audience and actors at the Phoenix or Cockpit. Shirley's *The Grateful Servant* had been well received at the Phoenix and its commenders, including Massinger, replied with attacks on Davenant's play as ribald and bombastic. Massinger further attacked Carew in the pointed prologue to the 1630 revival of his Phoenix play of 1621–2 *The Maid of Honour*. In a poem, probably by Davenant (No. 6), Carew was defended as author of 'ditties fit only for the eares of Kings', and Massinger attacked as a crude moralist and players' hireling. Massinger replied (No.7) by asserting his and the actors' professional integrity as against his opponent's cowardly anonymity and Carew's perceived right to judge as the 'Poets Tribune'.

The nub of the argument was not so much rivalry between two theatres – Massinger, although chief dramatist of the King's Men, took advantage of a revival to rally to the support of the Queen's company – as between different conceptions of the role and status of poets and playwrights. The three poems (Nos 5–7) are from Trumbull Add. MS 51, Berkshire Record Office, Reading, as edited by Peter Beal in 'Massinger at Bay: Unpublished Verses in a War of the Theatres', *YES*, vol. 10 1980, pp. 190–203.

Prologue to ye Mayde of honour

To all y^t are come hither, and haue brought
noe expectacon beyond the thought
of power in our performance; that this day
looke for noe more, nor lesse, then a newe play
May giue full satisfaccon for; a free
and happie welcome. May such euer bee
feasted with rarities. But to those that are
Resolu'd before they tast it, that noe fare
Cook'd or seru'd vp heere can giue content
Our Poet, in his owne strength Confident,
fforbids mee to presente a bended knee
or with one looke of seruile obsequye
to Court or grace or fauour. He well knowes
how much of care and vigilance that man owes
to such as would seeme Critiques of the age,
that Dares to 'expose his labours on ye stage,
And y^t one Poeme in this kind aske more
invention and iudgm^t: then a score
Of Chamber Madrigalls or loose raptures brought
In a Mart. booke from Italy and taught
To speake our Englishe Diale[c]t.* Nor are we

---

* 'Carew had lived in Italy in 1613–15 . . . A number of his lyrics were translations or imitations of Italian originals' (Beal, p. 30). 'Loose raptures' refers to Carew's erotic poem 'A Rapture'.

soe freighted wth a single Calumny,
publish[d] to our Disgrace, as to confesse,
by beeing silent, such a Guiltinesse
as wee are taxt with. Any sence that hee
or hath or can write in our deliuery
should loose noe lustre. But I doe forgett
The busines y^t I came for. Yo^u are mett
to see and heare a play. Doe soe and then
Wee strongely hope, iuditious Gentlemen,
you may report when yo^u haue look't vpon her
shee is a Maide compos'd of worth & hono^r./

6. William Davenant(?)

1630

'To my honored ffriend Mr Thomas Carew' is assumed to be the work of Davenant, defending Carew against Massinger as Carew had earlier championed him against Massinger's associate James Shirley (see headnote to No. 5). Davenant (1606–68) is known variously as Caroline playwright and masque librettist, royalist captain, author of *Gondibert* (1651), deviser of 1650s operatic spectacles, Restoration leader of the Duke's company, and adapter of Shakespeare.

Beal, 'Massinger at Bay', pp.193–5 (see No. 5).

To my honored ffriend Mr Thomas Carew at S^r: Richard Leightons house in Boswell Court these/

S^r: I haue mett wth a coppie of the Prologue
of the mayde of honour wherein it is apparant the
poet points at yo^u, yet I was tould yo^u wanted not
Confidence to heare it one ye stage whilst I forfeited
my patience but to reade it in my Chamber, w^{ch}
after a pause recou^{r}ing I thought fitt to convey

the opinion I hold of it and yo^u to yor owne hands
in these hastie leines./

Soe the rude Carpenter or Mason may
his axe or trowell in the ballance lay
With Euclides learned pen, & 'cause he frames
Circles & squares, nought knowinge but y^e names,
pretend to riuall him in his greate arte;
[so] this Mechanicke play=wright craue[s] a parte
in sacreet Poesey [&] bring[s] his flat
dull dialogues fraught w^{t}h insipit chatt
Into the scale with thy sweete Muse, wch sings
ditties fit only for the eares of Kings.
I knowe yo^u flinge not soe yor houres away
But I have read his workes, & by the bay
That crownes Apollo, I can nothinge finde
but a wilde desert, emptie aire & winde;
only some shreds of Seneca; rude
Modells of vice and virtue vnpursued;
no Character entire, but spight of arte
The ffishes fowle blacke tayle to thi'vpper parte
of a faire woeman ioyn[d]; lines forc[d], ruffe,
Botch'd & vnshap'd in fashion, Course in stuffe.
Yet hee this spurious issue poems calls.
Had I thy sleighted Chamber Madrigalls
Or [those] loose raptures wrote, I'de place my rimes
Equall wth any in our tounge or times.
There station they may Claime in ye first ranks
farre boue the humble forme of his lame blanks.
But thou art Charg'd wth an Italyan theft
and not tould where, noe meanes to purge thee left;
which howe can he impute, much lesse detect,
That neu^r vnderstood y^t dialect?
Yet they that reade thy naturall straines may knowe
thou nor for language Canst nor fancie owe.
But now not yo^u alone are wrong'd but all
Ingenious Gentlemen whose freedomes fall
by this his arte. Shall wee y^t feed ye knaues
ffor our owne sporte & pastime bee there slaues
That liue by vs, not dare to iudge but stand
in awe of such a Mercenary hand?

Yo^r Censure of those bawlers I dare sweare
is seconded by euery tunefull eare
That's not Engag'd like his. Alas, hee'le say
hee pleads his Masters cause, receiues the pay
And salary of a hirelinge, which brings
The oyle to grease his hinges when hee sings.
How poore a trade is there! Were it not more
Gentile to squire some prostitutes whore
Then bee a players Brauo? This excuse
frees him from blame & yo^u from all abuse.
I know such men as these haue made the name
of Poetts cheape, & quencht the risinge flame
of nobler witts; which might adorne this age
did not such roaringe whifflers keepe the stage.
I know yo^u fitt for a more glorious charge.
Yet till the state call, while yo^u liue at large,
spare not yor pen. This frontlese impudence
arriues not at yor heighth. Y^e difference
twixt yo^u & him will well be vnderstood
whil'st yo^u for pleasure sing, he sweats for food.
   I of the tribe of yor admirers ame
And but that title know noe other name./

7. Philip Massinger

1630

Massinger's reply to No. 6 should be seen not least as a blow in the battle to establish the respectability of writing public plays rather than private poems, following on the first volume of Jonson's controversially titled *Works* of 1616 and the Shakespeare folio of 1623 edited by the actor–sharers Heminge and Condell. At the same time, there is an anxiety that the theatre itself will be taken over by new, fashionable and immoral dramatists financed by patrons like

Carew. Massinger is defending professional playwrights, professional actors (though we do not know how far the King's Men liked their staple dramatist's championing of their rivals and attack on new drama produced at the Blackfriars), and his own conception of his moral and skilfully worked art.

Beal, 'Massinger at Bay', pp.196–9 (see No. 5).

A Charme for a Libeller/
I'me in my Circle & I haue thee here,
ragg of a Rime &, if thou dar'st, appeare,
son of the people, thinge wthout a name.
How shall I raise thee or wth what arte frame
an answeare to thy nothinge? Take what shape
thou can'st put on, Confirme thy selfe the ape
of thy admired Idoll, proude to bee
knowne for his parasite & profess't to bee;
or if soe habited thou'[r]t not secure
Come armed wth thine owne slaunders. Ile endure
thy seight & teach thy ignorance reasons why
Thou art oblig'd to giue thy selfe the lye.
As thou hast hope y^t thy greate patron shall
nod on thee from the stage, or, if there fall
a place of witt in's Colledge, to supply
The Roome due to his slauishe flattery,
or when he shall comaund thee to repeate
his verses in a Tau^rne for thy meate,
answeare my coniuracon & mainetaine
What thou hast writ wth full sail'd hopes to staine
My fame. Amongst good men will it not bee.
Must I make warr against an enemie
That dares not shew his face, a bird at night,
Whose t[w]o Calumnies* flye & abhore ye light?
Haue at thee howsoeuer and, though I
know thy base libell meritts noe replie,
but should in my iust scorne expire, I'le spare

---

*The two calumnies are clearly, as Beal suggests, p.200, Carew's verses for Davenant's *The Just Italian* and No. 6.

a vacant hower to stripp thy mallice bare
and naked to yᵉ world; nor shall the brand
of infamie stamp't on thee by my hand
be wash't of by thy Barbers subtillest arte
but still growe fresher (but if now I parte
with mine owne modest language let it bee
Imputed to yᵉ spurrulous subiect, thee).
Yoᵘ mett a coppie of my Prologue, true;
'Twas therefore writt. Why did it nettle yoᵘ,
Beinge Aim'de at an other? 'Twas my end
To haue it vnderstood. Yoʳ honored freind
hear[d] it vpon yᵉ stage with confidence
Like another Socrates, while yoʳ patience
was forefeited in yoʳ Chamber to reade that
In wᶜʰ yoᵘ found his reuerence pointed at
high treason to Apollo. Why is hee
The Poets Tribu[n]e, and authority
Conferr'd on him to free or to condemne
all that is writt or spoke by other men?
Was't death vnto my creditt but to fall
vpon his satire or not giue the wall
as it pass'd by tryvmphant? I ne're sawe
his patent nor can thinke I brake the lawe
of mannors or humanity to denie
What he affirmes to mine owne iniury.
Wᵗh mee his ipse dixit shall not passe
how e're yoᵘ hold him Pythagoras.
And sworne to this assertion this offence
drew yoʳ blacke Censure, wᵗʰ such violence
pronounced on mee & mine; but may I bee
Esteem'd thy equall (wᶜʰ is a decree
beneath all basenes) if for this abuse
Thou scap the whip of my incensed Muse.
Thy coarse comparison wᵗʰ the non=sence name
of a Mechanique playwright (to my shame
in thy vote in p[r]ose) nor yet thy flattery
Grose as thy Clownishe iudgmᵗ: fix one mee.
Nor Can thy witlesse malice ouerthrow
The buildinge of that Meritt whiche I owe
To knoweinge mens opinions. I should feare

my innocence if I found it any where
Protected by thy ignorance, for the praise
of such a buffon must impaire not raise
whats most by him comended; & 'twere fitt,
As hee will keepe ye credite of his witt,
That man of men who to thy wonders sings
Ditties fitt only for the eares of kings
Should charge thy toadelike muse vpon ye paine
of his displeasure ne're to croake againe.
That baye that crowneth yor Apollos head,
though safe from leightninge, would be withered
If thou sweare by it. Rather take ye name
of skenner in thy mouth or the greate fame
Purchas'[d] by Kendall;* & soe it may bee,
Yo^u being para[l]ells, the periury
may passe vnpunisht; or when next thou arte
to vent thy trumperies let them in some part
bee guilded o're wth seeminge truthes & not
deserue to haue all answear'd wth one blott
as what is writ of mee does. Therefore I
passe by it wth contempt & now applie
my selfe (though it is needles) to defend
my Masters cause, ye players. To what end
are they puok'd or why still knaues? What fee
or pension did they ere receiue from thee
Or such as though art? They are those indeed
to whom yo^u owe ye happines to feed.
The stage, yor accademy & what yo^u learne there
prepares yor entertainem^t: eur^y where.
Yo^u might sit dumbe & starue else. Is't in mee
And such as write a crime to take the fee
Due to our labours & deseru'd? Though thou
ar't not wth reason to bee won, allowe
What's warranted by example. Terrence (hee
whoe still liues famous for ye purity
of language) to ye willinge Ediles sould
That Comedy in wch tis said ye bold,
victorious and virtuous Scipio lent

*The references to 'skenner' and 'Kendall' are unexplained.

his odes; & tis affirmd wth one consent
of learned men that Statius, hauinge read
th'incestuous issue of Jocasta's bed
with admiracon, though ye benches were
Crack't wth the weight of such as throng'd to [h]eare
his noble Poem, had departed thence
with theire praise onely, but without defence
against ye stinge of hunger had not hee
with caution brought Agaues tragedies
To Paris and so found those wants supplied
By a prayer, wch the Romane Peeres denide
To his greate worke.* Champ on this bitt and then
Let it bee iudg'd whoe are the baser men:
Wee that descend from our owne height no more
Then those old Clasique Poets did before
or yo^u o' the wiser few. Indeed yo^u write
In corners and amonge yor selues recite
yor Compositions & [mutually],
The blind, the lame, you well agree
To crie vpon an other and soe rest,
not daringe to indure the publique test.
And what's yor frequent subiect? but to frame
seruile Encomions to some greate mans name
Or when hee's burn't vp with libidinous fires
like Panders to make way for his desires
With ruine of a chastety. And this
Y'are deerely paid for, & 'tis not amisse
yo^u feele noe scruple for it though I blush
To looke vpon yor scarlet and yor plushe
Thus got, & greiue to see such Rib'aulds flinge
There whorish filth into the virgine springe.
The Brauo's name in scorne to mee imputed
With a cudgell not my penn may be confuted;
And till then dabble one. The state noe doubte
Will nee're be preiudic'd though such snuffe stinke out
without imployment. Frontlesse impudence
To thinke it can need him, an Insolence

*The classical references are to Terence's *Andria* (according to Donatus) and to Statius' *Thebaid* and lost play *Agave* (to which Massinger had perhaps also alluded in *The Roman Actor*, I.i.1–2).

neighbouringe on treason! But yo^u are not worth
A Satire, or my Gall. Teeme and bringe forth
More prodigies, & hauinge tir'd the time
And all mens patience wth yor [pumpt] for rime,
To giue a period to yor infamie
Write yor Epita[p]h & sease to bee.

 Noe other mans admirer nor my owne,
 Conceale thy name, I feare not to bee knowen
  Phillip Massinger./

8. Sir Henry Herbert
1631, 1638

Sir Henry Herbert (1595–1673), half-brother of Lord Herbert of Cherbury and brother of George Herbert, was Master of the Revels from 1623.

Following the refusal in (a) Massinger changed the setting of *Believe As You List* from the modern to the ancient world, with King Antiochus' story replacing Sebastian's. The substitution of new names which are the metrical equivalents of the old suggests that the revision was minimal (see Charles J. Sisson (ed.), *Believe As You List*, Oxford, 1928, pp.xix–xx) and the parallel between its hero's plight and that of Frederick of Bohemia remains clear; nevertheless, Herbert licensed the new version for performance on 6 May 1631.

The speech from *The King and the Subject* quoted in (b) caused offence partly because of the evident allusion to the raising of forced loans. The play is lost.

Joseph Quincy Adams (ed.), *The Dramatic Records of Sir Henry Herbert*, New Haven and London, 1917, pp.19, 22–3.

(a)
This day being the 11 of Janu. 1630 [i.e. 1631], I did refuse to allow of a play of Messinger's because itt did contain dangerous matter, as the deposing of Sebastian king of Portugal, by Philip the [Second,] and ther being a peace sworen twixte the kings of England and Spayne.

(b)
Received of Mr. Lowens for my paines about Messinger's play called *The King and the Subject*, 2 June, 1638, 11. 0. 0.

The name of *The King and the Subject* is altered, and I allowed the play to bee acted, the reformations most strictly observed, and not otherwise, the 5th of June, 1638.

At Greenwich the 4 of June, Mr. W. Murray, gave mee power from the king to allowe of the play, and tould me that hee would warrant it.

> Monys? Wee'le rayse supplies what ways we please,
> And force you to subscribe to blanks, in which
> We'le mulct you as wee shall thinke fitt. The Caesars
> In Rome were wise, acknowledginge no lawes
> But what their swords did ratifye, the wives
> And daughters of the senators bowinge to
> Their wills, as deities, &c.

This is a peece taken out of Philip Messingers play, called *The King and the Subject*, and entered here for ever to bee remembered by my son and those that cast their eyes on it, in honour of Kinge Charles, my master, who readinge over the play at Newmarket, set his marke upon the place with his owne hande, and in thes words:

'This is too insolent, and to bee changed.'

Note, that the poett makes it the speech of a king, Don Pedro, king of Spayne, and spoken to his subjects.

9. William Heminge
1631–2

Heminge(s) (1602–>53) was a son of John Heminge, 'Shakespeare's friend and editor, the veteran leader of the King's company'; in 1630 he inherited his father's shares in the Globe and Blackfriars, but sold them in 1633 (Bentley, *JCS*, vol.4, pp.540–1). He wrote several plays including *The Fatal Contract* (*c.* 1638–9).

In the 'Elegy on Randolph's Finger' the Fairy Queen changes the severed finger of Heminge's friend the playwright Thomas Randolph (1605–35) into a maypole. The long and frequently irreverent list of her servants, who sing and dance a fairy ring around the pole, includes John Ford deep in his dump, 'the squibbing Middleton', the prolific Heywood, poor and red faced, and Brome (Broom) going before to sweep the way. Those listed below, near the beginning, fare rather better. Conceivably the compliment to Massinger is two-edged (cp. Introduction, p.6).

From a manuscript copy of a poem headed 'Mr Thomas Randall the Poett, his finger being cut of by a Riotous Gentleman, his friende m^r William Hemminge made this Eligie on the same', Bodleian Library MS Ashmole 38, fol.26.

The fluente Flettcher, Beaumonte riche In sence
for Complement and Courtshypes quintesence[,]
Ingenious Shakespeare, Messenger that knowes
the strength to wright or plott In verse or prose
whose easye pegasus Can Ambell ore
some threscore Myles of fancye In an hower[,]
Clowd grapling Chapman whose Aeriall mynde
soares att philosophye and strikes ytt blynd[.]

10. Sir Aston Cokaine
1632, 1640–58, 1647–58

Cokaine (1608–84), created a baronet in 1642, was 'evidently one of the gentlemanly patrons of the drama who were prominent in the audiences at the Blackfriars and Cockpit in the thirties' (Bentley, *JCS*, vol.3, p.167) and himself wrote two plays and a masque. In addition to the poems below he wrote a commendatory verse on *The Maid of Honour* in 1632 and mentioned Massinger favourably in his 'Præludium' to Richard Brome's *Five New Playes* of 1653. His joint epitaph on Fletcher and Massinger (b) and his protests at the folio editors' failure to acknowledge Massinger's share in the plays (c–d) show his concern for the fame of his friend, but (d) in particular makes clear that this is secondary to his enthusiasm for the potent and Massinger-excluding myth of the twin polestars Beaumont and Fletcher (see Introduction, p.10).

From *EG*, vol.3, p.405, and *A Chain of Golden Poems*, 1658, pp.186, 117 for 217, 91–3.

(a) To my worthy Friend, Mr. PHILIP MASSINGER, vpon his Tragæ-Comœdie, call'd *The Emperour of the East* (ll.5–18)

Thou more then Poet, our Mercurie *(that art*
Apollo's *Messenger, and do'st impart*
His best expressions to our eares) liue long
To purifie the slighted English tongue,
That both the Nymphes *of Tagus, and of* Poe,
May not henceforth despise our language so.
Nor could they doe it, if they ere had seene
The matchlesse features of the faerie Queene;
Read Iohnson, Shakespeare, Beaumont, Fletcher, *or*
Thy neat-limnd peeces, skilfull Massinger.
Thou knowne, all the Castillians *must confesse*

71

Vega de Carpio *thy foile, and blesse*
His language can translate thee, and the fine
Italian *witts, yeeld to this worke of thine.*

(b)   *An Epitaph on Mr.* John Fletcher, *and Mr.* Philip Massinger, *who lie buried both in one Grave in* St. Mary Overie's Church *in* Southwark

---

In the same Grave *Fletcher* was buried here
Lies the Stage-Poet *Philip Massinger*:
Playes they did write together, were great friends,
And now one Grave includes them at their ends:
So whom on earth nothing did part, beneath
Here (in their Fames) they lie, in spight of death.

(c)   *To Mr.* Humphrey Mosley, *and Mr.* Humphrey Robinson

In the large book of Playes you late did print
(In *Beaumonts* and in *Fletchers* name) why in't
Did you not justice? give to each his due?
For *Beaumont* (of those many) writ in few:
And *Massinger* in other few; the Main
Being sole Issues of sweet *Fletchers* brain.
But how came I (you ask) so much to know?
Fletchers chief bosome-friend inform'd me so.
Ith'next impression therefore justice do,
And print their old ones in one volume too:
For *Beaumonts* works, & *Fletchers* should come forth
With all the right belonging to their worth.

(d) From '*To my Cousin Mr. Charles Cotton*'

I wonder (Cousin) that you would permit
So great an Injury to *Fletcher's* wit,
Your friend and old Companion, that his fame
Should be divided to anothers name.

. . .

[Beaumont and Fletcher] were two wits, and friends, and who
Robs from the one to glorifie the other,
Of these great memories is a partial Lover.

. . .

And my good friend Old *Philip Massinger*
With *Fletcher* writ in some that we see there.

. . .

[Beaumont and Fletcher] were our *English* Polestars, and did beare
Between them all the world of fancie cleare:
But as two Suns when they do shine to us,
The aire is lighter, they prodigious;
So while they liv'd and writ together, we
Had Plays exceeded what we hop'd to see.
But they writ few; for youthful *Beaumont* soon
By death eclipsed was at his high noon.
Surviving *Fletcher* then did pen alone
Equal to both, (pardon Comparison)
And suffer'd not the *Globe*, and *Black-Friers* Stage
T'envy the glories of a former Age.
As we in humane bodies see that lose
An eye, or limbe, the vertue and the use
Retreats into the other eye or limb,
And makes it double; so I say of him:
Fletcher was *Beaumonts* Heir, and did inherit
His searching judgement, and unbounded Spirit.
His Plays are Printed therefore as they were,
Of Beaumont too, because his Spirit's there.

11. Wit's Recreations
1640

The first edition of the miscellany *Wit's Recreations* included anonymous epigrams or epitaphs on many of the dramatists of the day. Only pieces on Shakespeare and Jonson survived in the later editions. Colin Gibson notes that while 'Pleasure and admiration are the two key-notes of the literary epigrams . . . Jonson (Epigram III) and Massinger (Epigram VIII) are linked in eliciting the more temperate quality of respect'; the Massinger poem, couched in Roman terms, is possibly 'a response to Massinger's highly-wrought tragedy *The Roman Actor* (1626), since it hardly fits his romantic tragicomedies of the 1630s' (C.A. Gibson, 'Elizabethan and Stuart Dramatists in *Wit's Recreations* (1640)', *Research Opportunities in Renaissance Drama*, vol.29, 1986–7, p.21). The punning phrase '*Apollo's Messenger*' probably echoes Cokaine's use of it in No. 10(a).

Wits Recreations. Selected from the finest Fancies of Modern MUSES, London, 1640, B8r.

To Mr. Philip Massinger.

Apollo's Messenger, who doth impart
To us the edicts of his learned art,
We cannot but respect thee, for we know,
Princes are honour'd in their Legats so.

12. Abraham Wright
c. 1640

Abraham Wright (1611–90), clergyman and fellow of St John's College, Oxford, compiled a manuscript book of extracts from and comments on plays and chronicle histories for the benefit of his own style and the information of his son, the theatre historian James Wright (see *EG*, vol.1, pp.xlii–xliii and A.C. Kirsch, 'A Caroline Commentary on the Drama', *Modern Philology*, vol.66, 1968–9, pp.256–61). 'In his disappointment at Massinger's flow of unmetaphorical language, Wright strangely anticipates the burden of the complaint against Massinger's language running from Lamb to Eliot' (*EG*, vol.1, p.xliii). In his comments he also praises strength and intricacy of plotting; he particularly likes *Othello* and the work of James Shirley, and dislikes *Hamlet*.

I have inserted references for the extracts; it should be noted, however, that Wright is often paraphrasing rather than accurately quoting the original. From 'Excerpta quaedam per A.W. Adolescentem' (British Museum Add. MS 22608), fols 93–93v.

Out of ye new way to pay old debts, a Comedie by Phillip Massenger.

Act: 1. Noe bouze? nor noe Tobacco? xx some curate pend this inuective, and you studied it.
Mr Tapwell if I owe you anything shew it in chalke or Ile pay nothing, and you are to haue noe other register
S'rah, haue not I made purses for thee? then thou lickd my bootes: and thought your holy-day cloake too course to cleane them [I.i.1, 52–3, 25–6, 74–6].
A page. One y^t is scarce manumizd from ye *porters lodge* (ie, y^t is still subiect to ye porters lash) and yet sworn seruant to ye pantofle [I.i.136–7]. xx ye queene of flowers, ye glory of ye spring. ye sweetest comfort to our smell, ye rose sprang from an enuious brier; soe may a kind daughter from a churlish father [I.i. 146–51].
My ladies goe-beefore [I.ii.12]. Ie, a gentleman vsher. If such *fortifications* (Ie, such as cookes make.) had binne practisd at Breda, spinola might haue thrown his cap at it and nere tooke [it] [I.ii.25–8].
good s^r, doe soe much as remember pie-corner, and help mee to a peice of yt [I.iii.44]. (Ie ye corner of ye pie.
Why you slaues / created onely to make leggs, and cringe:

/ to carry a dish, and shift a trencher; yt haue noe soules onely to hope a blessing / beeyond black iacks and flagons [I.iii.59–63].

Act: 2 My duety suffers, if to please my selfe I should neglect my lord [II.ii.5–6].
sorrow followes ye flux of laughture [II.ii.138–9].

Act: 3 Hee eates till his belly's bracd vp like a drumme [III.i.23]. xx this is granted vnto few, but such as rise vp ye Kdomes glory [III.ii.81–2].
thou barathrum of ye shambles [III.ii.209]. Ie, a great eater. xx shees very willing, yet should wee take forts at ye first assaulte; twere poore in ye defendant [III.ii.229–32]. xx your bounties are soe great they rob mee, madam, of words to giue you thankes [III.ii.261–2]. (The rest not worth ye reading

A new way to pay old debts.
A silly play. ye plot but ordinary wch is the cheating of an vsurer beeing the plot of a great many plaies, at least a maine passage in them. but for ye lines they are very poore, noe expressions, but onely plaine downright relating ye matter; without any new dress either of language or fancy.

13. Philip Kynder

1656

Kynder (1597–<1665) was a physician, royal official, and friend of John Selden and Charles Cotton. Given his age in 1656, his acquaintance with *A New Way to Pay Old Debts* is not surprising, but the reference here does seem to presuppose a more general familiarity amongst Interregnum readers. This was an important period for the publication of plays – Humphrey Moseley's 'Beaumont and Fletcher' folio (1647) was followed in the 1650s by collections of

Cartwright, Brome, and Shirley, and Massinger's *Three New Playes* (1655).

The Surfeit (it is a surfeit 'Of reading men and books') debunks most branches of learning and belief while allowing that 'Your *Romances* and *Gazettes* are the only useful harmless readings'.

[Philip Kynder], *The Surfeit to ABC*, London, 1656, pp.57– 8.

The *Attick Archæologist* (full of reading, paines and learning) hath moulded up a piece of Antiquity, extracted for the most part from the Poets, *Lycophron, Sophocles, Aristophanes, Euripides* and the Scholiasts, and obtrudes upon us these to be the general customes of the *Athenians*: As if one in future age should make all *England* in ages past to be a *Bartholomew*-Faire, because *Ben. Johnson* hath writ it. Or that the condition of all our *English* women may be drawn out of *Shackespeers* merry wifes of *Windsor*; or the religion of the low-Countrimen from Mr. *Aminadab* [i.e. Ananias] in the *Alchymist*. Or from *Massingers* Mr. *Greedy*, a hungry Justice of Peace in *Nottingham*-shire: or *Will-doe* the Parson of *Gotham* the Condition of all the County. These may be applyed to *Rosinus* and *Goodwins* Roman Antiquities.*

14. Samuel Pepys

1661–8

The diary kept by Samuel Pepys (1633–1703) between 1660 and 1669 includes his many 'considering, though inconsistent' responses to the theatre productions he attended; with

---

*Joannes Rosinus, *Romanarum Antiquitatum Libri Decem*, Basle, 1583, and the much reprinted Thomas Godwin, *Romanae Historiae Anthologia. An English Exposition of the Romane Antiquities*, Oxford, 1614.

his enthusiasm and affection 'He alone, of all those who have left comments on the 17th-century theatre makes us feel the special excitement that the theatre can generate' (Richard Luckett, 'Plays', and Peter Holland, 'Theatre', in Robert Latham and William Matthews (eds), *The Diary of Samuel Pepys*, 11 vols, Cambridge, 1970–83, vol.10, pp.339, 445).

Pepys's emphasis on production indicates how essential and living a component of the early Restoration repertory were pre-1642 plays, but also reminds one how short-lived such popularity was likely to be as new plays entered the repertory and Massinger and most of his contemporaries became decreasingly available in print.

See Introduction, pp.11–12, for some reasons for the vogue for *The Bondman* and *The Virgin Martyr* in the 1660s.

Extracts from the Latham and Matthews edition.

(a) *The Bondman*

---

1 March 1661.
. . .to White-fryers and saw *The Bondman* acted – an excellent play and well done – but above all that ever I saw, Baterton doth the Bondman the best.

19 March 1661.
. . .to White-friers, where we saw *The Bondman* acted most excellently; and though I have seen it often, yet I am every time more and more pleased with Batterton's action.

26 March 1661.
I and my wife sat in the Pit . . . and saw *The Bondman* done to admiration.

25 May 1661.
. . .to the Theatre, where I saw a piece of *The Silent woman*, which pleased me. So homewards, and in my way bought *The Bondman* in Pauls church-yard.

4 November 1661.

...to the Opera, where we saw *The Bondman*, which of old we both did so doate on, and do so still; though, to both our thinking, not so well acted here (having too great expectacions) as formerly at Salsbury Court – but for Baterton; he is called by us both the best actor in the world.

2 April 1662.

...by water to the Opera and there saw *The Bondman* most excellently acted; and though we had seen it so often, yet I never liked it better than today, Ianthe [Mrs Saunderson, later Mrs Betterton] acting Cleora's part very well now Roxalana [Mrs Davenport] is gone.

28 July 1664.

...seeing *The Bondman* upon the posts, I consulted my oaths and find I may go safely this time without breaking it . . . [It] is true, for want of practice they had many of them forgot their parts a little, but Baterton and my poor Ianthe out-do all the world. There is nothing more taking in the world with me then that play.

2 November 1666.

...and so home, I reading all the way to make end of *The Bondman* (which the oftener I read, the more I like), and begin *The Duchesse of Malfy*, which seems a good play.

(b) *The Virgin Martyr*

---

16 February 1661.

...to the Theatre, where I saw *The Virgin=Martyr* – a good but too sober a play for the company.

27 February 1668.

...to the King's House to see *Virgin Martyr*, the first time it hath been acted a great while, and it is mighty pleasant; not that the play is worth much, but it is finely Acted by Becke Marshall; but that which did please me beyond anything in the whole world was the wind-musique when the Angell comes down, which is so sweet that it ravished me; and endeed, in a word, did wrap up my soul so that it made me really sick, just as I have formerly been when in love with my wife . . . so as I could not believe that ever any music hath that real command over the soul of man as this did upon me.

2 March 1668.

[*The Virgin Martyr*] doth mightily please me, but above all the Musique at the coming down of the Angell.

6 May 1668.

. . .to the King's playhouse and there saw *The Virgin Martyr* – and heard the music that I like so well.

15. Gerard Langbaine

1691

Langbaine (1656–92) is remembered for his early identification of many of the sources of Jacobean and Restoration plays. The general account of Massinger given here is followed by brief sections on each play including sources and evidence of success from title-pages and commendatory verses. Critical comment is limited: *The City Madam* is 'an Excellent old Play', *A New Way to Pay Old Debts* is 'deservedly commended' by Massinger's friends, and Massinger an 'Ingenious Poet'.

An Account of the English Dramatick Poets, Oxford, 1691, pp.352–4.

Philip MASSINGER.

This Author was born at *Salisbury*, in the Reign of King *Charles* the First; being Son to *Philip* [i.e. Arthur] Massinger, a Gentleman belonging to the Earl of *Montgomery* [i.e. Pembroke], in whose service after having spent many years happily, he Died. He bestow'd a liberal Education on our Author, sending him to the University of *Oxford*, at Eighteen years of Age *viz.* 1602. where he closely pursued his Studies in *Alban-Hall* for Three or Four years space. How he spent his Life afterwards I know not: but 'tis evident that he dedicated a great part of his Studies to Poetry, from several Plays which he has publisht, and which were highly esteem'd of the Wits of those times, for the purity of Stile, and the Oeconomy of their Plots; for which Excellency he is thus commended by an old Poet: [Quotes Heminge, No. 9]. He was extreamly belov'd by the Poets of that Age, and there were few but what took it as an Honour to club with him in a Play: witness *Middleton, Rowley, Field,* and *Decker*: all which join'd with him in several Labours. Nay, further to shew his Excellency, the ingenious *Fletcher,* took him as a Partner in several Plays, as I have already hinted, *p.*217. He was a Man of much Modesty and extraordinary Parts, and were it not that I fear to draw Envy on our Poets Memory, I could produce several Testimonials in confirmation of this truth: however I will give the Reader one Instance for many, being the Testimony of a Worthy Gentleman, Sir *Thomas Jay:* [Quotes No. 3(c)].

16. Anthony Wood

1691

Wood (1632–95) was historian of Oxford University and, in *Athenae Oxonienses,* of its writers and bishops. His Massinger is so unlike Langbaine's, and fits so little with the received impression of Massinger as a grave or dull moralist, that it has caused some perplexity.

From *Athenae Oxonienses,* 2 vols, Oxford, 1691–2, vol.1, p.536.

PHILIPP MASSINGER, Son of *Phil.* [i.e. Arthur] *Massinger* a servant belonging to the *Pembrochian* family, made his first entry on the stage of this vain world, within the City of *Salisbury,* was entred a Commoner of St. *Albans* hall, in the seventeenth year of his age 1601. where, tho incouraged in his studies by the Earl of *Pembroke*, yet he applied his mind more to Poetry and Romances for about four years or more, than to Logick and Philosophy, which he ought to have done, and for that end was patronized. Afterwards leaving the University without the honour of a degree, he retired to the great City to improve his fancy and studies by conversation. At length being sufficiently fam'd for several *specimens* of wit, wrote divers Comedies and Tragedies for the English Stage, (besides other things) much applauded and cryed up in their time, when acted and published. Their names are these. [Wood lists the plays then known, i.e. all but *The Parliament of Love* and *Believe As You List*, and also credits Massinger with not only the share in *The Old Law* now no longer attributed to him, but *Sejanus*.] As for our author *Ph. Massenger*, he made his last *exit* very suddenly, in his house on the *Bank-side* in Southwerk, near to [the] then play-house, for he went to bed well and was dead before morning. Whereupon his body, being accompanied by Comedians, was buried about the middle of that Ch. yard belonging to S. Saviours Church there, commonly called the *Bull-head Church yard*.

17. Nicholas Rowe
1703

Rowe (1674–1718), the first serious editor of Shakespeare (1709), Poet Laureate from 1715, and one of the most popular dramatists of the eighteenth century, was said to have contemplated an edition of Massinger (see the preface to *The Bondman*, 1719, quoted in *EG*, vol.1, p.xlviii) and certainly drew freely on the plot and situations of *The Fatal Dowry* in *The Fair Penitent* (1703). Rowe made the shape of his play more classical than that of its original, and its focus more marital and less on larger ethical questions (see Introduction, pp. 13–14).

From *The Fair Penitent. A Tragedy*, London, 1703.

(a)

As in *The Fatal Dowry* (IV.ii.60–126 and IV.iv) a new husband finds his wife with her lover (or, in Rowe, ex-lover) and kills him, and the girl's husband and father debate her punishment. But Rowe's 'Haughty, Gallant, Gay *Lothario*' (V.p.53), credited by Samuel Johnson with inspiring Richardson's Lovelace, is a much stronger and more menacing figure than Novall Junior. Conversely Altamont is weaker and less complex than Massinger's Charalois, who admits that his briskness of manner after the killing only staves off breakdown: 'My griefes are now, thus to be borne. / Hereafter ile finde time and place to mourne' (IV.ii.125–6). Subsequently in Massinger Beaumelle's husband and father debate her fate and the issues of justice and honour, but without the swings of purpose and spirals of emotion of Altamont, Sciolto, and Calista (Calista cannot 'bear to be outdone'). Beaumelle is soon to be executed by Charalois whereas Calista still has much to say before she eventually kills herself in Act Five.

Act IV, pp.41–4.

Loth. Thou hast ta'ne me somewhat unawares, 'tis true,
But Love and War take turns like Day and Night,
And little Preparation serves my turn,
Equal to both, and arm'd for either Field.
We've long been Foes, this Moment ends our Quarrel;
Earth, Heav'n and Fair *Calista* judge the Combat.

Cal. Distraction! Fury! Sorrow! Shame! and Death!

Alt. Thou hast talk'd too much, thy Breath is Poison to me,
It taints the ambient Air; this for my Father,
This for *Sciolto*, and this last for *Altamont*.
[*They Fight; Lothario is wounded once or twice, and then falls.*

Loth. Oh *Altamont*! thy Genius is the stronger,
Thou hast prevail'd! – My fierce, ambitious Soul
Declining droops, and all her Fires grow pale;
Yet let not this Advantage swell thy Pride,
I Conquer'd in my turn, in Love I Triumph'd:
Those Joys are lodg'd beyond the reach of Fate;
That sweet Revenge comes smiling to my Thoughts,

Adorns my Fall, and chears my Heart in Dying.

[*Dies.*

Cal.   And what remains for me? Beset with Shame,
Encompass'd round with Wretchedness, there is
But this one way, to break the Toil and 'scape.

[*She catches up* Lothario's *Sword, and offers to kill her self;* Altamont *runs to her, and wrests it from her.*

Alt.   What means thy frantick Rage?

Cal.   Off! let me go.

Alt.   Oh! thou hast more than murder'd me, yet still,
Still thou art here! and my Soul starts with Horror,
At thought of any Danger that may reach thee.

Cal.   Think'st thou I mean to live? to be forgiven?
Oh! thou hast known but little of *Calista*;
If thou hadst never heard my Shame, if only
The midnight Moon, and silent Stars had seen it,
I wou'd not bear to be reproach'd by them,
But dig down deep to find a Grave beneath,
And hide me from their Beams.

[*Sciolto within.*]   What ho! my Son!

Alt.   It is *Sciolto* calls; come near, and find me,
The wretched'st Thing of all my Kind on Earth.

Cal.   Is it the Voice of Thunder, or my Father?
Madness! Confusion! let the Storm come on,
Let the tumultuous Roar drive all upon me,
Dash my devoted Bark; ye Surges, break it;
'Tis for my Ruin that the Tempest rises.
When I am lost, sunk to the bottom low,
Peace shall return, and all be calm again.

Enter Sciolto.

. . .

Alt.   [S]ee that Body,
And guess my Shame! my Ruin! oh *Calista*!

Sci. It is enough! but I am slow to Execute,
And Justice lingers in my lazy Hand;
Thus let me wipe Dishonour from my Name,
And cut thee from the Earth, thou Stain to Goodness. –

[*Offers to kill* Calista, Altamont *holds him.*

Alt. Stay thee, *Sciolto*, thou rash Father stay,
Or turn the Point on me, and thro' my Breast,
Cut out the bloody Passage to *Calista*;
So shall my Love be perfect, while for her
I die, for whom alone I wish'd to live.

Cal. No, *Altamont*! my Heart, that scorn'd thy Love,
Shall never be indebted to thy Pity;
Thus torn, defac'd, and wretched as I seem,
Still I have something of *Sciolto*'s Virtue.
Yes! yes, my Father, I applaud thy Justice,
Strike home, and I will bless thee for the Blow;
Be merciful, and free me from my Pain,
'Tis sharp, 'tis terrible, and I cou'd curse
The chearful Day, Men, Earth, and Heav'n, and Thee,
Ev'n thee, thou venerable good Old Man,
For being Author of a Wretch like me.

Alt. Listen not to the Wildness of her Raving,
Remember Nature! Shou'd thy Daughter's Murder
Defile that Hand, so just, so great in Arms,
Her Blood wou'd rest upon thee to Posterity,
Pollute thy Name, and sully all thy Wars.

Cal. Have I not wrong'd his gentle Nature much?
And yet behold him pleading for my Life.
Lost as thou art, to Virtue, oh *Calista*!
I think thou canst not bear to be outdone;
Then haste to die, and be oblig'd no more.

Sci. Thy pious Care has giv'n me time to think,
And sav'd me from a Crime; then rest my Sword;
To Honour have I kept thee ever sacred,
Nor will I stain thee with a rash revenge;
But, mark me well, I will have Justice done;
Hope not to bear away thy Crimes unpunish'd,

MASSINGER

I will see Justice executed on thee,
Ev'n to a *Roman* strictness; and thou, Nature,
Or whatsoe'er thou art that plead'st within me,
Be still, thy tender Struglings are in vain.

[Calista again pleads to die rather than face a life of 'Scorn and fierce Upbraidings' from Sciolto. He banishes her from his sight to 'howl out the remainder of thy Life' in 'some dark Cell'.]

Cal.   Yes, I will fly to some such dismal Place,
And be more curst than you can wish I were;
This fatal Form that drew on my Undoing,
Fasting, and Tears, and Hardship shall destroy,
Nor Light, nor Food, nor Comfort will I know,
Nor ought that may continue hated Life.
Then when you see me meagre, wan, and chang'd,
Stretch'd at my Length, and dying in my Cave,
On that cold Earth I mean shall be my Grave,
Perhaps you may relent, and sighing say,
At length her Tears have wash'd her Stains away,
At length 'tis time her Punishment shou'd cease;
Die thou, poor suff'ring Wretch, and be at peace.

[*Exit* Calista.

(b)
In similarly pathetic strains, Altamont and his brother-in-law Horatio dilate on whether they can renew the close friendship broken when Altamont fought with him over his accusation of Calista. In *The Fatal Dowry* Horatio's equivalent is Romont, an uncomplicated and outspoken soldier who remains unflinchingly loyal to Charalois: even when rejected by him, Romont remains angry on his behalf more than with him. In the equivalent to this extract (V.ii.55f.) reconciliation is rapid and Romont is soon launched on a militant defence of his friend's action in killing his wife. There is no place for Rowe's Lavinia (Altamont's sister and Horatio's wife) who mediates between the two men but also stokes their histrionics with her own.

Act IV, pp.48–51

Alt.	Thou hast forgot me.
Hor.	No.
Alt.	Why are thy Eyes Impatient of me then, scornful and fierce?
Hor.	Because they speak the meaning of my Heart, Because they are honest, and disdain a Villain.
Alt.	I have wrong'd thee much, *Horatio*.
Hor.	True thou hast: When I forget it, may I be a Wretch, Vile as thy self, a false perfidious Fellow, An infamous, believing, *British* Husband.
Alt.	I've wrong'd thee much, and Heav'n has well aveng'd it. I have not, since we parted, been at Peace, Nor known one Joy sincere; our broken Friendship Pursu'd me to the last Retreat of Love, Stood glaring like a Ghost, and made me cold with Horror. Misfortunes on Misfortunes press upon me, Swell o'er my Head, like Waves, and dash me down. Sorrow, Remorse, and Shame, have torn my Soul, They hang like Winter on my youthful Hopes, And blast the Spring and Promise of my Year.
Lav.	So Flow'rs are gather'd to adorn a Grave, To lose their Freshness amongst Bones and Rottenness, And have their Odours stifled in the Dust. Canst thou hear this, thou cruel, hard *Horatio*? Canst thou behold thy *Altamont* undone? That gentle, that dear Youth! canst thou behold him, His poor Heart broken, Death in his pale Visage, And groaning out his Woes, yet stand unmov'd?
Hor.	The Brave and Wise I pity in Misfortune, But when Ingratitude and Folly suffers, 'Tis Weakness to be touch'd.
Alt.	I wo' not ask thee To pity or forgive me, but confess,

> This Scorn, this Insolence of Hate is just,
> 'Tis Constancy of Mind, and manly in thee.
> But oh! had I been wrong'd by thee, *Horatio*,
> There is a yielding Softness in my Heart
> Could ne'er have stood it out, but I had ran,
> With streaming Eyes, and open Arms, upon thee,
> And prest thee close, close!

Hor. I must hear no more,
The Weakness is contagious, I shall catch it,
And be a tame fond Wretch.

Lav. Where wou'dst thou go?
Wou'dst thou part thus? You sha' not, 'tis impossible;
For I will bar thy Passage, kneeling thus;
Perhaps thy cruel Hand may spurn me off,
But I will throw my Body in thy way,
And thou shalt trample o'er my faithful Bosom,
Tread on me, wound me, kill me e'er thou pass.

Alt. Urge not in vain thy pious Suit, *Lavinia*,
I have enough to rid me of my Pain.
Calista, thou hadst reach'd my Heart before;
To make all sure, my Friend repeats the Blow:
But in the Grave our Cares shall be forgotten,
There Love and Friendship cease.

[*Falls.*
[Lavinia *runs to him, and endeavours to raise him.*

[Lavinia sinks with Altamont; Horatio fears that 'My stubborn, unrelenting Heart has kill'd him', and, as the 'Youth' revives at the sound of his voice, begs and offers forgiveness. Horatio claims that he 'cannot speak', but is soon reflecting on his new-found sympathy and asking to bear Altamont's sorrows for him. The concluding speech of Act Four follows:]

Lav. Oh my Brother!
Think not but we will share in all thy Woes,
We'll sit all day, and tell sad Tales of Love,
And when we light upon some faithless Woman,
Some Beauty, like *Calista*, false and fair,
We'll fix our Grief, and our Complaining, there;

We'll curse the Nymph that drew the Ruin on,
And mourn the Youth that was like thee undone.

18. Oliver Goldsmith
1759

Goldsmith (?1730–74) wrote a considerable amount of journalism, especially at the beginning of his literary career. In his review of the Coxeter edition he is hostile to the reprinting of old plays, but also sceptical about the merits of 'cool and correct' modern ones.

The Critical Review, July 1759, pp.86–7.

Massinger was a dramatic poet, cotemporary with Beaumont and Fletcher, and about twenty years later than Shakespear; yet if we compare the stile of each, the former will seem more antient, at least by a century. We are to regard the time in which this poet wrote, as a period when polite learning was little encouraged; for school-philosophy, the foe of common sense, was still in fashion. A few of the nobility who had travelled, and whose taste had been formed in Italy, then the center of all politeness, gave our English writers, whom nevertheless they but slightly esteemed, some small encouragement. These patrons, however, were but a few, and the rest of the audience was composed of persons who came to a play with the same taste, and the same expectations, that we see the mob now repair to a puppet-shew. Those who went by the name of the learned, laymen as well as divines, were engaged in controversial divinity, neglected poetry as a trifling amusement, and regarded plays, unless they were wrote in Latin, with the utmost contempt. What therefore could be expected from performances calculated to amuse such an audience? Nothing less than a genius like Shakespear's could make plays wrote to the taste of those times, pleasing now; a man whose beauties seem rather the result of chance than design; who, while he laboured to satisfy his audience with monsters and mummery, seemed to throw in his inimitable beauties as trifles into the bargain. Massinger, however, was not such a man; he seldom rises to any pitch of sublimity, and yet it must be owned is never so incorrigibly absurd, as we often find his predecessor. His performances are all crowded with incident, but want character, the genuine mark of genius in a dramatic poet. In our days it is probable he might make a very judicious poet; he might preserve every unity, prepare his incidents, work up his plot, and give us a piece as cooly correct, or as unfeelingly boisterous, as the best tragedy-maker of them all. What mighty reason our editor had to disturb his repose, we cannot see at present, especially as his best plays have been already published in Dodsley's collection. A poet, whose works have been forgotten so soon after publication, when his language was modern, and his humour new, must surely cut but an indifferent figure, brought back to light again in an age when his diction is become antiquated, and the highest sallies of his humour forced, for want of models to compare them by. There are, however, a set of readers, who being half critics, and half antiquarians, will be apt to regard what may be displeasing to others, as beauties. Such will lay his antiquity against his faults, and pardon the one for the sake of the other. With regard to the present edition, the text seems tolerably correct, yet still admits of some obvious emendations; and as for the editor's notes, it is not severity to say, that they will admit of several emendations also.

19. George Colman
1761

George Colman the Elder (1732–94) was at the beginning of his career as a dramatist when he addressed his *Critical Reflections* to David Garrick. Subsequently he collaborated with Garrick in *The Clandestine Marriage* (1766) (and quarrelled with him as a result) and was manager of Covent Garden (1767–74) and later of the Haymarket. His adaptations of Renaissance drama included *Philaster* (1763) and *Bonduca* (1778).

Colman has been arguing for some pages that Shakespeare's contemporaries, including Massinger, are unjustly neglected by Garrick and the public. If Shakespeare can break the rules without violating 'Nature', so can others.

Critical Reflections on the Old English Dramatick Writers, in Thomas Coxeter (ed.), *The Dramatic Works of Philip Massinger*, London, 4 vols, 1761, vol.1, pp.12–16, 22–4.

Nothing can be more fantastick, or more in the extravagant Strain of the *Italian* Novels, than this Fiction [the introduction of the magic picture in *The Picture*, I.i.109–85]: And yet the play, raised on it, is extremely beautiful, and abounds with affecting Situations, true Character, and a faithful Representation of Nature.

. . .

The fiction of *the* PICTURE being first allowed, the most rigid Critick will, I doubt not, confess, that the Workings of the human Heart are accurately set down in the above Scene [IV.i.1–91, where Mathias's faith in Sophia's chastity is shattered by the change in her picture]. The Play is not without many others, equally excellent, both before and after it; nor in those Days, when the Power of Magick was so generally believed, that the severest Laws were solemnly enacted against Witches and Witchcraft, was the fiction so bold and extravagant, as it may seem at present. Hoping that the Reader may, by this Time, be somewhat reconciled to the Story, or even interested in it, I will venture to subjoin to the long Extracts I have already made from the Play one more Speech, where *the* PICTURE is mentioned very beautifully . . . [Quotes IV.iv.64–82, where Mathias rejects adultery with Honoria and compares life to the picture, each retaining 'the just proportion' only while virtue is adhered to].

These several Passages will, I hope, be thought by the judicious Reader to be written in the true Vein of a true Poet, as well as by the exact Hand of a faithful Disciple of Nature.

. . .

But to conclude:

Have I, Sir, been wasting all this Ink and Time in vain? Or may it be hoped that you will extend some of that Care to the rest of our Old Authors, which you have so long bestowed on *Shakespeare*, and which you have so often lavished on many a worse Writer, than the most inferior of those here recommended to You? It is certainly your Interest to give Variety to the Publick Taste, and to diversify the Colour of our Dramatick Entertainments. Encourage new Attempts; but do Justice to th Old! The Theatre is a wide Field. Let not one or two Walks of it alone be beaten, but lay open the Whole to the Excursions of Genius! This, perhaps, might kindle a Spirit of Originality in our modern Writers for the Stage; who might be tempted to aim at more Novelty in their Compositions, when the Liberality of the Popular Taste rendered it less hazardous. That the Narrowness of theatrical Criticism might be enlarged I have no Doubt. Reflect, for a Moment, on the uncommon Success of *Romeo and Juliet* and *Every Man in his Humour*! and then tell me, whether there are not many other Pieces of as antient a Date, which, with the like proper Curtailments and Alterations, would produce the same Effect? Has an industrious hand been at the Pains to scratch up the Dunghill of *Dryden's Amphitryon* for the few Pearls that are buried in it, and shall the rich Treasures of *Beaumont* and *Fletcher*, *Jonson*, and *Massinger*, lie (as it were) in the Ore, untouched and disregarded? Reform your List of Plays! In the Name of *Burbage*, *Taylor*, and *Betterton*, I conjure you to it! Let the veteran Criticks once more have the Satisfaction of seeing *the Maid's Tragedy*, *Philaster*, *King and no King*, &c. on the Stage! – Restore *Fletcher's Elder Brother* to the Rank unjustly usurped by *Cibber's Love makes a Man*! and since you have wisely desisted from giving an annual Affront to the City by acting the *London Cuckolds* on Lord-Mayor's Day, why will you not pay them a Compliment, by exhibiting *the City Madam* of *Massinger* on the same Occasion?

If after all, Sir, these Remonstrances should prove without Effect, and the Merit of these great Authors should plead with You in vain, I will here fairly turn my Back upon You, and address myself to the Lovers of Dramatick Compositions in general. They, I am sure, will peruse those Works with Pleasure in the Closet, though they lose the Satisfaction of seeing them represented on the Stage: Nay, should They, together with You, concur in determining that such Pieces are unfit to be acted, You, as well as They, will, I am confident, agree, that such Pieces are, at least, very worthy to be read. There are many Modern Compositions, seen with Delight at the Theatre, which sicken on the Taste in the Perusal . . . The Excellencies of our Old Writers are, on the contrary, not confined to Time and Place, but always bear about them the Evidences of true Genius.

Massinger is perhaps the least known, but not the least meritorious of any of the old Class of Writers. His Works declare him to be no mean Proficient in the same School. He possesses all the Beauties and Blemishes common to the Writers of that Age. He has, like the rest of them, in Compliance with the Custom of the Times, admitted Scenes of a low and gross Nature, which might be omitted with no more Prejudice to the Fable, than the Buffoonry in *Venice Preserved*. For his few Faults he makes ample Atonement. His Fables are, most of them, affecting; his Characters well conceived, and strongly supported; and his Diction, flowing, various, elegant, and manly. His two Plays, revived by *Betterton, the Bondman*, and *the Roman Actor*, are not, I think, among the Number of his best. *The Duke of Milan, the Renegado, the Picture, the Fatal Dowry, the Maid of Honour, A New Way to pay Old Debts, the Unnatural Combat, the Guardian, the City Madam*, are each of them, in my Mind, more excellent. He was a very popular Writer in his own Times, but so unaccountably, as well as unjustly, neglected at present, that the accurate Compilers of a Work called *The Lives of the Poets*, published under the learned Name of the late Mr. *Theophilus Cibber*, have not so much as mentioned him. He is, however, take him for all in all, an Author, whose Works the intelligent Reader will peruse with Admiration: And that I may not be supposed to withdraw my Plea for his Admission to the Modern Stage, I shall conclude these Reflections with one more Specimen of his Abilities; submitting it to all Judges of Theatrical Exhibitions, whether the most masterly Actor would not here have an Opportunity of displaying his Powers to Advantage. [Quotes *The Duke of Milan*, I.iii.266–381, where Sforza has Francisco swear to kill Marcelia if he fails to return from his interview with the Emperor.]

20. Thomas Davies
1779

Davies (c.1712–85), unsuccessful actor turned bookseller, was a friend of Samuel Johnson and Thomas Warton. He did much to encourage interest in Massinger as publisher of the editions of 1761 and 1779 and as author of this enthusiastic essay included in the 1779 edition and also published separately. See also his *Dramatic Micellanies* (sic), 3 vols, London, 1784, vol.1, p.51.

In the later part of the essay Davies extends the historicist approach sometimes present in the work of Oldys, Dodsley, and Colman into a detailed political analysis of the sort only rarely undertaken by most of his nineteenth-century successors.

Some Account of the Life of Philip Massinger, in John Monck Mason (ed.), *The Dramatick Works of Philip Massinger*, 4 vols, London, 1779, vol.1, pp.lxxvii–xcii.

In *Massinger*, Nature and Art are so happily connected, that the one never seems to counteract the other, and in whatever Rank he may be plac'd by the Criticks, yet this Praise cannot be refused him, that his Genius operates equally in every Part of his Composition; for the Powers of his Mind are impartially diffused through his whole Performance; no Part is purposely degraded to Insipidity, to make another more splendid and magnificent; one Act of a Play is not impoverished to enrich another. All the Members of the Piece are cultivated and disposed as Plot, Situation, and Character require.

The Editor very justly observes, that *Massinger* excels *Shakespeare* himself in an easy constant flow of harmonious Language; nor should it be forgotten, that the Current of his Style is never interrupted by harsh, and obscure Phraseology, or overloaded with figurative Expression. Nor does he indulge in the wanton and licentious Use of mixed Modes in Speech; he is never at a Loss for proper Words to cloath his Ideas. And it must be said of him with Truth, that if he does not always rise to *Shakespeare*'s

Vigour of Sentiment, or Ardor of Expression, neither does he sink like him into mean Quibble, and low Conceit.

There is a Discrimination in the Characters of *Massinger*, by which they are varied as distinctly as those of *Shakespeare*. The Hero, the Statesman, the Villain, the Fop, the Coward, the Man of Humour, and the Gentleman, speak a Language appropriated to their several Personages.

Sometimes he takes Pleasure in smoothing the Features of a Villain, and concealing his real Character, till his Wickedness breaks out into Action; nor is this Peculiarity in our Author effected by any constrained or abrupt Conduct, but strictly conformable to Dramatick Truth, and the Oeconomy of his Fable. *Francisco*, in the *Duke of Milan*, assumes, during the first Act, such a Face of Honesty and Fidelity, that the Reader must be surprized, though not shocked at the Change of his Behaviour in the second Act. The Villains of *Massinger* are not Monsters of Vice, who sin merely from the Delight they feel in the Practice of Wickedness. *Francisco*, like Dr. *Young*'s *Zanga* [in Edward Young's *The Revenge*, 1721], carries his Resentment beyond the Limits of his Provocation; but a Sister dishonoured, is by an *Italian*, supposed to be a sufficient Cause for Pursuing the deepest Revenge.

. . .

Massinger is equally skilful in producing Comick and Tragick Delight; his Characters in both Styles are stamped by the Hand of Nature. *Eubulus*, in the *Picture*, is as true a Portrait of honest Freedom, shrewd Observation, and singular Humour, as *Shakespeare*'s *Ænobarbus*, in *Antony and Cleopatra*. *Durazzo*, in the *Guardian*, is inferior to no Character of agreeable Singularity in any Author. Joyous in Situations of the utmost Peril, he is an impartial Lover of Valour, in Friend or Foe; he pardons the Follies of Youth, by a generous Recollection of his own. *Durazzo* forgives every Thing but Cowardice of Spirit and Meanness of Behaviour; a more animated and picturesque Description of Field Sports than that given by *Durazzo* is not to be found in any Author.

. . .

MASSINGER

That *Massinger* was no mean Scholar every Reader of Taste will discern; his Knowledge in Mythology, and History antient and modern, appears to have been extensive; nor was he a mere Smatterer in Logic, and Philosophy, though *Wood* informs us that he did not apply himself to the Study of these Sciences when he was at the University. That he was very conversant with the *Greek* and *Roman* Classics, his frequent Allusions to poetical Fable, and his interweaving some of the choicest Sentiments of the best antient Writers in his Plays, sufficiently demonstrate. What he borrowed from the Classics he paid back with Interest, for he dignified their Sentiments by giving them a new Lustre; while *Jonson*, the superstitious Idolater of the Antients, deforms his Style by affected Phraseology and verbal Translation; his Knowledge was unaccompanied by true Judgment and Elegance of Taste.

. . .

Massinger, though inferior in pointed Satire to *Shakespeare*, seizes every Opportunity to crush rising Folly, and repel incroaching Vice.

When this Author lived, Luxury in Eating and Finery in Dress universally prevailed, to the most enormous Excess. – These Perversions of natural Appetite and decent Custom he combated with an uncommon Ardor of Resentment, and applied to them the force of Ridicule wherever he fairly met them. In his *City Madam* he attacks the Pride, Extravagance, and Affectation of the Citizens and their Wives; he fixes the Boundaries between the gay Splendors of a Court, and the sober Customs of the City.

. . .

Massinger does not, like *Shakespeare* and *Jonson*, sport with Cowardice and Effeminacy; he considers them not only as Defects of Character but as Stains of Immorality: *Romont*'s Reproof to *Noval*, a Coward and a Fop, is singular and bitter. [Quotes *The Fatal Dowry*, III.i.112–21.]

But, besides the occasional Censure which *Massinger* passed upon the growing Vices of the Times in which he lived he aimed at higher Game. He boldly attacked the Faults of Ministers and of Kings themselves. He pointed his Arrows against *Carr* and *Buckingham*, against *James* and *Charles* the First.

. . .

Massinger, though from the general Tenor of his Writings, he appears to have been a firm Friend of Monarchy, and warmly attached to Government in Church and State, was not a Favourer of Arbitrary Power, or inclined to put an implicit Faith in the Word of Kings; he was averse from embracing the Doctrines of Passive Obedience and Non-Resistance, so much inculcated by *James*, in his Speeches to Parliament, and his Court Divines in their Sermons. *Massinger* was a good Subject, but not like other Poets, his Contemporaries, a slavish Flatterer of Power, and an Abettor of despotick Principles.

Our Poet, in his play of the *Maid of Honour*, under the Characters of *Roberto*, King of *Sicily*, and *Fulgentio* his Favourite, undoubtedly drew the Portraits of *James* and his Minion, *Carr* or *Buckingham*, or perhaps both.

The Duke of *Urbino*, by his Ambassador, craves the Assistance of the King of *Sicily*. – *Roberto* pleads in his Refusal, the Injustice of the Duke's Cause. – *James* too, would not own the Title of his Son-in-Law to *Bohemia*, though he was chosen by the free Votes of the Estates of that Kingdom; nor would he permit him to receive the Honours due to his high Rank, from pretended Scruples of Conscience or Motives of Honour. *Bertoldo*, from many spirited Arguments, urges the King to grant the Duke the requested Aid. The following Speech will, I believe, confirm my Conjecture of the *Sicilian* Prince's Resemblance to our *British* Monarch. [Quotes *The Maid of Honour*, I.i.215–35.]

When this animated Speech was first delivered by the Actor, I cannot doubt but that it was heard by the Audience with Rapture, and universally applauded. The Poet spoke the genuine Sense of the Nation. *James*, unhappily for himself and his Posterity, instead of giving free Liberty to the generous Spirit of his Subjects, and indulging the favourite Passion of the Nation in the brisk Prosecution of a foreign War, by which he might have gained their Love and secured their Allegiance, cherished the Cockle of Discontent and Sedition, which broke out with Violence in the Reign of his Successor, and caused the Ruin of the King and Kingdom.

Of *Fulgentio*, King *Roberto*'s Favourite, *Bertoldo* speaks with the utmost Contempt:

– Let him keep his Smiles
For his State Catamite
[I.i.270–1]

Though *James* was supposed to be averse from the Fair Sex, and was unsuspected of any Intrigue with Women, yet he was extremely solicitous to gratify the amorous Passions of his two great Favourites . . . [I]f we may credit Sir *Edward Peyton, James* carried his Complaisance to his Minion *Buckingham* . . . even to a shameful Degree of Pandarism. [Quotes examples from Peyton's *Divine Catastrophe of the Kingly House of Stuarts*, 1652.]

In the same Play of the *Maid of Honour*, King *Roberto*, willing to second the Passions of his Favourite *Fulgentio*, employs his Influence to forward his Match with *Camiola*. For that Purpose, he sends her a Ring by the Minion himself; but the Lady treats Fulgentio with that proper Contempt which his Character deserves: [Quotes II.ii.132–57 (with omissions)].

But *Massinger* did not confine his Censure to personal Defects or Vices in the Prince and his Ministers. He extended his Satire to an open Attack upon Mal-administration, and the Abuses of Government.

. . .

In the *Emperor of the East*, a Play acted by the Command of *Charles* I, *Massinger* vindicates the Cause of the Nation against unjust and exorbitant Impositions, and the Excesses of regal and ministerial Authority. A Scene between the Projectors and *Pulcheria*, the Guardian of the Kingdom, in whose Character I think he intended a Compliment to the Memory of Queen *Elizabeth*, gave the Author an Opportunity to speak the public Sense upon the Stage: [Quotes I.ii.237–53].

The Reader of public Transactions, during the whole Reign of *James*, and the greatest Part of *Charles* I. will acknowledge the Justice of *Massinger's* Censure.

. . .

In a peculiar Strain of Eloquence, and most pathetick Art of Persuasion, *Massinger* equals, if not excells, all Dramatick Writers, ancient and modern; whether he undertakes the Defence of injured Virtue, avenges the Wrongs of suffering Beauty, or pleads the Cause of insulted Merit; would he sooth, by gentle Insinuation, or prevail by Strength of Argument, and the Irradiations of Truth! – Does he arraign, supplicate, reproach, threaten or condemn! – He is equally powerful, victorious and triumphant. What are all the laboured Defences of the Stage, when compared to *Paris*'s eloquent Vindication of scenical Exhibition before the *Roman* Senate, in the Tragedy of the *Roman Actor*? Would the Reader feel the Effects of filial Piety, in its most amiable and enthusiastick Excess, let him read *Charolois* pleading in Behalf of his dead Father, and claiming a Right to his Body, by giving up his own in Exchange, in the *Fatal Dowry*. The same *Charolois*, justifying himself from the Charge of Cruelty, in putting to Death an adulterous Wife, exhibits a still stronger Proof of that inimitable Art, which our Author so perfectly enjoyed, to move the Passions, by an irresistible Stream of eloquent and pathetick Language.

Massinger is the avowed Champion of the Fair Sex . . . The Females of *Beaumont* and *Fletcher* are for the most Part violent in their Passions, capricious in their Manners, licentious, and even indecent in their Language. *Massinger's* Fair Ones are cast in a very different Mold; they partake just so much of the male Virtues, Constancy and Courage, as to render their feminine Qualities more amiable and attractive.

. . .

Though it must be granted, that *Massinger*, in Compliance with the Times in which he lived, and in Conformity to the practice of contemporary Writers, did occasionally produce low Characters, and write Scenes of licentious and reprehensible Dialogue; yet we must remember to his Honour, that he never sports with Religion by prophane Rants or idle Jesting; nor does he once insult the Clergy, by petulant Witticism or Common-place Abuse.

21. Reviews of *The Bondman*
1779

Versions by Richard Cumberland (see No. 24) of *The Bondman* and *The Duke of Milan* were performed at Covent Garden in the autumn of 1779. The texts have not survived, but in the case of *The Bondman* 'from the newspaper accounts it would seem that the original play was not materially changed' (*EG*, vol.1, p.309).

The reviews show little sympathy with the scholarly primitivism which had helped Massinger's works to three printings in twenty years.

(a) *The Westminster Magazine*, vol.7, 1779, p.504.

The business of rummaging old libraries, and reviving Plays which have been long consigned to oblivion, or to Circulating Libraries, has ever appeared to us a miserable expedient in the management of a Play-House; at this time, especially, when the best Theatre-Writers are either complaining of ill-usage, or, in consequence of a paultry neglect, publishing Pieces which ought to have been performed, to have recourse to the expedient of Revival is not very excuseable.

Massinger's Plays are well known; and most of our readers are acquainted with *The Bondman*. It is contrived like a garment, made plain, simple, and neat, and then ornamented with every thing grotesque and extravagant which the tailor could pin upon it. Mr. Cumberland has thought proper to take off some of these ornaments, but he has stopped his hand too soon; perhaps from a judicious consideration of the taste of his audience.

The Play was well received, principally on account of some striking political passages in it. [Quotes, as 'received with great applause', much of I.iii.12–18, 89–102, 171–210.] The performers in general did justice to their parts.

(b) *The Town and Country Magazine*, vol.11, 1779, pp.517–18.

Though this piece is strongly tinged with the improprieties of character and dialogue that prevailed at the time of its being written, there are many judicious observations upon life and manners, which afford some scenic situations that produce a very happy effect.

. . .

Mr. Aickin in Timoleon gave uncommon satisfaction. His animadversions on the character of the Syracusans met with the warmest applause, as great part of the audience judged them applicable to the present times. The passages alluded to are the following: [Quotes a shortened version of I.iii.178–86 which is, however, given in full by *The Westminster Magazine*, and I.iii.171–7].

. . .

Mr. Hull spoke the Prologue, which turned upon the martial disposition that now prevails through all ranks of people. The idea was a good one, but we cannot add it was happily pursued.

22. Henry Bate
1783

The Reverend Henry Bate (1745–1824), later Sir Henry Bate Dudley, was a journalist and author of comic operas 'well known as a man of pleasure' (*DNB*). His alteration of *The Picture*, which was performed seven times at Covent Garden in 1783–4, changed the role of magic to render 'the whole fable more consistent with dramatic probability' (*The Critical Review*, vol.56, 1783, p.396) and introduced four songs and many local variations (in the last scene, for instance, the 'rampant valour' of Ricardo and Ubaldo (V.iii.149) becomes their 'gallantry' (p.92) and Sophia blames Eugenius for dealing with magic ''gainst your reason' (p.93) where she had blamed Mathias for dealing with it ''gainst your religion' (V.iii.176–7)).

From the Advertisement, *The Magic Picture, a Play [Altered from Massinger]*, London, 1783, A3–A3v.

To prepare MASSINGER's Tragi-Comedy, THE PICTURE, for a modern entertainment, proved a more arduous task than was at first conceived. After giving a different turn to the drama, by making the changes of the Picture, the effects of *Eugenius*'s jealousy, instead of the magic art of *Baptista*, and expunging the gross indelicacies which overran the play, it was found that most of the characters required a little fresh modelling to complete the design of the present undertaking. Hence the necessity of new-writing no inconsiderable part of the dialogue, in imitation of the old Dramatist. Though enamoured with the beauties of the antique structure, the Alterer set about its reparation with the utmost diffidence, fearing, like an unskilful architect, he might destroy those venerable features he could not improve! What has been his success, the public decision must determine.

The same kind of irregular and broken measure, through necessity still prevails, except where the language could be reduced to the heroic verse without impairing the spirit of the dialogue.

As to the *unities*, – being so totally disregarded by MASSINGER himself, no use could possibly be made of them in the present alteration.

23. Reviews of *The Magic Picture*
1783

On Bate's revision of *The Picture* see headnote to No. 22. While generally favourable, the reviews continue to demand a high level of probability and propriety.

(a) *The Town and Country Magazine*, vol.15, 1783, pp.603–4 (a review of the Covent Garden production)

This production is an alteration of Massinger's comedy of the Picture, and appears in its present shape, improved by the pen of Mr. Bate. The original has ever been considered as a good acting play: but the main incident on which the whole plot turned, namely, the magical properties of Sophia's picture, though teeming with great dramatic effect, has been generally pronounced as so violently offensive to probability, that it has defeated the design of the author. Besides this circumstance, there was a still more formidable objection to the representation of this comedy, the grossness of its language, and indelicacy of its allusions, which were the vices of dramatic writers about the time of Massinger.

These objections formed the ground-work of the present alteration; and it must be acknowledged the Editor has not missed his aim, for the impurities are removed, and probability restored. The enchantment no longer subsists . . . The greater part of the original is new written, and the style much modernized and polished . . . The comedy was received with great applause, and it will probably, in its new garb, turn out a stock play.

(b) *The English Review, or an Abstract of English and Foreign Literature*, vol.2, 1783, p.471 (a review of the printed text)

The Magic Picture as written by Massinger abounds in absurdities and indelicacies. The task of an alterer was difficult. Mr. Bate however has shewn great judgment in re-writing many parts of the play, the new scenes so happily resembling the manner and stile of Massinger, that to a Reader not acquainted with the original, it would not be easy to say which is which. As it stands now, however, it is better calculated for stage effect than for the closet. There is too much farce in many of the characters. Eugenius and Sylvia are the principal, and are pourtrayed with the hand of a master. The jealousy of Eugenius is well displayed, and in the character of Eubulus and Hillario there is great attention to nature and consistency. Mr. Bate has added a few airs to heighten the interest of the piece with the audience. The prologue is very indifferent indeed. The principal objection to the alteration is the retention of some nasty allusions to a disorder not fit to be mentioned in decent company. [See *The Picture*, IV.ii.56–72 and *The Magic Picture*, IV.p.65.] These the Author might have well left out.

24. Richard Cumberland

1786

Cumberland (1732–1811), the prolific author of Sentimental comedies whom Sheridan satirizes as Sir Fretful Plagiary in *The Critic* (1779), mocking Cumberland's first tragedy *The Battle of Hastings* (1778), was also variously a politician, Greek scholar, novelist, poet, and pamphleteer. His most famous comedy was *The West Indian* (1771). In 1779 his adaptations of *The Duke of Milan* and *The Bondman* had been staged at Covent Garden (see No. 21). On the importance of his detailed comparison between Rowe's *The Fair Penitent* (No. 17) and Massinger and Field's *The Fatal Dowry* see Introduction, pp.18–19.

The Observer: Being a Collection of Moral, Literary and Familiar Essays, 5 vols, London, 1786–91, vol.3, pp.263–302.

N° LXXXVIII.

[T]he high degree of public favour in which [*The Fair Penitent*] has long stood, has ever attracted the best audiences to it, and engaged the talents of the best performers in its display. As there is no drama more frequently exhibited, or more generally read, I propose to give it a fair and impartial examination, jointly with the more unknown and less popular tragedy from which it is derived.

The Fair Penitent is in fable and character so closely copied from *The Fatal Dowry*, that it is impossible not to take that tragedy along with it; and it is matter of some surprize to me that Rowe should have made no acknowledgement of his imitation either in his dedication or prologue, or any where else that I am apprised of.

This tragedy of *The Fatal Dowry* was the joint production of Massinger and Nathaniel [*i.e.* Nathan] Field; it takes a wider compass of fable than *The Fair Penitent*, by which means it presents a very affecting scene at the opening, which discovers young Charalois attended by his friend Romont, waiting with a petition in his hand to be presented to the judges, when they shall meet, praying the release of his dead father's body . . . Massinger, to whose share this part of the tragedy devolved, has managed this pathetic introduction with consummate skill and great expression of nature; a noble youth in the last state of worldly distress, reduced to the humiliating yet pious office of soliciting an unfeeling and unfriendly judge to allow him to pay the solemn rites of burial to the remains of an illustrious father, who had fought the country's battles with glory, and had sacrificed life and fortune in defence of an ingrateful state, impresses the spectators mind with pity and respect, which are felt through every passage of the play: One thing in particular strikes me at the opening of the scene, which is the long silence that the poet has artfully imposed upon his principal character (Charalois) who stands in mute sorrow with his petition in his hand, whilst his friend Romont, and his advocate Charmi, urge him to present himself to the judges and solicit them in person . . . The judges point him out to each other; they lament the misfortunes of his noble house . . . It is in vain; the opportunity passes off, and Charalois opens not his mouth, nor even silently tenders his petition.

I have, upon a former occasion, both generally and particularly observed upon the effects of dramatic silence [*The Observer*, essay XLV?]; the stage cannot afford a more beautiful and touching instance than this before us: To say it is not inferior to the silence of Hamlet upon his first appearance, would be saying too little in its favour. I have no doubt but Massinger had this very case in his thoughts, and I honour him no less for the imitating, than I should have done for striking out a silence so naturally and so delicately preserved. What could Charalois have uttered to give him that interest in the hearts of his spectators, which their own conclusions during his affecting silence have already impressed? No sooner are the judges gone, than the ardent Romont again breaks forth –

> *This obstinate spleen*
> *You think becomes your sorrow, and sorts well*
> *With your black suits.*

This is Hamlet himself, his *inky cloak*, and *customary suits of solemn black*. The character of Charalois is thus fixed before he speaks; the poet's art has given the prejudice that is to bear him in our affections through all the succeeding events of the fable; and a striking contrast is established between the undiscerning fiery zeal of Romont, and Charalois' fine sensibility and high-born dignity of soul.

A more methodical and regular dramatist would have stopped here, satisfied that the impression already made was fully sufficient for all the purposes of his plot; but Massinger, according to the busy spirit of the stage for which he wrote, is not alarmed by a throng of incidents, and proceeds to open the court and discuss the pleadings on the stage: The advocate Charmi in a set harangue moves the judges for dispensing with the rigour of the law in favour of creditors, and for rescuing the Marshal's corpse out of their clutches; he is brow-beaten and silenced by the presiding judge old Novall: The plea is then taken up by the impetuous Romont, and urged with so much personal insolence, that he is arrested on the spot, put in charge of the officers of the court, and taken to prison. This is a very striking mode of introducing the set oration of Charalois; a son recounting the military atchievments of a newly deceased father, and imploring mercy from his creditors and the law towards his unburied remains, now claims the attention of the court, who had been hitherto unmoved by the feeble formality of a hired pleader, and the turbulent passion of an enraged soldier. Charalois' argument takes a middle course between both; the pious feelings of a son, tempered by the modest manners of a gentleman: The creditors however are implacable, the judge is hostile, and the law must take its course. [Quotes I.ii.195–219.]

[In the remainder of essay LXXXVIII Cumberland continues to follow the introduction of characters amidst the 'cluster of incidents' of Act Two.]

N° LXXXIX:

We have now expended two entire acts of *The Fatal Dowry* in advancing to that period in the fable, at which the tragedy of *The Fair Penitent* opens. If the author of this tragedy thought it necessary to contrast Massinger's plot, and found one upon it of a more regular construction, I know not how he could do this any otherwise than by taking up the story at the point where we have now left it, and throwing the antecedent matter into narration; and though these two prefatory acts are full of very affecting incidents, yet the pathos, which properly appertains to the plot and conduces to the catastrophe of the tragedy, does not in strictness take place before the event of the marriage. No critic will say that the pleadings before the judges, the interference of the creditors, the distresses of Charalois, or the funeral of the Marshal, are necessary parts of the drama; at the same time no reader will deny (and neither could Rowe himself overlook) the effect of these incidents: He could not fail to foresee that he was to sacrifice very much of the interest of his fable, when he was to throw that upon narration, which his original had given in spectacle; and the loss was more enhanced by falling upon the hero of the drama; for who that compares Charalois, at the end of the second act of Massinger, with Rowe's Altamont at the opening scene of *The Fair Penitent*, can doubt which character has most interest with the spectators? We have seen the former in all the offices which filial piety could perform . . . Altamont presents himself before us in his wedding suit, in the splendour of fortune and at the summit of happiness; he greets us with a burst of exaltation –

Let this auspicious day be ever sacred . . .

The rest of the scene is employed by him and Horatio alternately in recounting the benefits conferred upon them by the generous Sciolto; and the very same incident of the seizure of his father's corpse by the creditors, and his redemption of it, is recited by Horatio.

It is not however within the reach of this, or any other description, to place Altamont in that interesting and amiable light, as circumstances have already placed Charalois; the happy and exulting bridegroom may be an object of our congratulation, but the virtuous and suffering Charalois engages our pity, love and admiration. If Rowe would have his audience credit Altamont for that filial piety, which marks the character he copied from, it was a small oversight to put the following expression into his mouth –

Oh, great Sciolto! Oh, my more than father!

A closer attention to character would have reminded him that it was possible for Altamont to express his gratitude to Sciolto without setting him above a father, to whose memory he had paid such devotion.

From this contraction of his plot, by the defalcation of so many pathetic incidents, it became impossible for the author of *The Fair Penitent* to make his Altamont the hero of his tragedy, and the leading part is taken from him by Horatio, and even by Lothario, throughout the drama. There are several other reasons, which concur to sink Altamont upon the comparison with Charalois, the chief of which arises from the captivating colours in which Rowe has painted his libertine: On the contrary, Massinger gives a contemptible picture of his young Novall; he makes him not only vicious, but ridiculous; in foppery and impertinence he is the counterpart of Shakespear's Osrick; vain-glorious, purse-proud, and overbearing amongst his dependants; a spiritless poltroon in his interview with Romont. *Lothario* (as Johnson observes [in his *Life of Rowe*]) *with gaiety which cannot be hated, and bravery which cannot be despised, retains too much of the spectator's kindness.* His high spirit, brilliant qualities and fine person are so described, as to put us in danger of false impressions in his favour, and to set the passions in opposition to the moral of the piece: I suspect that the gallantry of Lothario makes more advocates for Calista than she ought to have. There is another consideration, which operates against Altamont, and it is an indelicacy in his character, which the poet should have provided against: He marries Calista with the full persuasion of her being averse to the match; . . . it fixes a meanness upon him, which prevails against his character throughout the play. Nothing of this sort could be discovered by

Massinger's bridegroom, for the ceremony was agreed upon and performed at the very first interview of the parties; Beaumelle gave a full and unreserved assent, and though her character suffers on the score of hypocrisy on that account, yet Charalois is saved by it: Less hypocrisy appears in Calista, but hers is the deeper guilt, because she was already dishonoured by Lothario, and Beaumelle's coquetry with Novall had not yet reached the length of criminality. Add to this, that Altamont appears in the contemptible light of a suitor, whom Calista had apprized of her aversion, and to whom she had done a deliberate act of dishonour, though his person and character must have been long known to her. The case is far otherwise between Charalois and Beaumelle, who never met before, and every care is taken by the poet to save his hero from such a deliberate injury, as might convey contempt; with this view the marriage is precipitated; nothing is allowed to pass, that might open the character of Charalois to Beaumelle: She is hurried into an assignation with Novall immediately upon her marriage; every artifice of seduction is employed by her confidante Bellaperte, and Aymer the parasite of Novall, to make this meeting criminal; she falls the victim of passion, and when detection brings her to a sense of her guilt, she makes this penitent and pathetic appeal to Charalois – [Quotes IV.iv.48–62, 68–75]. Compare this with the conduct of Calista, and then decide which frail fair-one has the better title to the appellation of a *Penitent*, and which drama conveys the better moral by its catastrophe.

There is indeed a grossness in the older poet, which his more modern imitator has refined; but he has only sweetened the poison, not removed its venom; nay, by how much more palatable he has made it, so much more pernicious it is become in his tempting sparkling cup, than in the coarse deterring dose of Massinger.

Rowe has no doubt greatly outstepped his original in the striking character of Lothario, who leaves Novall as far behind him as Charalois does Altamont: It is admitted then that Calista has as good a plea as any wanton could wish to urge for her criminality with Lothario, and the poet has not spared the ear of modesty in his exaggerated description of the guilty scene; every luxurious image, that his inflamed imagination could crowd into the glowing rhapsody, is there to be found, and the whole is recited in numbers so flowing and harmonious, that they not only arrest the passions but the memory also, and perhaps have been, and still can be, as generally repeated as any passage in English poetry. Massinger with less elegance, but not with less regard to decency, suffers the guilty act to pass within the course of his drama; the greater refinement of manners in Rowe's day did not allow of this, and he anticipated the incident; but when he revived the recollection of it by such a studied description, he plainly shewed that it was not from moral principle that he omitted it; and if he has presented his heroine to the spectators with more immediate delicacy during the compass of the play, he has at the same time given her greater depravity of mind; her manners may be more refined, but her principle is fouler than Beaumelle's. Calista, who yielded to the gallant gay Lothario, *hot with the Tuscan grape*, might perhaps have disdained a lover who addressed her in the holiday language which Novall uses to Beaumelle – [Quotes II.ii.62–6, 68–71, 'Best day to Nature's curiosity! / Star of Dijon, the lustre of all France! . . .'].

. . .

N° XC.

[Cumberland contrasts the improbabilities and exaggerations of Horatio's conduct and manner in his confrontations with Lothario and Calista with Romont's more straightforward 'warmth suitable to his zeal' in dealing with Novall and Beaumelle. He now turns to the scenes in which Horatio informs Altamont, and Romont informs Charalois, of their betrayal by their wives.]

I can only express my surprize, that the author of *The Fair Penitent*, with this scene before him, could conduct his interview between Altamont and Horatio upon a plan so widely different, and so much inferior: I must suppose he thought it a strong incident to make Altamont give a blow to his friend, else he might have seen an interview carried on with infinitely more spirit, both of language and character, between Charalois and Romont, in circumstances exactly similar, where no such violence was committed, or even meditated. Was it because Pierre had given a blow to Jaffier [in Otway's *Venice Preserv'd*, 1682], that Altamont was to repeat the like indignity to Horatio, for a woman, of whose aversion he had proofs not to be mistaken? Charalois is a character at least as high and irritable as Altamont, and Romont is out of all comparison more rough and plain-spoken than Horatio: Charalois might be deceived into an opinion of Beaumelle's affection for him; Altamont could not deceive himself into such a notion, and the lady had testified her dislike of him in the strongest terms, accompanied with symptoms which he himself had described as indicating some rooted and concealed affliction: Could any solution be more natural than what Horatio gives? Novall was a rival so contemptible, that Charalois could not, with any degree of probability, consider him as an object of his jealousy; it would have been a degradation of his character, had he yielded to such a suspicion: Lothario, on the contrary, was of all men living the most to be apprehended by a husband, let his confidence or vanity be ever so great. Rowe, in his attempt to *surprize*, has sacrificed nature and the truth of character for stage-effect; Massinger, by preserving both nature and character, has conducted his friends through an angry altercation with infinitely more spirit, more pathos and more dramatic effect, and yet dismissed them with the following animated and affecting speech from Charalois to his friend: [Quotes III.i.484–97, '*Thou'rt not my friend; / Or being so, thou'rt mad . . .*'].

. . .

It now remains only to say a few words upon the catastrophe, in which the author varies from his original, by making Calista destroy herself with a dagger, put into her hand for that purpose by her father . . . Rage and instant revenge may find some plea; sudden passion may transport even a father to lift his hand against his own offspring; but this act of Sciolto has no shelter but in heathen authority –

> *'Tis justly thought, and worthy of that spirit,*
> *That dwelt in antient Latian breasts, when Rome*
> *Was mistress of the world.*

Did ever poetry beguile a man into such an allusion? And to what does that piece of information tend, *that Rome was mistress of the world?* If this is human nature, it would almost tempt one to reply in Sciolto's own words –

> *I cou'd curse nature.*

But it is no more like nature, than the following sentiments of Calista are like the sentiments of a *Penitent*, or a Christian –

> *That I must die it is my only comfort; . . .*
> *Death is the privilege of human nature,*
> *And life without it were not worth our taking –*

And again,

> *Yet Heav'n, who knows our weak imperfect natures,*
>
> . . .
>
> *is aton'd by penitence and prayer.*
> *Cheap recompence! here 'twou'd not be receiv'd;*
> *Nothing but blood can make the expiation.*

Such is the catastrophe of Rowe's *Fair Penitent*, such is the representation he gives us of human nature, and such the moral of his tragedy.

I shall conclude with an extract or two from the catastrophe of *The Fatal Dowry*; and first, for the *penitence* of Beaumelle, I shall select only the following speech, addressed to her husband:

> *I dare not move you*
> *To hear me speak. I know my thought is far*
> *Beyond qualification or excuse;*
> *That 'tis not fit for me to hope, or you*
> *To think of mercy; only I presume*
> *To intreat you wou'd be pleas'd to look upon*
> *My sorrow for it, and believe these tears*
> *Are the true children of my grief, and not*
> *A woman's cunning.*
>
> [IV.iv.11–19]

I need not point out the contrast between this and the quotations from Calista. It will require a longer extract to bring the conduct of Rochfort in comparison with that of Sciolto: The reader will observe that Novall's dead body is now on the scene, Charalois, Beaumelle, and Rochfort her father, are present. The charge of adultery is urged by Charalois, and appeal is made to the justice of Rochfort in the case. [Quotes IV.iv.117–39.] In consequence of this the husband strikes her dead before her father's eyes: The act indeed is horrid; even tragedy shrinks from it, and Nature with a father's voice instantly cries out – *Is she dead then?* – *and you have kill'd her?* – Charalois avows it, and pleads his sentence for the deed; the revolting, agonized parent breaks forth into one of the most pathetic, natural and expressive lamentations, that the English drama can produce – [Quotes IV.iv.157–76]. What conclusions can I draw from these comparative examples, which every reader would not anticipate? Is there a man, who has any feeling for real nature, dramatic character, moral sentiment, tragic pathos or nervous diction, who can hesitate, even for a moment, where to bestow the palm?

25. Charles Lamb

1796–1808

Lamb (1775–1834) has had extensive influence on the valuation of English Renaissance plays between his day and the present through his *Specimens* of 1808, which was reprinted six times between 1813 and 1907. It retains some of the earlier enthusiasm for Massinger, Beaumont and Fletcher, apparent in (a)–(c), but Lamb now finds them lacking in the intensity and sublimity of Webster, Ford, and *The Revenger's Tragedy*, Chapman's passion, Dekker's 'poetry enough for any thing' and the sweetness and gentleness of Heywood. Lamb's brief, memorable, impressionistic remarks affected readers and critics as monumental editions did not. On the stage Massinger long continued to please audiences, but Lamb was one of the chief disseminators of the idea that true poetry was not to be sought in the theatre; already in (c) below he finds Cooke both ideally suited to Overreach and an unsatisfactory speaker of poetry.

(a) to (d) from Edwin W. Marrs, Jr (ed.), *The Letters of Charles and Mary Anne Lamb*, Ithaca and London, 3 vols, 1975–8, vol.1, pp.30–1, 35; vol.2, pp.8, 146–7; (e) from *Specimens of English Dramatic Poets, Who Lived About the Time of Shakspeare*, London, 1808, pp.vi–vii, 424, 430, 441, 453.

MASSINGER

(a) To Samuel Taylor Coleridge, 14 June 1796

Are you acquainted with Massinger? At a hazard I will trouble you with a passage from a play of his called 'A Very Woman'. The lines are spoken by a lover (disguised) to his faithless mistress. You will remark the fine effect of the double endings. You will by your ear distinguish the lines, for I write 'em as prose. [Quotes, with omissions, IV.iii.124–61, now generally attributed to Fletcher] . . . But don't you conceive all poets after Shakspeare yield to [Beaumont and Fletcher] in variety of genius? Massinger treads close on their heels; but you are most probably as well acquainted with his writings as your humble servant.

(b) To Samuel Taylor Coleridge, 29 June 1796

I writhe with indignation, [whe]n in books of Criticism, where common place quotation is heaped upon quotation, I find no mention of such men as Massinger or B. & Fl. men with whom succeeding Dramatic Writers (otway alone excepted) can bear no manner of Comparison. Stupid Knox hath noticed none of 'em amongst his extracts [Vicesimus Knox's *Elegant Extracts*, 1785].

(c) To Robert Lloyd, 26 June 1801.

[George Frederick Cooke's] manner is strong, coarse & vigorous, and well adapted to some characters. – But the lofty imagery and high sentiments and high passions of *Poetry* come black & prose-smoked from his prose Lips. – I have not seen him in *Over Reach*, but from what I remember of the character, I think he could not have chosen one more fit! I thought the play a highly finished one, when I read it sometime back. I *remember* a most noble image. Sir Giles drawing his sword in the last scene, says

> Some undone widow sits upon mine arm,
> And takes away the use on't.

This is horribly fine, and I am not sure, that it did not suggest to me my conclusion of Pride's Cure; but my imitation is miserably inferior.

> This arm was busy in the day of *Naseby*:
> Tis paralytic now, & knows no use of weapons –

[Marrs points out that these lines were later deleted from *Pride's Cure*.]

(d) To William Wordsworth, 13 October 1804 (In reply to Wordsworth's 'commissions' for books. Wordsworth had in fact already acquired 'three volumes of Massinger' in 1798 (Ernest de Selincourt (ed.), *The Letters of William and Dorothy Wordsworth* (revised by Chester L. Shaver, Mary Moorman, and Alan G. Hill), 5 vols, Oxford, 1967–79, vol.1, pp.217–18))

Ben Jonson is a Guinea Book. Beaumont & Fletcher in folio, the right folio, not now to be met with; the octavos are about £3. – As to any other old dramatists, I do not know where to find them except what are in Dodsly's old plays, which are about £3 also: Massinger I never saw but at one shop, but it is now gone, but one of the editions of Dodsley contains about a fourth (the best) of his plays. – Congreve and the rest of King Charles's moralists are cheap & accessible . . . Marlow's plays & poems are totally vanished; only one edition of Dodsley retains one, & the other two, of his plays: but John Ford is the man after Shakespear.

MASSINGER

(e) From *Specimens of English Dramatic Poets* (1808)

Another object which I had in making these selections was, to bring together the most admired scenes in Fletcher and Massinger, in the estimation of the world the only dramatic poets of that age who are entitled to be considered after Shakespeare, and to exhibit them in the same volume with the more impressive scenes of old Marlowe, Heywood, Tourneur, Webster, Ford, and others. To shew what we have slighted, while beyond all proportion we have cried up one or two favourite names.

. . .

[On *The City Madam*, IV.iv.39–135 (Luke reprehends '*The extravagance of the City Madams aping court fashions*'; the interjections by Milliscent and Holdfast are omitted as are some of Lady Frugal's).] This bitter satire against the city women for aping the fashions of the court ladies must have been peculiarly gratifying to the females of the Herbert family and the rest of Massinger's noble patrons and patronesses.

[On *The Picture*, I.i.1–90, where Mathias '*in parting with his wife, shews her substantial reasons why he should go*'.] The good sense, rational fondness, and chastised feeling, of this dialogue, make it more valuable than many of those scenes in which this writer has attempted a deeper passion and more tragical interest. Massinger had not the higher requisites of his art in any thing like the degree in which they were possessed by Ford, Webster, Tourneur, Heywood, and others. He never shakes or disturbs the mind with grief. He is read with composure and placid delight. He wrote with that equability of all the passions, which made his English style the purest and most free from violent metaphors and harsh constructions, of any of the dramatists who were his contemporaries.

[On *The Virgin Martyr*, II.i.174–218.] This scene has beauties of so very high an order that, with all my respect for Massinger, I do not think he had poetical enthusiasm capable of furnishing them. His associate Decker, who wrote Old Fortunatus, had poetry enough for any thing. The very impurities which obtrude themselves among the sweet pieties of this play (like Satan among the Sons of Heaven) and which the brief scope of my plan fortunately enables me to leave out, have a strength of contrast, a raciness, and a glow, in them, which are above Massinger. They set off the religion of the rest, somehow as Caliban serves to shew Miranda.

[On *The Old Law*, a play not now believed to contain any work by Massinger.] There is an exquisiteness of moral sensibility, making one to gush out tears of delight, and a poetical strangeness in all the improbable circumstances of this wild play, which are unlike any thing in the dramas which Massinger wrote alone. The pathos is of a subtler edge. Middleton and Rowley, who assisted in this play, had both of them finer geniuses than their associate.

[Lamb also extracted, without comment, *The City Madam*, III.iii.1–43 (Luke enraptured by his new riches), *A New Way to Pay Old Debts*, IV.i.56–133 ('Over-reach . . . treats about marrying his daughter with Lord Lovell'), *The Parliament of Love*, IV.ii.1–102 (the duel between Cleremond and Montross), *A Very Woman* (the scene by Fletcher referred to in (a) above), *The Unnatural Combat*, II.i.114–216 (Malefort and his son 'parley' and then fight), and *The Fatal Dowry*, II.i.1–143 (the funeral scene now accepted as Field's).]

26. William Gifford
1805

Gifford (1756–1826) was the first editor of *The Quarterly Review*, from 1809 to 1824. He translated Juvenal and Persius, and was the author of two satirical poems – *The Baviad* (1794) and *The Maeviad* (1795) – and a notable editor of Massinger (1805 and 1813), Jonson (1816), Ford (1827), and Shirley (1833, completed by Alexander Dyce). While the high standard of Gifford's editing did much to keep Massinger central to early nineteenth-century discussions of Jacobean drama, both Gifford's introduction and notes and the appended essays of Dr John Ireland helped identify Massinger as essentially an establishment figure, worthy of respect rather than enthusiasm, rhetorical rather than poetic (see Introduction, pp.21–2).

The Plays of Philip Massinger, 4 vols, London, 1805, vol.1, pp.xlvii–li.

All the writers of his life unite in representing him as a man of singular modesty, gentleness, candour, and affability; nor does it appear that he ever made or found an enemy. He speaks indeed of opponents on the stage, but the contention of rival candidates for popular favour must not be confounded with personal hostility. With all this, however, he seems to have maintained a constant struggle with adversity; since not only the stage, from which, perhaps, his natural reserve presented him from deriving the usual advantages, but even the bounty of his particular friends, on which he chiefly relied, left him in a state of absolute dependance. Jonson, Fletcher, Shirley, and others, not superiour to him in abilities, had their periods of good fortune, their bright as well as their stormy hours; but Massinger seems to have enjoyed no gleam of sunshine; his life was all one wintry day, and 'shadows, clouds, and darkness' [Addison's *Cato*, V.i], rested upon it.

Davies finds a servility in his dedications which I have not been able to discover: they are principally characterised by gratitude and humility, without a single trait of that gross and servile adulation which distinguishes and disgraces the addresses of some of his contemporaries. That he did not conceal his misery, his editors appear inclined to reckon among his faults; he bore it, however, without impatience, and we only hear of it when it is relieved. Poverty made him no flatterer, and, what is still more rare, no maligner of the great: nor is one symptom of envy manifested in any part of his compositions.

His principles of patriotism appear irreprehensible: the extravagant and slavish doctrines which are found in the dramas of his great contemporaries make no part of his creed, in which the warmest loyalty is skilfully combined with just and rational ideas of political freedom. Nor is this the only instance in which the rectitude of his mind is apparent; the writers of his day abound in recommendations of suicide; he is uniform in the reprehension of it, with a single exception, to which, perhaps, he was led by the peculiar turn of his studies.* Guilt of every kind is usually left to the punishment of divine justice: even the wretched Malefort excuses himself to his son on his supernatural appearance, because the latter was not *marked out by heaven* for his mother's avenger; and the young, the brave, the pious Charalois accounts his death fallen upon him by the will of heaven, because 'he made himself a judge in his own cause'.

But the great, the glorious distinction of Massinger, is the uniform respect with which he treats religion and its ministers, in an age when it was found necessary to add regulation to regulation, to stop the growth of impiety on the stage. No priests are introduced by him 'to set on some quantity of barren spectators' to laugh [*Hamlet*, III.ii.41–2] at their licentious follies; the sacred name is not lightly invoked, nor daringly sported with; nor is Scripture profaned by buffoon allusions lavishly put into the mouths of fools and women.

. . .

Mr. M. Mason has remarked the general harmony of his numbers, in which, indeed, Massinger stands unrivalled. He seems, however, inclined to make a partial exception in favour of Shakspeare; but I cannot admit of its propriety. The claims of this great poet on the admiration of mankind are innumerable, but rhythmical modulation is not one of them: nor do I think it either wise or just to hold him forth as supereminent in every quality which constitutes genius: Beaumont is as sublime, Fletcher as pathetick, and Jonson as nervous: – nor let it be accounted poor or niggard praise, to allow him only an equality with these extraordinary men in their peculiar excellencies, while he is admitted to possess many others, to which they make no approaches. Indeed, if I were asked for the discriminating quality of Shakspeare's mind, that by which he is raised above all competition, above all prospect of rivalry, I should say it was WIT. To wit Massinger has no pretensions, though he is not

*Gifford's note suggests that *The Duke of Milan*, I.iii.209–15 is to be linked with the church debates on whether suicide was permissible to avoid rape 'on the irruption of the barbarians into Italy'.

without a considerable portion of humour; in which, however, he is surpassed by Fletcher, whose style bears some affinity to his own: there is, indeed, a morbid softness in the poetry of the latter, which is not visible in the flowing and vigorous metre of Massinger, but the general manner is not unlike.

27. The Edinburgh Review
1808

Before the main analysis of Massinger extracted here, this review of Gifford's edition acknowledges his editorial skills but censures his occasional mistakes, his asperity towards his predecessors, and his inclusion of Ireland's moralizing remarks. While begging leave to disagree with 'the excessive praise which Mr. Gifford has lavished on Massinger', it treats the author with considerable seriousness and respect for his 'eloquence'.

The Edinburgh Review, vol.12, April–July 1808, pp.113–18.

Massinger, in our unprejudiced (though perhaps mistaken) opinion, is an eloquent writer; but an indifferent dramatist. His comedies have no wit; his tragedies no propriety. In his Bondman (one of the best) . . . Pisander, for the sake of showing his own continence to his beloved Cleora, excites the slaves who remained in Syracuse to revolt, and in pure good humour to ravish all the wives and daughters, and scourge all the fops, who were left behind in the city. At the end of the play, when Timoleon returns with the army, Pisander . . . receives Cleora for his bride with the good-will of all the Syracusans; and the facetious ravishing of their wives and daughters is passed over lightly, as having been a wholesome lesson to the proud dames of Sicily.

There is not, according to the best of our recollection, a single pathetic scene in all the writings of Massinger; there is not a passage, amidst all the butchery which he displays, that can draw a tear of sympathy from the audience; and he appears to have been conscious of his inability to represent a tender emotion, which he has scarcely ever attempted. In the Unnatural Combat, a tragedy in which every horror that the mind can imagine has been accumulated, and which is by no means destitute of terrific beauties, two opportunities offered themselves for the representation of the deepest emotion and distress, and both are completely neglected. The one, where Theocrine hears that her father has killed her brother in single combat; the other where Belgarde [i.e. Beaufort] finds his beloved Theocrine (who had been ravished by a ruffian, and turned out half naked in a tempestuous night) lying dead beside her father. A more dreadful scene cannot be conceived; but the only observations of [Beaufort] on this occasion are as follows:

> All that have eyes to weep
> Spare one tear with me. Theocrine's dead.

And afterwards,

> Here's one retains
> Her native innocence, that never yet
> Call'd down Heaven's vengeance.
> [V.ii.331-2, 336-8]

With these few words from [Beaufort], and a dry moral from his father, the play concludes. An author, who could dismiss such circumstances of distress, without aiming at a single expression of emotion, must have felt himself incompetent 'to ope the sacred source of sympathetic tears', and have shrunk from the attempt. 'The gates of horror' he has set wide open [see Gray's 'Progress of Poesy', ll.92-4].

Massinger's talents appear to have been better fitted by nature for heroic than dramatic writing: he excels in dignified scenes; he describes both character and passion with skill; but is unable to give them appropriate language and expression: he is eloquent, indeed, in every species of description; but his flowing, stately periods, are perhaps too lofty for the stage, and contribute to render his plays heavy and wearisome to the reader; while those of Beaumont and Fletcher, with equal faults, are far more diverting. [Quotes 'specimens of Massinger's eloquent language' including

The Duke of Milan, I.i.80–93, *The Unnatural Combat*, II.i.15–44 and III.ii.31–9, and *The Virgin Martyr* (a play full of horrors, absurdities and obscurity but containing many fine passages, and where 'Decker is less fluent and stately, hath more of conceit, and admits occasional rhymes'), V.ii.120–60.]

28. William Gifford
1813

Part of Gifford's lengthy reply to *The Edinburgh* (extracted in No. 27; whence the quotations).

The Plays of Philip Massinger, 2nd edition, London, 1813, 'Advertisement', pp.xxxi–xxxii.

'Perhaps . . . Mr. Gifford will be offended at the little ceremony with which we have treated his favourite dramatist.' Not in the least. Judgement is free to all, and the decision rests with the public. In the present case, indeed, if the anxious call for another Edition be permitted to stand for any thing, they have already determined the question in my favour. At any rate, Massinger has taken his place on our shelves; he is noticed by those who overlooked him in the blundering volumes of Coxeter and M. Mason, and cannot again be thrown entirely out of the estimate of our ancient literature.

. . .

This 'cursory dismission of the circumstance' [at the end of *The Unnatural Combat*] is attributed to the incompetency of Massinger to call forth a tear: and certain it is, that a modern writer would have *yelled out many syllables of dolour* [*Macbeth*, IV.ii.7–8] on the occasion. But this was not Massinger's mode; and it yet remains to be proved that the modern writer would be right.

THE CRITICAL HERITAGE

29. Samuel Taylor Coleridge
1809–34

Lamb mentioned Massinger to Coleridge in letters of 1796 (No. 25(a)–(b)); Coleridge (1772–1834) 'borrowed Mason's Massinger from the Bristol Library in 1797 or 1798 and presumably began that intent and affectionate study of Massinger's verse which seems to have continued right up to his death' (*EG*, vol.1, p.lvi). For further examples of this interest not included here see the index to Roberta Florence Brinkley (ed.), *Coleridge on the Seventeenth Century*, Durham, N.C., 1955, and Kathleen Coburn (ed.), *The Notebooks of Samuel Taylor Coleridge*, 3 vols, London, 1957–73, sections 3187, 3446, and 4212.

My reading of the manuscript material has been checked against those of Brinkley and the usually more exact George Whalley and R.A. Foakes in the relevant volumes of Kathleen Coburn (general editor), Bart Winer (associate editor), and others, *The Collected Works of Samuel Taylor Coleridge*, 9 vols so far, Princeton, 1969–88. Dates given for the marginalia are those suggested by the Princeton editors.

(a) Note from the flyleaves of John Barclay, *Argenis*, Amsterdam, 1659 (*c.* July–December 1809)

Of dramatic Blank Verse we have many & various Specimens – ex. gr. Shakspere's as compared with Massinger's – both excellent in their kind.

(b) Marginalia from Peter Whalley and George Colman (eds), *The Dramatic Works of Ben Jonson and Beaumont and Fletcher*, 4 vols, London, 1811, vol.2, flyleaf and p.12 (*c.*late 1817–spring 1819)

Massinger . . . might be reduced to a rich and yet regular metre. But then the *Regulæ* must be first known – tho' I will venture to say, that he who does not find a line (not corrupted) of Massinger's flow to the *Time total* of an Iambic Pentameter Hyperacatalectic, i.e. four Iambics (˘-) and an Amphibrach (˘-˘) has not read it aright. By power of this last principle (ret[ardation] and accel[eration] of time) we have even proceleusmatics (˘˘˘˘) and Dispondœuses (----) not to mention the Choriambics, the Ionics, the Pæons and the Epitrites. Since Dryden the metre of our Poets leads to the Sense: in our elder and more genuine Poets the Sense, including the Passion, leads to the metre. Read even Donne's Satires as he meant them to be read and as the sense & passion demand, and you will find in the lines a manly harmony.

. . .

It is worth noticing that of the three greatest tragedians, Massinger was a Democrat, B + F. the most servile jure divino Royalist – Shakespear a Philosopher – if any thing, an Aristocrat/

(c) Notes for lecture 'On Ben Jonson, Beaumont and Fletcher, and Massinger' given on 17 February 1818. From British Library Add. MS 34225, fols 62–7, except section 2 ('I do not mean' onwards) and the final paragraph ('I like Massinger's comedies . . .'), which are supplied from the longer version in Henry Nelson Coleridge (ed.), *The Literary Remains of Samuel Taylor Coleridge*, 2 vols, London, 1836, vol.1, pp.108–9, 111–12

Hence Massinger and Ben Jonson both more perfect in their kind than Beaumont & Fletcher – the former more to story and affecting incidents, the latter more to manners and peculiarities & whims in language and vanities of appearance –

. . .

1. Massinger – Vein of *Satire* on the *Times* – i.e. not as in Shakespear the Natures evolving themselves according to their incidental disproportions, from excess, deficiency, or mislocation of one or more of the component elements – but what is attributed to them by others. –

2 His excellent metre – a better model for Dramatists in general (even tho' a dramatic Taste existed in the Frequenters of the Stage, and could be gratified in the present size and management (or rather managerment [Foakes reads '[mis] management']) of the two patent Theatres). I do not mean that Massinger's verse is superior to Shakespeare's or equal to it. Far from it; but it is much more easily constructed and may be more successfully adopted by writers in the present day. It is the nearest approach to the language of real life at all compatible with a fixed metre. In Massinger, as in all our poets before Dryden, in order to make harmonious verse in the reading, it is absolutely necessary that the meaning should be understood; – when the meaning is once seen, then the harmony is perfect. Whereas in Pope and in most of the writers who followed in his school, it is the mechanical metre which determines the sense.
3. Impropriety, indecorum of Demeanor in his favorite characters: as in Bertoldo who is a *swaggerer* – who talks to his Sovereign what no sovereign could endure, & to gentlemen what no gentlemen would answer but by pulling his nose –
4. Shakespear's Sir Andrew Ague-Cheek & Osric displayed by others – in the course of social intercourse, as by the mode of their performing some office in which they are employed – but Massinger['s] *Sylli* comes forward to declare himself a fool, ad arbitrium authoris, and so the diction always needs the subintelligitur (the man looks *as if he thought* so and so) expressed in the language of the satirist not of the man himself – Ex. gr. [*The Maid of Honour*, II.i.33–6] Astutio to Fulgentio. The Author mixes his own feelings & judgements concerning him – but the man himself, till mad, fights up against them & betrays by the attempt to modify [a]n activity & copiousness of thought, Image and expression which belongs not to Sylli but to a man of wit making himself merry with his character.
5. Utter want of preparation – as in Camiola, the Maid of Honour – Why? because the Dramatis Personae were all planned, *each by itself* but in Sh. the Play is a *syngenesia*, each has indeed a life of it's own, & is an individuum of itself; but yet an organ to the whole – as the Heart & the Brain – &c/.– *The* Heart &c of *that* particular Whole. – S. a comparative anatomist.

Hence Massinger & all indeed but Sh. take a dislike to their

own characters, and spite themselves upon them by making them talk *like fools* or *monsters* – so Fulgentio in his visit to CAMIOLA [II.ii]. Hence too the continued *Flings* at Kings, Courtiers, and all the favorites of Fortune, like one who had enough of intellect to see the *disproportion* & injustice of his own inferiority in the share of the good things of life, but not genius enough to rise above it & forget himself – envy democratic. B. and F. the same vice in the opposite Pole – Servility of Sentiment – partizanship of the monarchical Faction –
6. From the want of Character, of a guiding Point, in Massinger's Characters you never know what they are about.
7. Soliloquies = with all the connectives and arrangements that have no other purpose but our fear lest the person to whom we speak should not understand us.
8. Neither a one effect produced by the spirit of the whole, as in 'as you like it' – nor by any one indisputably prominent as in the Hamlet – 'Which you like, Gentlemen!' [Foakes suggests that this puzzling reference is to *Hamlet*, I.v. where Hamlet twice uses 'gentlemen'.]
9. Unnaturally irrational passions that deprive the Reader of all sound interest in the Character, as in Mathias in the Picture –
10. The comic Scenes in Massinger not only do not harmonize with the tragic, not only interrupt the feeling, but degrade the characters that are to form any Part in the action of the Piece so as to render them unfit for any *tragic interest* – as when a gentleman is insulted by a mere Black-guard – it is the same as if any other accident of nature had occurred, as if a Pig had run [and] made his horse throw him/ –

I like Massinger's comedies better than his tragedies, although where the situation requires it, he often rises into the truly tragic and pathetic. He excells in narration, and for the most part displays his mere story with skill. But he is not a poet of high imagination; he is like a Flemish painter, in whose delineations objects appear as they do in nature, have the same force and truth, and produce the same effect upon the spectator. But Shakespeare is beyond this; – he always by metaphors and figures involves in the thing considered a universe of past and possible experiences; he mingles earth, sea, and air, gives a soul to every thing, and at the same time that he inspires human feelings, adds a dignity in his images to human nature itself. [Quotes Sonnet 33, 'Full many a glorious morning have I seen . . .'.]

(d) Notes from a copy of Gifford's 1805 edition of Massinger (see Ralph J. Coffman, *Coleridge's Library*, Boston, 1987, p.138) in [W.G.T.] Shedd (ed.), *The Complete Works of Samuel Taylor Coleridge*, 7 vols, New York, 1871–5 [1854], vol.4, p.262 (date uncertain)

Two or three tales, each in itself independent of the others, and united only by making the persons that are the agents in the story the *relations* of those in the other, as when a bind-weed or thread is twined round a bunch of flowers, each having its own root – and this novel narrative in *dialogue* – such is the *character* of Massinger's plays. – That the juxtaposition and the tying together by a common thread, which goes round this and round that, and then round them all, twine and intertwine, are contrived ingeniously – that the component tales are well chosen, and the whole well and conspicuously told; so as to excite and sustain the mind by kindling and keeping alive the curiosity of the reader – that the language is most pure, equally free from bookishness and from vulgarism, from the peculiarities of the School, and the transiencies of fashion, whether fine or coarse; that the rhythm and metre are incomparably good, and form the very model of dramatic versification, flexible and seeming to rise out of the passions, so that whenever a line sounds immetrical, the speaker may be certain he has recited it amiss, either that he has misplaced or misproportioned the emphasis, or neglected the acceleration or retardation of the voice in the pauses (all which the mood or passion would have produced in the real Agent, and therefore demand from the Actor or translator / emulator and that read aright the blank verse is not less smooth than varied, a rich harmony, puzzling the fingers, but satisfying the ear – these are Massinger's characteristic merits.

(e) *Table Talk*, 17 February, 5 and 24 April 1833; 15 March 1834, from Shedd's edition (see (d)), vol.6, pp.426–7, 433–4, 445, 506.

The styles of Massinger's plays and the Samson Agonistes are the two extremes of the arc within which the diction of dramatic poetry may oscillate. Shakspeare in his great plays is the midpoint. In the Samson Agonistes, colloquial language is left at the greatest distance, yet something of it is preserved, to render the dialogue probable: in Massinger the style is differenced, but differenced in the smallest degree possible, from animated conversation, by the vein of poetry.

There's such a divinity doth hedge our Shakspeare round, that we can not even imitate his style. I tried to imitate his manner in the Remorse, and, when I had done, I found I had been tracking Beaumont and Fletcher and Massinger instead. It is really very curious. At first sight, Shakspeare and his contemporary dramatists seem to write in styles much alike; nothing so easy as to fall into that of Massinger and the others; while no one has ever yet produced one scene conceived and expressed in the Shaksperian idiom. I suppose it is because Shakspeare is universal, and, in fact, has no *manner*; just as you can so much more readily copy a picture than Nature herself.

The first act of the Virgin Martyr is as fine an act as I can remember in any play. The Very Woman is, I think, one of the most perfect plays we have. There is some good fun in the first scene between Don John, or Antonio, and Cuculo, his master; and can any thing exceed the skill and sweetness of the scene between him and his mistress, in which he relates his story? [Both scenes are now regarded as Fletcher's.] The Bondman is also a delightful play. Massinger is always entertaining; his plays have the interest of novels.

But, like most of his contemporaries, except Shakspeare, Massinger often deals in exaggerated passion. Malefort senior, in the Unnatural Combat, however he may have had the moral will to be so wicked, could never have actually done all that he is represented as guilty of, without losing his senses. He would have been in fact mad.

Except in Shakspeare, you can find no such thing as a pure conception of wedded love in our old dramatists. In Massinger, and Beaumont and Fletcher, it really is on both sides little better than sheer animal desire. There is scarcely a suitor in all their plays, whose *abilities* are not discussed by the lady or her waiting-women. In this, as in all things, how transcendent over his age and his rivals was our sweet Shakspeare!

Ben Jonson's blank verse is very masterly and individual, and perhaps Massinger's is even still nobler. In Beaumont and Fletcher it is constantly slipping into lyricisms.

30. Sir James Bland Burges

1810

Burges (1752–1824), a politician who turned to literature in his later years, 'founded' his *Riches* on *The City Madam*. It enjoyed a good deal of theatrical success. There were fourteen performances of the first production in 1810, Kean played Luke with acclaim at intervals from 1814 to 1830, and Macready between 1810 and 1841 (see Rudolf Kirk (ed.), *The City-Madam*, Princeton, 1934, pp.45–50). For Macready's view of the play see Introduction, p.32.

Burges used less than half of Massinger's lines and made various plot alterations which increased the concentration on Luke. In the last act, for instance, the Indian disguises and 'magic' are removed. At the end Luke, largely silent in the original, is first abject and then eloquently defiant. When the play first appeared in 1810 *The Monthly Mirror* (vol.29, pp.154–5) pointed out how much more wronged and sympathetic Luke had become; later reviewers accordingly talked less of Luke's hypocrisy than of those moments of histrionic and psychological impact in which Kean skilfully 'maintained the equivocal tone of the character' (Hazlitt in *The Morning Chronicle*, 26 May 1814). *The Theatrical*

Observer, No.2534 (26 January 1830), noted admiringly that Kean's 'departing curse was delivered with an energy perfectly appalling'.

The extract starts with Luke addressing Sir Maurice Lacey and Lady Traffic (Massinger's Lord Lacie and Lady Frugal); Sir Maurice had reported that Sir John had committed suicide rather than, as in the original, retiring to a monastery.

Riches; or the Wife and Brother, Cumberland's British Theatre, vol.24, London, [1830], pp.61–3.

LUKE. Rail on, vain dotard! Thou art in my pow'r,
And soon shall feel it. As for you, proud madam,
I'll make you feel it, too; you shall perceive
I am the master of your fate; each hour
Shall teach you what dependence upon me is.

LADY TRAFFIC. I am prepar'd for all; it will but make me
Contrast more strongly my lamented husband
With this degenerate heritor.

LUKE. Your husband!
Could he but know the treatment I will give thee,
My vengeance would be full. Oh! that the grave
Would yield him up again, such as he was,
Complete in all his senses and affections,
Here would I stand, and as his eyes met mine –
Have mercy! save me!

[*Hides his face, staggers, and falls into a chair, c. – Lady Traffic falls on her knees.*]

Enter SIR JOHN TRAFFIC, SIR MAURICE LACEY, HEARTWELL, *and* EDWARD LACEY, R.

SIR JOHN [*Crossing to Lady Traffic.*]
Rise, I am thy husband,

| | Thy living husband. Once more in mine arms |
| | I hold thee, and receive thee as my treasure! |

MARIA
& }   My father!
ELIZA.

SIR JOHN.   Let me hold you to my heart.

LADY TRAFFIC. Am I awake? – Art thou, art thou, indeed,
Restor'd? – Alas! and can you condescend
To notice one who has so ill deserv'd
Your tenderness?

SIR JOHN.   Be all forgotten, love!
That can allay our present happiness.

[The young lovers are happily reunited.]

SIR MAURICE. That's well. Now turn thee from this scene of joy,
And look at that fall'n wretch. – Arouse thee, man!
Behold th'avenger of thy crimes before thee.

SIR JOHN.   Rise, brother!

LUKE [Sitting, C.].
No – I cannot look upon thee –
I'll fall yet lower – thus, upon the ground
My fittest place, I will lie humbly prostrate,
And supplicate for pardon and for favour.
[Kneels.

SIR JOHN.   Pardon thou hast; but look not for my favour;
Thou hast offended, Luke, beyond remission.
I've known thy practices, thy tyranny,
Thy dark dissimulation. Those who suffer'd
By thine oppression, are again set free:
But, though thy wish was foil'd, thy base intent
Bears everlasting testimony 'gainst thee.

LUKE. Let me implore you to look kindly on me!
I am a poor weak man, who will obey you,
Live but in your good favour –

SIR JOHN. I have said.

LUKE. Do you bereave me, then, of ev'ry hope?
Am I cast off for ever and abandon'd?

SIR JOHN. Give o'er, for shame. – I've answer'd thee already.

LUKE [Rising.]
Hope, then, is gone, and I'm once more myself!
There! triumph o'er the wreck you see before you!
Heap insult upon insult! – I defy you!
Bar not my way! – The world is wide enough
For all to range in. I will find my part,
And work my way in't. Curses light upon you!
[Exit Luke, L.

SIR JOHN. What strange obduracy! – But come, my love!
Let us retire, and, pondering on what's past,
May we be taught to estimate our blessings,
And shun those arts, which still defeat their aim,
And lead their vot'ries to contempt and shame.

LADY TRAFFIC. Sure, I have liv'd in one eventful day
More than an age, and bought such rich experience
As must preserve me humble. I have seen
In that bad man the image of myself;
I'll lay it to my heart: henceforth to thee,
Thou best of men, I dedicate my life, –
My proudest title, thy obedient wife.

31. Sir Walter Scott
1813, 1819

Scott (1771–1832) mentions or quotes from Massinger (chiefly *A New Way* but also *The Unnatural Combat*) fourteen times in letters between 1803 and 1827, including six jocular variations on *A New Way*, III.ii.71–2, 'Let it be dumpl'd / Which way thou wilt' (see H.J.C. Grierson (ed.), *The Letters of Sir Walter Scott*, 12 vols, London, 1932–7). His enthusiasm seems to have been based principally on an awareness of theatrical rather than poetic qualities in the plays; in (a) his unequivocal approval of George Frederick Cooke should be contrasted with Lamb's attitude (see No. 25(c) and headnote); in (b) he judges Massinger on the grounds of strength of plot and character.

(a) From a letter to Joanna Baillie, 13 March 1813 (*Letters*, vol.3, pp.236–7).

My great amusement here [Edinburgh] this some time past has been going almost nightly to see John Kemble who certainly is a great artist . . . But sudden turns and natural bursts of passion are not his forte. I saw him play Sir Giles Overreach (the Richd. III. of middling life) last night. But he came not within a hundred miles of Cooke whose terrible visage and short abrupt and savage utterance gave a reality almost to that extraordinary scene in which he boasts of his own successful villany to a nobleman of worth and honor of whose alliance he is so ambitious. Cooke contrived somehow to impress upon the audience the idea of such a monster of enormity as had learned to pique himself even upon his own atrocious character. But Kemble was too handsome too plausible and too smooth to admit its being probable that he should be blind to the unfavourable impression which these extraordinary Vaunts are likely to make on the person whom he is so anxious to conciliate.

(b) From 'Essay on the Drama', in *The Miscellaneous Prose Works of Sir Walter Scott, Bart.*, 6 vols, Edinburgh, 1827, vol.6, pp.407–9 (first published in *The Encyclopaedia Britannica*, 1819)

Although incalculably superior to his contemporaries, Shakspeare had successful imitators, and the art of Jonson was not unrivalled. Massinger appears to have studied the works of both, with the intention of uniting their excellencies. He knew the strength of plot; and although his plays are altogether irregular, yet he well understood the advantage of a strong and defined interest; and in unravelling the intricacy of his intrigues, he often displays the management of a master. Art, therefore, not perhaps in its technical, but in its most valuable sense, was Massinger's as well as Jonson's; and, in point of composition, many passages of his plays are not unworthy of Shakspeare. Were we to distinguish Massinger's peculiar excellence, we should name that first of dramatic attributes, a full conception of character, a strength in bringing out, and consistency in adhering to it. He does not, indeed, always introduce his personages to the audience, in their own proper character; it dawns forth gradually in the progress of the piece, as in the hypocritical Luke, or in the heroic Marullo. But, upon looking back, we are always surprised and delighted to trace from the very beginning, intimations of what the personage is to prove, as the play advances. There is often a harshness of outline, however, in the characters of this dramatist, which prevents their approaching to the natural and easy portraits bequeathed us by Shakspeare.

32. *The Times*

1816

In January 1816 and for years afterwards Edmund Kean's Sir Giles Overreach was a *succès de scandale*. This review, with those of Hazlitt and Reynolds (Nos 33(a), 34(b)), must stand here for a wealth of similar detailed responses (see further *Ball*, pp.59–97 and Introduction, pp.27–9).

The Times, 13 January 1816.

This play, though occasionally brought into notice within the memory of those who still frequent the Drama, has, through some misfortune, or want of management – some failure in the acting, or corruption of the public feeling, never kept steady possession of the stage. We are happy to offer it as our decided judgment that it has now reappeared under such favourable circumstances as will ensure to the London audience a long course of rich and rational delight, and to the name of MASSINGER a full, however tardy, measure of justice. Of Mr. KEAN'S performance of the character of *Sir Giles Overreach*, we have some fear of being charged with the ordinary fault of exaggeration, if we attempt to convey to others our own conception of its excellence. We think it by many degrees his grandest and most noble effort. The character, indeed, belongs in the strictest sense, to tragedy; it is a vivid picture of terrific and untameable passions, leading to the commission of the most odious crimes. SHAKESPEARE, perhaps, has scarcely ever sketched a more daring portrait. The subtle, malignant, and ironical oppressor; the hardy bravo that maintains by his sword the wrongs he offers – the miser, loaded with the spoils of triumphant avarice, dressing up to himself a second idol in ambition, that he may be refreshed by the acquisition of a double stimulus, to the accomplishment of further wickedness; all these are thrown together by a vigorous and luxuriant invention, and go to form, in the person of *Sir Giles Overreach*, a model which could only have sprung from a mind profoundly conversant in human nature, and gifted with an extraordinary power of generalizing and combining its observations. Mr. KEAN gave to this character throughout, a complexion of the deadliest hue. He gave it all its subtlety, coarseness, and ferocity. Tyrant and destroyer were written as legibly on his brow, as ever they sat upon the countenance of *Richard*. His occasional relaxation into an assumed and designing levity was not the least striking instance of his skill, and was in frightful harmony with the schemes he meditated, and the passions he but half concealed. The tone of severe though almost involuntary sarcasm, with which he never failed to utter the title of 'Lord', and the epithet 'Right Honourable', had something in it strikingly characteristic of a spirit that mocked the puerility of its own ambition. His finest scenes were his first communication to his daughter of her intended marriage with *Lord Lovell* – his avowal to that Nobleman of his disdain for every upright principle, and moral obligation – and the last – in which his villanies were detected – his schemes disappointed – his nephew liberated from his gripe – and his daughter married, under the authority of his own signature, to *Allworth*. The variety, and at the same time the intensity of passion, which burned within him throughout this high-wrought scene, has never been surpassed by any actor. The whirlwind of rage and vengeance sweeping before it every creature within its reach – was succeeded by despair so terrible – and concluded by a torpor so fixed and shocking, that the look which accompanied his removal from the stage bore no resemblance to any thing we ever witnessed, except the expression which sometimes remains upon the human countenance when a violent death has imprinted there the image of its final agonies. As a proof of the force with which this impression was communicated by Mr. KEAN to others beside ourselves, Mrs. GLOVER, who stood near him immediately before he was carried off, was so far overcome by it, as to sink into a chair beside her . . . This Play must surely become a favourite, and will, we trust, encourage the Managers to bring into circulation many other treasures from the same mine.

33. William Hazlitt

1816–20

The theatre criticism ((a)–(b) below) of Hazlitt (1778–1830) 'rests on the assumption that a play is composed of a series of "moments", crises in which the chief character is called upon to respond imaginatively to strong external influences' (Joseph W. Donohue, Jr, *Dramatic Character in the English*

Romantic Age, Princeton, 1970, p.327). Kean's Sir Giles provided him satisfactorily with such moments. But, once outside the theatre (see especially (d) below) he is unable to discover the sort of complexity which would adequately account for Sir Giles's responses. Twice he seeks out the realistic explanation for Massinger's improbabilities and gloating villains that 'such may be a true picture of the mixed barbarity and superstition of the age in which Massinger wrote'.

The comparative minuteness of Hazlitt's analysis at once provides ammunition for more hostile later nineteenth-century critics and attests his own period's sheer fascination with *A New Way to Pay Old Debts*.

P.P. Howe (ed.), *The Complete Works of William Hazlitt*, 21 vols, London, 1930–4.

(a) Review of *A New Way to Pay Old Debts* at Drury Lane, *The Examiner*, 21 January 1816 (Howe, vol.5, p.277; Hazlitt had first reviewed the production on 14 January – Howe, vol.5, pp.273–4)

The admirable comedy of a New Way to Pay Old Debts, continues to be acted with increased effect. Mr. Kean is received with shouts of applause in Sir Giles Overreach. We have heard two objections to his manner of doing this part, one of which we think right and the other not. When he is asked, 'Is he not moved by the orphan's tears, the widow's curse?' he answers – 'Yes – as rocks by waves, or the moon by howling wolves' [see IV.i.111–16]. Mr. Kean, in speaking the latter sentence, dashes his voice about with the greatest violence, and howls out his indignation and rage. Now we conceive this is wrong: for he has to express not violence, but firm, inflexible resistance to it, – not motion, but rest. The very pause after the word *yes*, points out the cool deliberate way in which it should be spoken. The other objection is to his manner of pronouncing the word 'Lord, – Right Honourable Lord' [see IV.i.44–5, 100], which Mr. Kean uniformly does in a drawling tone, with a mixture of fawning servility and sarcastic contempt. This has been thought inconsistent with the part, and with the desire which Sir Giles has to ennoble his family by alliance with a 'Lord, a Right Honourable Lord'. We think Mr. Kean never shewed more genius than in pronouncing this single word, *Lord*. It is a complete exposure (produced by the violence of the character), of the elementary feelings which make up the common respect excited by mere rank. This is nothing but a cringing to power and opinion, with a view to turn them to our own advantage with the world. Sir Giles is one of those knaves, who 'do themselves homage' [*Othello*, I.i.54]. He makes use of Lord Lovell merely as the stalking-horse of his ambition. In other respects, he has the greatest contempt for him, and the necessity he is under of paying court to him for his own purposes, infuses a double portion of gall and bitterness into the expression of his self-conscious superiority. No; Mr. Kean was perfectly right in this, he spoke the word 'Lord' *con amore*. His praise of the kiss, 'It came twanging off – I like it' [III.ii.181–2], was one of his happiest passages. It would perhaps be as well, if in the concluding scene he would contrive not to frighten the ladies into hysterics. But the whole together is admirable.

(b)   Review of *The Duke of Milan* at Drury Lane, *The Examiner*, 17 March 1816 (Howe, vol.5, pp.289–91). (The first part of the review, omitted here, includes remarks on the play incorporated in the lecture of 1820, (d) below)

The peculiarity of Massinger's vicious characters seems in general to be, that they are totally void of moral sense, and have a gloating pride and disinterested pleasure in their villanies, unchecked by the common feelings of humanity. Francesco, in the present play, holds it out to the last, defies his enemies, and is 'proud to die what he was born'. At other times, after the poet has carried on one of these hardened unprincipled characters for a whole play, he is seized with a sudden qualm of conscience, and his villain is visited with a judicial remorse. This is the case with Sir Giles Overreach, whose hand is restrained in the last extremity of rage by 'some widow's curse that hangs upon it', and whose heart is miraculously melted 'by orphan's tears' [see V.i.362–5]. We will not, however, deny that such may be a true picture of the mixed barbarity and superstition of the age in which Massinger wrote. We have no doubt that his Sir Giles Overreach, which some have thought an incredible exaggeration, was an actual portrait. Traces of such characters are still to be found in some parts of the country, and in classes to which modern refinement and modern education have not penetrated; – characters that not only make their own selfishness and violence the sole rule of their actions, but triumph in the superiority which their want of feeling and of principle gives them over their opponents or dependants. In the time of Massinger, philosophy had made no progress in the minds of country gentlemen: nor had the theory of moral sentiments, in the community at large, been fashioned and moulded into shape by systems of ethics continually pouring in upon us from the Universities of Glasgow, Edinburgh, and Aberdeen. Persons in the situation, and with the dispositions of Sir Giles, cared not what wrong they did, nor what was thought of it, if they had only the power to maintain it. There is no calculating the advantages of civilization and letters, in taking off the hard, coarse edge of rusticity, and in softening social life. The vices of refined and cultivated periods are *personal* vices, such as proceed from too unrestrained a pursuit of pleasure in ourselves, not from a desire to inflict pain on others.

Mr. Kean's Sforza is not his most striking character; on the contrary, it is one of his least impressive, and least successful ones. The mad scene was fine, but we have seen him do better. The character is too much at cross-purposes with itself, and before the actor has time to give its full effect to any impulse of passion, it is interrupted and broken off by some caprice or change of object. In Mr. Kean's representation of it, our expectations were often excited, but never thoroughly satisfied, and we were teased with a sense of littleness in every part of it. It entirely wants the breadth, force, and grandeur of his Sir Giles.

One of the scenes, a view of the court-house at Milan, was most beautiful. Indeed, the splendour of the scenery and dresses frequently took away from the effect of Mr. Kean's countenance.

(c) Prefatory Remarks to *A New Way to Pay Old Debts*, from *The New English Drama*, ed. William Oxberry, vol.1, London, 1818 (Howe, vol.10, pp.63–6)

This is certainly a very admirable play, and highly characteristic of the genius of its author, which was hard and forcible, and calculated rather to produce a strong impression than a pleasing one. There is considerable unity of design and a progressive interest in the fable, though the artifice by which the catastrophe is brought about (the double assumption of the character of favoured lovers by Wellborn and Lovell) is somewhat improbable and out of date; and the moral is peculiarly striking, because its whole weight falls upon one who all along prides himself in setting every principle of justice and all fear of consequences at defiance.

The character of Sir Giles Overreach (the most prominent feature of the play, whether in the perusal, or as it is acted) interests us less by exciting our sympathy than our indignation. We hate him very heartily, and yet not enough; for he has strong, robust points about him that repel the impertinence of censure, and he sometimes succeeds in making us stagger in our opinion of his conduct, by throwing off any idle doubts or scruples that might hang upon it in his own mind, 'like dew-drops from the lion's mane' [*Troilus and Cressida*, III.iii.224]. His steadiness of purpose scarcely stands in need of support from the common sanctions of morality, which he intrepidly breaks through, and he almost conquers our prejudices by the consistent and determined manner in which he braves them. Self-interest is his idol, and he makes no secret of his idolatry: – he is only a more devoted and unblushing worshipper at this shrine than other men. Self-will is the only rule of his conduct, to which he makes every other feeling bend: or rather, from the nature of his constitution, he has no sickly, sentimental obstacles to interrupt him in his headstrong career. He is a character of obdurate self-will, without fanciful notions or natural affections; one who has no regard to the feelings of others, and who professes an equal disregard to their opinions. He minds nothing but his own ends, and takes the shortest and surest way to them. His understanding is clear-sighted, and his passions strong-nerved. Sir Giles is no flincher, and no hypocrite: and he gains almost as much by the hardihood with which he avows his impudent and sordid designs as others do by their caution in concealing them. He is the demon of selfishness personified; and carves out his way to the objects of his unprincipled avarice and ambition with an arm of steel, that strikes but does not feel the blow it inflicts. The character of calculating, systematic self-love, as the master-key to all his actions, is preserved with great truth of keeping and in the most trifling circumstances. Thus ruminating to himself, he says, 'I'll walk, to get me an appetite: 'tis but a mile; and exercise will keep me from being pursy!' [II.iii.61–2] – Yet to show the absurdity and impossibility of a man's being governed by any such pretended exclusive regard to his own interest, this very Sir Giles who laughs at conscience, and scorns opinion, who ridicules everything as fantastical but wealth, solid, substantial wealth, and boasts of himself as having been the founder of his own fortune by his contempt for every other consideration, is ready to sacrifice the whole of his enormous possessions – to what? – to a title, a sound, to make his daughter 'right honourable', the wife of a lord whose name he cannot repeat without loathing, and in the end becomes the dupe and falls a victim to that very opinion of the world which he despises!

The character of Sir Giles Overreach has been found fault with as unnatural; and it may, perhaps, in the present refinement of our manners, have become in a great measure obsolete. But we doubt whether even still, in remote and insulated parts of the country, sufficient traces of the same character of wilful selfishness, mistaking the inveteracy of its purposes for their rectitude, and boldly appealing to power as justifying the abuses of power, may not be found to warrant this an undoubted original – probably a facsimile of some individual of the poet's actual acquaintance. In less advanced periods of society than that in which we live, if we except rank, which can neither be an object of common pursuit nor immediate attainment, money is the only acknowledged passport to respect. It is not merely valuable as a security for want, but it is the only defiance against the insolence of power. Avarice is sharpened by pride and necessity . . . When he who is not 'lord of acres' is looked upon as a slave and a beggar, the soul becomes wedded to the soil by which its worth is measured, and takes root in it in proportion to its own strength and stubbornness of character. – The example of Wellborn may be cited in illustration of these remarks. The loss of his land makes all the difference between 'young master Wellborn' and 'rogue Wellborn'; and the treatment he meets with in this latter capacity is the best apology for the character of Sir Giles. Of the two it is better to be the oppressor than the oppressed.

Massinger, it is true, dealt generally in extreme characters, as well as in very repulsive ones. The passion is with him wound up to the height at first, and he never lets it down afterwards. It does not gradually arise out of previous circumstances, nor is it modified by other passions. This gives an appearance of abruptness, violence, and extravagance to all his plays. All Shakespeare's characters act from mixed motives, and are made what they are by various circumstances. All Massinger's characters act from single motives, and become what they are, and remain so, by a pure effort of the will, in spite of circumstances. This last author endeavoured to embody an abstract principle, labours hard to bring out the same individual trait in its most exaggerated state; and the force of his impassioned characters arises for the most part from the obstinacy with which they exclude every other feeling. Their vices look of a gigantic stature from their standing alone. Their actions seem extravagant, from their having always the same fixed aim – the same incorrigible purpose. The fault of Sir Giles Overreach, in this respect, is less the excess to which he pushes a favourite propensity, than in the circumstance of it being unmixed with any other virtue or vice.

We may find the same simplicity of dramatic conception in the comic as in the tragic characters of this author. Justice Greedy has but one idea or subject in his head throughout. He is always eating, or talking of eating . . . He is a very amusing personage; and in what relates to eating and drinking, as peremptory as Sir Giles himself. – Marrall is another instance of confined comic humour, whose ideas never wander beyond the ambition of being the implicit drudge of another's knavery or good fortune. He sticks to his stewardship, and resists the favour of a salute from a fine lady as not entered in his accounts. The humour of this character is less striking in the play than in Munden's personification of it. The other characters do not require any particular analysis. They are very insipid, good sort of people.

(d) From *Lectures Chiefly on the Dramatic Literature of the Age of Elizabeth*, London and Edinburgh, 1820 (Howe, vol.6, pp.265–8)

I must hasten to conclude this Lecture with some account of Massinger and Ford, who wrote in the time of Charles 1. I am sorry I cannot do it *con amore*. The writers of whom I have chiefly had to speak were true poets, impassioned, fanciful, 'musical as is Apollo's lute' [see *Love's Labour's Lost*, IV.iii.339–40]; but Massinger is harsh and crabbed, Ford finical and fastidious. I find little in the works of these two dramatists, but a display of great strength and subtlety of understanding, inveteracy of purpose, and perversity of will. This is not exactly what we look for in poetry, which, according to the most approved recipes, should combine pleasure with profit, and not owe all its fascination over the mind to its power of shocking or perplexing us. The Muses should attract by grace or dignity of mien. Massinger makes an impression by hardness and repulsiveness of manner. In the intellectual processes which he delights to describe, 'reason panders will' [*Hamlet*, III.iv.88]: he fixes arbitrarily on some object which there is no motive to pursue, or every motive combined against it, and then by screwing up his heroes or heroines to the deliberate and blind accomplishment of this, thinks to arrive at 'the true pathos and sublime of human life' [Burns, 'Epistle to Dr Blacklock']. That is not the way. He seldom touches the heart or kindles the fancy. It is vain to hope to excite much sympathy with convulsive efforts of the will, or intricate contrivances of the understanding, to obtain that which is better left alone, and where the interest arises principally from the conflict between the absurdity of the passion and the obstinacy with which it is persisted in. For the most part, his villains are a sort of *lusus naturæ*; his impassioned characters are like drunkards or madmen. Their conduct is extreme and outrageous, their motives unaccountable and weak; their misfortunes are without necessity, and their crimes without temptation, to ordinary apprehensions. I do not say that this is invariably the case in all Massinger's scenes, but I think it will be found that a principle of playing at cross-purposes is the ruling passion throughout most of them. This is the case in the tragedy of the Unnatural Combat, in the Picture, the Duke of Milan, A New Way to Pay Old Debts, and even in the Bondman, and the Virgin Martyr, &c. In the Picture, Matthias nearly loses his wife's affections, by resorting to the far-fetched and unnecessary device of procuring a magical portrait to read the slightest variation in her thoughts. In the same play, Honoria risks her reputation and her life to gain a clandestine interview with Matthias, merely to shake his fidelity to his wife, and when she has gained her object, tells the king her husband in pure caprice and fickleness of purpose. The Virgin Martyr is nothing but a tissue of instantaneous conversions to and from Paganism and Christianity. The only scenes of any real beauty and tenderness in this play, are those between Dorothea and Angelo, her supposed friendless beggar-boy, but her guardian angel in disguise, which are understood to be by Deckar. The interest of the Bondman turns upon two different acts of penance and self-denial, in the persons of the hero and heroine, Pisander and Cleora. In the Duke of Milan (the most poetical of Massinger's productions), Sforza's resolution to destroy his wife, rather than bear the thought of her surviving him, is as much out of the verge of nature and probability, as it is unexpected and revolting, from the want of any circumstances of palliation leading to it. It stands out alone, a pure piece of voluntary atrocity, which seems not the dictate of passion, but a start of phrensy; as cold-blooded in the execution as it is extravagant in the conception.

Again, Francesco, in this play, is a person whose actions we are at a loss to explain until the conclusion of the piece, when the attempt to account for them from motives originally amiable and generous, only produces a double sense of incongruity, and instead of satisfying the mind, renders it totally incredulous. He endeavours to seduce the wife of his benefactor, he then (failing) attempts her death, slanders her foully, and wantonly causes her to be slain by the hand of her husband, and has him poisoned by a nefarious stratagem, and all this to appease a high sense of injured honour, that 'felt a stain like a wound' [Burke, *Reflections on the Revolution in France*] and from the tender overflowings of fraternal affection, his sister having, it appears, been formerly betrothed to, and afterwards deserted by, the Duke of Milan. Sir Giles Overreach is the most successful and striking effort of Massinger's pen, and the best known to the reader, but it will hardly be thought to form an exception to the tenour of the above remarks.

[Appends as a note (c) above.] The same spirit of caprice and sullenness survives in Rowe's Fair Penitent, taken from this author's Fatal Dowry.

34. John Hamilton Reynolds
1816

Reynolds (1796–1852) was Keats's friend and correspondent, a poet, and a journalist.

In addition to the pieces below, Reynolds wrote a review of Kean's *The Duke of Milan* (*The Champion*, 17 March 1816), praising particularly 'The melancholy and almost hopeless tone of his voice . . . well assisted by the eagerness of his eyes and the earnestness of his features' in V.ii.

Leonidas M. Jones (ed.), *Selected Prose of John Hamilton Reynolds*, Cambridge, Mass., 1966, pp.36–8, 132–5.

(a) From 'On the Early Dramatic Poets, I', *The Champion*, 7 January 1816

Massinger is a poet of very great ability. [Quotes Gifford (No. 26) on Massinger's 'very pathetic and interesting passage on the misfortunes of the poet'.] His plots are admirably managed; – and characters and manners are strongly drawn by him. He gives the most delicate portraitures of female gentleness and fidelity, – and depicts an elevated mind in the most commanding and dignified manner. His versification is exquisitely beautiful, and is generally one continual flow of harmony; – it resembles the calm and majestic gliding of a river. In these days, it would not be possible to refine the language of his best passages; they have in them an imperishable sweetness – the changes of time and manners touch them not. But the wit of Massinger is by no means so brilliant, as that of many of his contemporaries, – nor is his humour so chaste: and it is perhaps owing to these deficiencies that his impurities are more glaring: – he is also destitute of passion. His descriptions of nature, – and his finished and faithful delineations of noble minds, – and his general eloquence of sorrow, place him, however, amongst the finest poets of his age: though inferior to some of them in wit, he is seldom beneath them in stateliness and grace.

. . .

The following description from '*The Great Duke of Florence*,' – which, by the way, is the finest specimen of elegant comedy, that our language can boast, – is highly beautiful. [Quotes I.i.233–44, Giovanni to Lidia on the natural delights they might have continued to share, and goes on to quote from *The Fatal Dowry*, II.i (by Field), the 'very fine' 'complaint against slavery' in *The Bondman*, IV.ii.67–78, and the 'very beautiful' 'speech of Sforza, over the body of Marcelia' in *The Duke of Milan*, V.ii.60–9.]

(b) From 'Drury Lane Theatre. From A New Way to Pay Old Debts', *The Champion*, 14 January 1816

Sir Giles Overreach is the *Richard* of common life [cp. Scott, No. 31(a)]: He has all the latter's enthusiasm, and industry, and personal courage, – with, perhaps, less of subtlety and reflection, he has more of vanity, and avarice, and naked ferocity. *Overreach* is, indeed, avowedly brutal to his closest relatives, and unguardedly talkative on the subject of his crimes; *Richard*, on the contrary, is seemingly kind to those about him, and wholly reserved in his villainies: – the first calculates only on present occurrences, – the last looks out after future mishaps and successes . . . [Kean's] delineation of *Overreach* is second only to *Richard*. From the moment that Mr. Kean appeared on the stage, we felt that he was at home in the character, – his eye told us so . . . Mr. Kean was excellent in the scene in which *Sir Giles* urges his daughter to throw out lures to *Lord Lovell*: – he walked around her, – and fed his eyes upon her splendour and her beauty, – and inwardly gladdened, as if secure in his hopes: nothing could be more dreadful than the loose and heartless manner with which he bade her to be free of her favours to the young Lord, or the fierceness with which he treated her modesty and sorrow. The moment that *Lovell* appears, Sir Giles casts aside his violence and meets him smilingly: – Mr. Kean's quick change of voice and manner was admirable, – he turned from frowning to fawning in an instant, and subdued the harsh loudness of his tone, to a sound of gentleness and courtesy the most winning. When the young Lord salutes *Margaret*, the savage delight with which he spoke the following words was inimitable;

> That kiss
> Came twanging off, – I like it.
> [III.ii.181–2]

. . .

We were electrified by this great actor's style of delivering the following lines, in answer to a question touching his conscience –

> *Lov.* Are you not frighted with the imprecations
> And curses of whole families, made wretched
> By your sinister practises?
> *Over.* Yes, as rocks are,
> When foamy billows split themselves against
> Their flinty ribs; or as the moon is moved,
> When wolves, with hunger pined, howl at her brightness.
> [IV.i. 111–16]

But in the last act, Mr. Kean rose above every thing that we have mentioned. He became all energy. His heart seemed to live on its hopes of grandeur and nobility; and as he failed in his plots against *Wellborn*, his fury maddened itself into a restless joy at the prospect of his daughter's marriage. We never heard any thing spoken more exultingly than the following.

> – They come! I hear the music,
> A lane there for my Lord!
> [V.i.260–1]

His last look at *Margaret*, when he finds that she has married contrary to his wish and expectation, was full of hatred, fierceness, and hopelessness: – his clinging gaze left her not, till all his vital powers were withered up, and he sunk lifeless into the arms of his servants.

35. *Beauties of Massinger*
1817

The tone of this 'Advertisement' to an extensive and morality-centred selection of the plays is partly dictated by the need for sales (and indeed the book went through two editions in 1817). But it does suggest something both of the extraordinary esteem in which Massinger was held at this time, and of the vulnerability of his position. His growing popularity has not removed the deep-seated objection that the old plays are full of 'ribaldry and looseness'. And his reputation is not helped by his being compared only with Shakespeare, everywhere regarded as an exception, rather than with his other no less ribald, but more slowly rediscovered, contemporaries (cp. headnote to No. 48).

Beauties of Massinger, London, 1817, pp. v–vi.

[In spite of Gifford's admirable efforts] the enjoyment of Massinger's beauties is confined to the literary few: – his name indeed begins to be more popular, and the idea of his excellencies is certainly advancing; but the ribaldry and looseness, with which his plays are supposed to be interspersed, operate as a spell of exclusion from many libraries, into which their undoubted merit would otherwise be a certain introduction. The charge however is greatly exaggerated; but, even allowing its truth to a certain extent, may we not ask whether Shakespeare is not guilty of a similar fault? Yet who looks on his immortal works with other feelings than those with which all men of true taste view a naked statue? It may seem venturous to bring Massinger's name into such competition; but Dr. Ferriar, the author of the Essay on his Writings, mentions him as 'not often much inferior, and sometimes nearly equal to that wonderful poet': and many are the passages which justify the critic's opinion, and atone for the grossness, for which the age, rather than the poet, is accountable.

However difficult it may be to contend against prejudice, the following selections are published in the hope of assisting in its removal, and of bringing the poet into greater estimation, by exhibiting some of the beauties which adorn his pages, without offending the eye with the indecency which blemishes them.

. . .

The editor . . . feels convinced that the readers of the following partial selection will seek for further enjoyment in the perusal of the Plays themselves, and he anticipates the time when to be well acquainted with Massinger will be nearly as common as it now is to have an intimate knowledge of his immortal contemporary.

36. John Keats
1819

Keats clearly read Massinger with his habitual attentiveness. It has been suggested, for instance, that there is an echo of *The Duke of Milan* in a letter to Fanny Keats of 23 August 1820 ('The Seal-breaking business is over blown' inspired by 'this tempest is well ouerblowne', III.i.248) – see Hyder E. Rollins (ed.), *The Letters of John Keats 1814–1821*, 2 vols, Cambridge, Mass., 1958, vol.2, p.329, n.2. Standing in for Reynolds, he also reviewed *Riches* (No. 30, based on *The City Madam*), together with *Richard III*, in 'Mr Kean', *The Champion*, 21 December 1817 (H. Buxton Forman (ed.), revised by Maurice Buxton Forman, *The Poetical Works and Other Writings of John Keats*, New York, 1938–9, vol.5, pp.227–32). Most of the article, unfortunately, is about Kean's Richard rather than his Luke.

Text from the Rollins edition of the letters, vol.2, pp.123–4, 180.

(a) To Fanny Brawne, 1 July 1819

In case of the worst that can happen, I shall still love you – but what hatred shall I have for another! Some lines I read the other day are continually ringing a peal in my ears:

> To see those eyes I prize above mine own
> Dart favors on another –
> And those sweet lips (yielding immortal nectar)
> Be gently press'd by any but myself –
> Think, think, Francesca, what a cursed thing
> It were beyond expression!

[*The Duke of Milan*, I.iii.203–8, with substitutions including 'press'd' for 'touch'd', Francesca for Marcelia, and 'it were' for 'I were', and omitting 'though compell'd' from the second line.]

(b) To Charles Wentworth Dilke, 22 September 1819

Rooms like the gallants legs in massingers time 'as good as the times allow, Sir.' [*A Very Woman*, III.i.103. The line is now generally accepted as Fletcher's.]

37. George Gordon, Lord Byron
1819

Byron (1788–1824) mentions Massinger favourably in *English Bards and Scotch Reviewers* (1809), 1.592, and in letters of 13 June 1813 and 25 January 1819. Replying to a complimentary letter from Gifford on 18 June 1813, he intimates acquaintance with his edition. But Byron's interest in Massinger seems mainly to have been inspired by seeing Kean in *A New Way* and, as with many of his contemporaries, to have been restricted to this play. He quotes briefly from it in letters of 1 August 1819 and 8 October 1820, *The Vision of Judgement* (1821) cv and *Don Juan* (1823) IX.lxiii. Thomas Medwin reports that 'the Noble Poet was not very well read in the Old Plays' and, besides, disliked 'those old *ruffiani*, the old dramatists, with their tiresome conceits, their jingling rhymes, and endless play upon words' (Ernest J. Lovell, Jr (ed.), *Medwin's 'Conversations of Lord Byron'*, Princeton, 1966, pp.98, 93).

Leslie A. Marchand (ed.), *Byron's Letters and Journals*, 12 vols, London, John Murray, 1973–82, vol.6, p.206 (letter to John Murray, 12 August 1819).

Last night I went to the representation of Alfieri's Mirra – the two last acts of which threw me into convulsions. – I do not mean by that word – a lady's hysterics – but the agony of reluctant tears – and the choaking shudder which I do not often undergo for fiction. – This is but the second time for anything under reality, the first was on seeing Kean's Sir Giles Overreach.

38. Thomas Campbell

1819

The poet Thomas Campbell (1777–1844) included in the third volume of his *Specimens* 'Marcelia tempted by Francisco' from *The Duke of Milan*, 'Giovanni . . . taking leave of Lidia' from *The Great Duke of Florence*, Field's *The Fatal Dowry*, II.i, and five extracts from *The Bondman*: Leosthenes' parting from and return to Cleora, 'Pisander declaring his passion for Cleora' and parleying with 'the chiefs of Syracuse', and 'The Court of Justice'.

Campbell speaks for many of his more conservative contemporaries in his esteem for all that is rational in Massinger and, later in the essay, his disapproval of Webster (whose 'Pegasus is like a nightmare'; see Introduction, pp.23–4), the over-ingenious Donne, and his followers with their preposterous metaphors.

Essay on English Poetry, in *Specimens of the British Poets*, 7 vols, London, 1819, vol.1, pp.203–10.

Massinger is distinguished for the harmony and dignity of his dramatic eloquence. Many of his plots, it is true, are liable to heavy exceptions. The fiends and angels of his Virgin Martyr are unmanageable tragic machinery; and the incestuous passion of his Ancient Admiral [*The Unnatural Combat*] excites our horror. The poet of love is driven to a frightful expedient, when he gives it the terrors of a maniac passion breaking down the most sacred pale of instinct and consanguinity. The ancient Admiral is in love with his own daughter. Such a being, if we fancy him to exist, strikes us as no object of moral warning, but as a man under the influence of insanity. In a general view, nevertheless, Massinger has more art and judgment in the serious drama than any of the other successors of Shakspeare. His incidents are less entangled than those of Fletcher, and the scene of his action is more clearly thrown open for the free evolution of character. Fletcher strikes the imagination with more vivacity, but more irregularly, and amidst embarrassing positions of his own choosing. Massinger puts forth his strength more collectively. Fletcher has more action and character in his drama, and leaves a greater variety of impressions upon the mind. His fancy is more volatile and surprising, but then he often blends disappointment with our surprise, and parts with the consistency of his characters even to the occasionally apparent loss of their identity. This is not the case with Massinger. It is true that Massinger excels more in description and declamation than in the forcible utterance of the heart and in giving character the warm colouring of passion. Still, not to speak of his one distinguished hero (Sir Giles Overreach) in comedy, he has delineated several tragic characters with strong and interesting traits. They are chiefly proud spirits. Poor himself, and struggling under the rich man's contumely, we may conceive it to have been the solace of his neglected existence to picture worth and magnanimity breaking through external disadvantages, and making their way to love and admiration. Hence his fine conceptions of Paris, the actor, exciting by the splendid endowments of his nature the jealousy of the tyrant of the world; and Don John and Pisander, habited as slaves, wooing and winning their princely mistresses. He delighted to show heroic virtue stripped of all adventitious circumstances, and tried, like a gem, by its shining through darkness. His Duke of Milan is particularly admirable for the blended interest which the poet excites by the opposite weaknesses and magnanimity of the same character . . . The fever of Sforza's diseased heart is powerfully described, passing from the extreme of dotage to revenge, and returning again from thence to the bitterest repentance and prostration, when he has struck at the life which he most loved, and has made, when it is too late, the discovery of her innocence. Massinger always enforces this moral in love; – he punishes distrust, and attaches our esteem to the unbounded confidence of the passion. But while Sforza thus exhibits a warning against morbidly-selfish sensibility, he is made to appear, without violating probability, in all other respects a firm, frank, and prepossessing character. When his misfortunes are rendered desperate by the battle of Pavia, and when he is brought into the presence of Charles V., the intrepidity with which he pleads his cause disarms the resentment of his conqueror; and the eloquence of the poet makes us expect that it should do so. [Quotes III.i.106–18, 127–32, 143–63.]

If the vehement passions were not Massinger's happiest element, he expresses fixed principle with an air of authority. To make us feel the elevation of genuine pride was the master-key which he knew how to touch in human sympathy; and his skill in it must have been derived from deep experience in his own bosom.

39. Thomas Lovell Beddoes
1824–30

Beddoes (1803–49), poet and verse dramatist, drew on *The Duke of Milan* for a poisoning in *The Brides' Tragedy* (1822) (see H.W. Donner (ed.), *The Works of Thomas Lovell Beddoes*, London, 1935, p.234).

Four letters, all to Thomas Forbes Kelsall, from Donner's edition, pp.593, 595, 640, 650.

(a) 8 November 1824

The four first acts of the fatal Dowry have improved my opinion of Massinger: he is a very effective 'stage-poet' after all.

(b) 11 January 1825

The fatal dowry has been cobbled, I see, by some purblind ultracrepidarian. McReady's friend, Walker, very likely [in fact either R.L. Sheil or J.S. Knowles; see No. 40] – but nevertheless I maintain 'tis a good play – & might have been rendered very effective by docking it of the whole fifth Act, which is an excrescence – re-creating Novall – & making Beaumelle a good deal more ghost-gaping & moonlightish – The cur-tailor has taken out the most purple piece in the whole weft – the end of the 4th act – & shouldered himself into toleration thro' the prejudices of the pit, when he should have built his admiration on their necks.

THE CRITICAL HERITAGE

(c) 27 February 1829

Is it not really a ridiculous fact, that of our modern dramatists none, (for who can reckon Mr. Rowe now a days?) has approached in any degree to the form of play delivered to us by the founders of our stage? All – from Massinger & Shirley down to Sheil & Knowles – more or less French: and how could they expect a lasting or a real popularity? The people are in this case wiser than the critics; instinct and habit a truer guide than the half & half learning & philosophy of Ramblers, Quarterlys, and Magaziners.

(d) 19 July 1830

Tieck [(Johann) Ludwig Tieck (1773–1853), *Das altenglischer Theater*, in *Kritische Schriften*, 2 vols, Berlin, 1848, vol.1, pp.316–17] has translated the 2nd Maidens Trag: and attributes it to Massinger, I must ask him, Why? the poisoning and painting is somewhat like him but also like Cyril Tourneur – & it is too imaginative for old Philip.

40. Richard Lalor Sheil(?)
1825

The adaptor of *The Fatal Dowry* in 1825 may have been either James Sheridan Knowles (1784–1862), well known for his tragedy *Virginius* (1820), or the dramatist and politician Richard Lalor Sheil (1791–1851). According to Macready's memoirs it was Sheil who 'undertook the task of its purification' from grossness .(Sir Frederick Pollock (ed.), *Macready's Reminiscences*, 2 vols, London, 1875, vol.1, p.301); the first production starred Macready as Romont at Drury Lane in January and April 1825 and he played the part again in 1827. There were other revivals in 1825, 1829, and 1845, for which see *EG*, vol.1, pp.11–12.

The 'Advertisement' to the adaptation states its intention of 'substituting the manly and racy poetry of the Shaksperian age, with all its fine characterising power, for the tumour and vapidness of Rowe's harmoniously sounding lines'. In its sentimental anguishings, however, the new version retains some similarity with *The Fair Penitent* (No. 17). In the 1825 version as in the original, Charalois himself kills Beaumelle, but there was no precedent for the sensational way in which he reveals the fact to her father in this extract. In general the emphasis is more emotional than ethical; there is no discussion, for instance, of the rightness or wrongness of taking the law into one's own hands.

The Fatal Dowry, London, 1825, V.ii, pp.62–5.

Roch. She must not live, and if no hand but mine
Would strike the blow – myself would do it.

Chara. Then –
Behold what is here –

[*Takes off the black cloth from the grave of his father.* BEAUMELLE *discovered dead upon it.*]

Roch. [*Starting up.*] Almighty Heaven, my child! –

Rom. It is a spectacle interprets nobly
The symbol [*i.e.* blood], that thy hand was steep'd withal.
Now, by thy father's memory, thou could'st not
Have offered him a higher sacrifice,
And his great spirit does rejoice to see
The fearful immolation.

Roch. Oh, my child!

Rom.	Why stare you, sirs, amaz'd, as 'twere a crime You were spectators to? He hath but given To blind and slow-pac'd justice wings and eyes To seek and overtake impieties, Which from a cold proceeding had received Indulgence, or protection.
Roch.	Beaumelle, my dear child! and is she dead then?
Chara.	Yes, sir, this is her heart-blood.
Roch.	You have kill'd her?
Chara.	I should have done it by your doom.
Roch.	I spoke it as a judge only: As a friend to justice, I broke all ties of nature, and cut off The love and soft affection of a parent; I looked on you as a wronged husband, but You closed your eyes against me as a father. Beaumelle! my daughter!
Rom.	Now by all my love of Charalois and honour, I lament That reverend old man's fortune.
Roch.	Why did you take me With such a stratagem?
Beau.	Pray you remember To use the temper, which to me you promised.
Roch.	Angels themselves must break, Beaumont that promise Beyond the strength and patience of angels! But I have done – I pray you pardon me, A weak old man. And pray you, add to that A miserable father. – Can you then blame me If I forget to suffer like a man, Or rather, act the woman!

Chara. Honoured Rochfort, before
I laid your daughter on that silent stone,
Where rests my buried father, I did give her
Occasion for repentance; – I called up
The memory of virtue in her heart,
And, as the tears at last began to gush,
In the security, that she should find
Beyond the limits of mortality
That, which I could not grant her – I did strike
The pogniard to her heart, and with a prayer
As earnest as thine own, do I implore
Rest to her sinful spirit. Ha! who comes?

Rom. There is a flare of torches.
           [*Noise of voices without.*
           'This way; this way.'
Chara. I am prepared.

[Old Novall and his followers arrive, seeking to punish Charalois for the death of Young Novall. Romont's statement of the mitigating 'injuries he sustained' goes unheeded.]

Old N. Why bring you not the rack forth?
Wherefore stands the murderer unbound?

Rom. Bonds! rack, and bonds! Oh, Charalois, my friend,
Is there no way? Thou butcher of the law,
    [*To* OLD NOVALL.

Thou sanctified assassin! would'st thou dare
Coerce those arms, trenched o'er with honoured scars
To keep thine own from chains?
Since to die, Charalois, is the worst,
Bare we our naked breasts to their keen swords
And sell our lives to advantage.

Chara.   Friend, forbear!
What have I left worthy the wish to live for?
Yet I'll not fall ignobly –
Lord Rochfort and Novall, and you, that here

          Stand the spectators of this tragic act,
          This is my father's sword – I slew with it
          The man that wronged me, and 'tis red besides
          With the warm blood of one that well I loved.
          Behold the last good office, that it e'er
          Shall render unto Charalois.   [*Stabs himself.*

Rom.   Oh! Charalois!

Chara. Mourn not for me, Romont, receive
          The only legacy I can bequeath, this sword;
          Wear it in memory of the man you loved,
          And sometimes think on the unhappy Charalois.   [*Dies.*

Rom.   He is dead.
          These tears, that I was never given to shed,
          Flow from me like a woman's. – I have now
          No task left to fulfil except – to earth
          Resign thee with a fitting epitaph,
          That shall record thy virtue and my friendship.
          Oh! Charalois, in that the world esteems
          A precious gift from fortune, – in the wealth
          And beauty of thy bride, didst thou receive
          To thee and to thy friend A FATAL DOWRY.

41. Henry Neele

1827

Neele (1798–1828) delivered his lectures in 1827. His other publications include his collected poems and *The Romance of English History* (both 1827).

From *Lectures on English Poetry*, in *The Literary Remains of the Late Henry Neele*, London, 1829, pp. 129–31.

The public are much better acquainted with the writings of Massinger than with those of most of his contemporaries; for which distinction he is mainly indebted to the admirable manner in which he has been edited by Mr. Gifford, and to the circumstances of some of his Plays having been illustrated on the Stage by the talents of a popular Actor. I cannot, however, quite agree with Mr. Gifford, when he ranks this Author immediately after Shakspeare. He certainly yields in versatility of talent to Beaumont and Fletcher, whose Comic genius was very great; and in feeling and nature, I by no means think his Tragedies equal to their's, or to Ford's, or Webster's. Massinger excelled in working up a single scene forcibly and effectively, rather than in managing his plots skilfully, or in delineating characters faithfully, and naturally. His catastrophes are sometimes brought about in a very improbable and unnatural manner; as in the '*Bondman*', where the Insurrection of the slaves is quelled by their masters merely shaking their whips at them; and in '*A new Way to pay old Debts*', where *Overreach*, about to murder his daughter, suddenly drops his weapon, and says, 'Some undone Widow sits upon my arm, and takes away the use of't'. I am aware that the first incident is said to be an historical fact; but even if it be so, it is not a probable and effective incident in a Drama. 'Le vrai n'est pas toujours le vraisemblable' ['Le Vrai peut quelquefois n'estre pas vraisemblable' – Boileau, *L'Art poétique*, 3.48]. His characters are certainly drawn with amazing power, especially those in which the blacker passions are depicted; but they are generally out of nature. At least he wanted the art of shading his pictures: he gives us nothing but the bold, prominent features; we miss all the delicate tints of the back ground.

With all these drawbacks, the genius of Massinger is unquestionably great. The sweetness and purity of his style, was not surpassed even in his own days. His choice and management of imagery is generally very happy; excepting that he is apt to pursue a favourite idea too long. His descriptive powers were also very considerable, the clearness and distinctness with which he places objects before our eyes, might furnish models for a Painter. In single scenes too, as I before observed, his genius is great and original. The battle between the Father and Son in the '*Unnatural Combat*', and the dreadful parley which precedes it, are as powerfully expressed, as they are imagined. Indeed, the genius of

Massinger is, perhaps, more conspicuous in this Play, with all its faults, than in any other. The character of *Old Malefort*, although possessing all the defects which I have pointed out, is a masterly delineation, and ably sustained. Like Ford's *Giovanni*, he is the victim of a guilty passion; but instead of an enthusiastic, romantic, and accomplished scholar, we have here a veteran warrior, and the perpetrator of many crimes. The flash of lightning by which he is destroyed is another of Massinger's violent catastrophes; but such a catastrophe is finer and more effective in this Play than in some others, as it seems to harmonise with the tremendous tone of the whole picture.

42. Henry Hallam

1839

Henry Hallam (1777–1859), father of Tennyson's friend Arthur Hallam, was well known as a historian. Neo-classical values are upheld in his comprehensive history of literature, which values dignity and intelligibility of language, and strength of characterization, in preference to the poetic intensity sought by many of his contemporaries.

An Introduction to the Literature of Europe, During the Fifteenth, Sixteenth, and Seventeenth Centuries, London, 4 vols, 1837–9, vol.3, pp.609–15.

Massinger was a gentleman, but in the service, according to the language of those times, of the Pembroke family; his education was at the university, his acquaintance both with books and with the manners of the court is familiar, his style and sentiments are altogether those of a man polished by intercourse of good society.

Neither in his own age nor in modern times, does Massinger seem to have been put on a level with Fletcher or Jonson . . . He is however far more intelligible than Fletcher; his text has not given so much embarrassment from corruption, and his general style is as perspicuous as we ever find it in the dramatic poets of that age. The obscure passages in Massinger, after the care that Gifford has taken, are by no means frequent.

. . .

A shade of melancholy tinges the writings of Massinger; but he sacrifices less than his contemporaries to the public taste for superfluous bloodshed on the stage. In several of his plays, such as the Picture, or the Renegado, where it would have been easy to determine the catastrophe towards tragedy, he has preferred to break the clouds with the radiance of a setting sun. He consulted in this his own genius, not eminently pathetic, nor energetic enough to display the utmost intensity of emotion, but abounding in sweetness and dignity, apt to delineate the loveliness of virtue, and to delight in its recompence after trial.

. . .

The most striking excellence of this poet is his conception of character; and in this I must incline to place him above Fletcher, and, if I may venture to say it, even above Jonson. He is free from the hard outline of the one, and the negligent looseness of the other. He has indeed no great variety, and sometimes repeats, with such bare modifications as the story demands, the type of his first design. Thus the extravagance of conjugal affection is pourtrayed, feeble in Theodosius, frantic in Domitian, selfish in Sforza, suspicious in Mathias; and the same impulses of doting love return upon us in the guilty eulogies of Mallefort on his daughter. The vindictive hypocrisy of Montreville in the Unnatural Combat, has nearly its counterpart in that of Francesco in the Duke of Milan, and is again displayed with more striking success in Luke. This last villain indeed, and that original, masterly, inimitable conception, Sir Giles Overreach, are sufficient to establish the rank of Massinger in this great province of dramatic art. But his own disposition led him more willingly to pictures of moral beauty. A peculiar refinement, a mixture of gentleness and benignity with noble daring, belong to some of his favourite characters, to Pisander in the Bondman, to Antonio in A Very Woman, to Charolois in the Fatal Dowry. It may be readily supposed that his female characters are not wanting in these graces. It seems to me that he has more variety in his women than in the other sex, and that they are less mannered than the heroines of Fletcher. A slight degree of error or passion in Sophia, Eudocia, Marcelia, without weakening our sympathy, serves both to prevent the monotony of perpetual rectitude, so often insipid in fiction, and to bring forward the development of the story.

. . . .

Next to the grace and dignity of sentiment in Massinger, we must praise those qualities in his style. Every modern critic has been struck by the peculiar beauty of his language. In his harmonious swell of numbers, in his pure and genuine idiom, which a text, by good fortune and the diligence of its last editor, far less corrupt than that of Fletcher, enables us to enjoy, we find an unceasing charm. The poetical talents of Massinger were very considerable; his taste superior to that of his contemporaries; the colouring of his imagery is rarely overcharged; a certain redundancy, as some may account it, gives fullness, or what the painters call *impasto*, to his style, and if it might not always conduce to effect on the stage, is on the whole suitable to the character of his composition.

The comic powers of this writer are not on a level with the serious; with some degree of humorous conception he is too apt to aim at exciting ridicule by caricature, and his dialogue wants altogether the sparkling wit of Shakspeare and Fletcher. Whether from a consciousness of this defect, or from an unhappy compliance with the viciousness of the age, no writer is more contaminated by gross indecency. It belongs indeed chiefly, though not exclusively, to the characters he would render odious; but upon them he has bestowed this flower of our early theatre with no sparing hand. Few, it must be said, of his plays are incapable of representation merely on this account, and the offence is therefore more incurable in Fletcher.

Among the tragedies of Massinger, I should incline to prefer the Duke of Milan. The plot borrows enough from history to give it dignity, and to counterbalance in some measure the predominance of the passion of love which the invented parts of the drama exhibit. The characters of Sforza, Marcelia, and Francesco, are in Massinger's best manner; the story is skilfully and not improbably developed; the pathos is deeper than we generally find in his writings; the eloquence of language, especially in the celebrated speech of Sforza before the Emperor, has never been surpassed by him. Many, however, place the Fatal Dowry still higher. This tragedy furnished Rowe with the story of his Fair Penitent. The superiority of the original, except in suitableness for representation, has long been acknowledged. In the Unnatural Combat, probably among the earliest of Massinger's works, we find a greater energy, a bolder strain of figurative poetry, more command of terror and perhaps of pity, than in any other of his dramas. But the dark shadows of crime and misery which overspread this tragedy belong to rather an earlier period of the English stage than that of Massinger, and were not congenial to his temper. In the Virgin Martyr, he has followed the Spanish model of religious Autos, with many graces of language and a beautiful display of Christian heroism in Dorothea; but the tragedy is in many respects unpleasing.

The Picture, The Bondman, and A Very Woman may perhaps be reckoned the best among the tragi-comedies of Massinger. But the general merits as well as defects of this writer are perceptible in all; and the difference between these and the rest is not such as to be apparent to every reader. Two others are distinguishable as more English than the rest; the scene lies at home, and in the age; and to these the common voice has assigned a superiority. They are A New Way to Pay Old Debts, and The City Madam. A character drawn, as it appears, from reality, and though darkly wicked, not beyond the province of the higher comedy, Sir Giles Overreach, gives the former drama a striking originality and an impressive vigour. It retains, alone among the productions of Massinger, a place on the stage. Gifford inclines to prefer the City Madam; which, no doubt, by the masterly delineation of Luke, a villain of a different order from Overreach, and a larger portion of comic humour and satire than is usual with this writer, may dispute the palm. It seems to me that there is more violent improbability in the conduct of the plot, than in A New Way to Pay Old Debts.

Massinger, as a tragic writer, appears to me second only to Shakspeare; in the higher comedy, I can hardly think him inferior to Jonson. In wit and sprightly dialogue, as well as in knowledge of theatrical effect, he falls very much below Fletcher. These however are the great names of the English stage.

THE CRITICAL HERITAGE

43. Hartley Coleridge
1840

Hartley Coleridge (1796–1849), poet and essayist, was the eldest son of Samuel Taylor Coleridge. His edition of Massinger and Ford, reprinted in 1848 and 1851, was much used in the mid nineteenth century. The introduction, one of Coleridge's most substantial completed works, contains some of the period's most extreme examples of biographical speculation or 'fancy'. Even the frontispiece – an elegant engraved prospect of Wilton House – emphasizes his view of Massinger's aristocratic background and later melancholy at his separation from it.

The Dramatic Works of Massinger and Ford, London, 1840, pp.xi, xxvii–xxxviii, xliii–xlv, li–liv.

[O]ur elder dramatists have told us little about themselves, and their contemporaries have told us little about them. Letters they must occasionally have written . . . There is, indeed, a short and melancholy note [No. 1], in which the name of Massinger is joined with those of Field and Daborne; a memorial of poverty, only less afflicting than poor Burns' death-bed supplication for the same trifle of five pounds.

. . .

Of the childhood and boyhood of Massinger no record remains. It has been said, indeed, that he was brought up in the family of his father's patron . . . Could it indeed be proved that the child Massinger wandered in the marble halls and pictured galleries of Wilton, that princely seat of old magnificence, where Sir Philip Sidney composed his *Arcadia*; that his young eyes gazed upon those panels whereon the story of Mopsa and Dorcas, and Musidorus and Philoclea, were limned in antique tracery; that he was dandled in his babyhood by the fair Countess of the *Arcadia*, and shared the parting kiss of Sir Philip when he set forth for those wars from which he was never to return, – with what

165

accumulated interest should we read his dramas, several of which display an intimacy with the details of noble housekeeping, not likely to have been acquired in the latter periods of the poet's existence! Is it not possible that Sir Philip may have been his godfather, and given him his name? The conjecture is in strict accordance with the manners of that age, and almost derives a plausibility from the sequel of Massinger's fortunes. It is a common trick of Fate to flatter the infancy of those whose manhood is written in her black book . . . Many a dawn of golden beauty harbingers a day of troubled dimness: many a one has smiled in the cradle on the fair, the good, the great, and the wise, whose death-bed was without a comfort or a comforter.

. . .

Somewhere or other Massinger obtained a classical education. That his works evince . . . But his learning is no way scholastic or profound: it is that of a reader, rather than of a student. His classical allusions are frequent, but not like those of Ben Jonson, recondite, nor like those of Shakspeare and of Milton, amalgamated and consubstantiated with his native thought. They float, like drops of oil on water, on the surface of his style, and have too much the air of quotations. What erudition he possessed he was not shy of displaying; no more was Shakspeare: Jonson was not a whit more of a pedant than his contemporaries; he showed more reading, because he had more to show.

. . .

Whatever might be Massinger's tenets [i.e. whether or not he was a Roman Catholic], his works are strongly tinctured with religious feeling. He had manifestly read and thought much on religious subjects, and sometimes ventures upon topics, which might be deemed fitter for the pulpit than the stage. Gifford has highly and justly commended his reverence for holy things, and his abstinence from jocular allusions to Scripture. But I doubt whether the simple perversion of words found in the Bible to a ludicrous sense, however offensive to taste and decorum, would so much shock a modern hearer, as solemn appeals to Heaven, and discourses on the most awful mysteries, uttered by a painted player, or a boy in petticoats, upon a stage but just vacated by a buffoon or ribald rake. This incongruous mixture, derived from the old miracle-plays and moralities, is far more frequent in Massinger than could be wished. Even were his scenes entirely purged of their licence and scurrility, there would still remain an insuperable objection to prayers not meant to be prayed, but acted; and preaching, which however serious or tragic, could hardly be in earnest. Some people complain of the want of religion in plays; I complain of its superabundance. In palliation, however, of what cannot be justified, let it be remembered, that our ancestors . . . were upon much more familiar terms with their religion than we are wont to be with ours.

. . .

Massinger seems to have been of a shy, reserved, and somewhat melancholy nature. Nothing in his writings betokens the exuberant life and dancing blood of Shakspeare and Fletcher. This defect of animal spirits, perhaps, prevented him from following the example set by Peele, Marlow, Middleton, Rowley, Decker, Heywood, and Shakspeare himself, of uniting the functions of actor and author.

. . .

Mr. Gifford asks, could the play for which the small advance was solicited [in the 'tripartite letter'] be the 'Fatal Dowry'? . . . There is strong internal evidence, in the earlier scenes . . . that it was written by a man in debt, – for their direct tendency is to make creditors odious, and to hold up the laws of debtor and creditor to detestation. But it is not the only play in which Massinger has betrayed how keenly he felt 'The world was not his friend, nor the world's *law*' [see Wordsworth's *Guilt and Sorrow*, 1.505]. He seldom slips an opportunity of glancing at the abuses of the courts, and the corruption of justice. The topic was, indeed, popular, – but he handles it with the sore sincerity of a sufferer. The 'City Madam' sets forth with fearful vividness the miseries to which the mere turn of trade might reduce an honest man, and the worse than despotic power which the law put into the hands of the obdurate – allowing the same individual to be at once plaintiff, judge, and executioner. I cannot but think, that in penning the pathetic pleadings of *Luke* in behalf of the unfortunate merchants, he forgot that he was putting his own afflicted heart into the mouth of a villain. The 'New Way to Pay Old Debts', by its very title, indicates an embarrassed author; and the whole piece is a keen and powerful satire on the mis-government which furnishes arms to the wicked.

My revered father, in a lecture which I shall never forget, with an eloquence of which the Notes published in his Remains convey as imperfect an impression as the score of Handel's Messiah upon paper compared to the Messiah sounding in multitudinous unison of voices and instruments beneath the high embowered roof of some hallowed Minster, contrasted the calm, patriotic, constitutional loyalty of Shakspeare, with the ultra-royalism of Fletcher on the one hand, and the captious whiggism of Massinger on the other. He should have remembered that Shakspeare was a prosperous man, of a joyous poetic temperament, while Massinger's native melancholy was exacerbated by sorrow and disappointment.

. . .

In all probability he never married; and if he loved, he has left not a stanza nor a hint of his success or rejection. Sometimes I have imagined that, like Tasso, he fixed his affections too high for hope, as his fortunes were certainly too low for marriage. I ground this fancy, – for it is but a fancy, – on the 'Bondman', the 'Very Woman', and the 'Bashful Lover', in all of which high-born ladies become enamoured, as they suppose, of men of low degree. . . . Methinks, he soothed his despondency with a visionary unsphering of those stellar beauties, whose effluence was predominant over his affections, though they hardly consoled him with so much as 'collateral light' [*All's Well that Ends Well*, I.i.88]. He dreamed and shut his eyes, and tried to dream again – a dream he willed not to see realized, for whatever might be his political bias, he was sufficiently aristocratic in all that comes home, (and concerns our 'business and bosoms'). His social morals were derived from chivalry and feudal days . . . The reverence for descent and degree, always stronger and longer strong, in the retainers of great houses than in the great themselves, was transfused from Arthur to Philip, and betrays itself in an aversion to *parvenu* wealth and civic ostentation, worthy a forfeited Highland chief of '45, or a French marquis of the old régime. Charles Lamb remarks how acceptable his *showing-up* of the City must have been to the haughty females of the Pembroke family.

But it is only *poor* gentility that really enjoy such exhibitions, even as the rich vulgar gloat upon caricature representations of that esoteric school of fashion, in whose secrets they are uninitiate.

Massinger, who fell short of Shakspeare in his veneration for constituted authority, had a far more exclusive devotion to rank and blood. His menial and plebeian characters are, with hardly an exception, worthless, disagreeable, and stupid – stupider than he meant them to be; as he had no turn for low comedy, nor indeed for comedy of any sort, if comedy be that which 'tendeth to laughter' [*Henry IV*, Part Two, I.ii.8]; for of all dull jokers he would have been the dullest, if Ford had not contrived to be still more dull. His fools are 'fools indeed' [Edward Young, *Love of Fame*, satire 2, 1.282], and bores and blockheads into the bargain. His attempts at drollery painfully remind you of 'Sober Lanesborough dancing in the gout' [Pope's *Moral Essays*, Epistle 1, 1.251]. What is much more grievous, he puts his worst ribaldry into the mouths of females. His chastest ladies are very *liberal* of speech, even according to the standard of his age, but some of his 'humble companions' and waiting-gentlewomen would disgrace a penitentiary. I speak not of such as *Calipso* in the 'Guardian', who only talk *professionally*, but of those in whom some regard to modesty and their mistresses' ears would not have been *dramatically* improper. It is a comfort that they resemble no *real* women of any sort, and that *no* women had to act them.

. . .

Complaint [in his dedications] seems to have become habitual to him, like the sickly tone of a confirmed valetudinarian, who thinks you unfeeling if you tell him he is looking well. We are accustomed to hear of the peaceful days of Charles, as days when the sister Muses sang together in the warm light of a Christian Phoebus. Yet Massinger continually talks of his 'despised quality', and addresses each successive dedicatee as his sole and last hope. Gifford says, 'all Massinger's patrons were persons of worth and consideration'. He never degraded himself, like poor Otway, by dedicating to a titled courtezan [*Venice Preserv'd* (1682) was dedicated to Charles II's mistress, the Duchess of Portsmouth]; but his principal patron, Philip of Pembroke and Montgomery, has left a stain upon the name of Herbert which no dedication can wash away. His ignorance and cowardice have, no doubt, been much exaggerated; but of his brutality, meanness, and ingratitude, there can be no doubt at all . . . Is it not lamentable to see a man like Massinger, whom we would preserve in everlasting remembrance, constrained to write nonsense [in 'Sero, Sed Serio'] for a poor pittance from one who deserved not the impunity of oblivion?

. . .

Massinger did feel, painfully feel his humiliation. The degradation of patronage ate into his soul . . . To inward disquietude, and a desire to utter in falsetto what his poverty forbade him to speak in his natural tones, rather than to any sincere sympathy with the nascent republicanism of his age, we must ascribe the angry dislike of kings, and courts, and ministers, which is so obtrusive in Massinger's plays, and the unnecessary, – unpoetical baseness of many of his characters. His political sentiments, abstractedly considered, are, for the most part, just; but they are thrust in head and shoulders, where there is no dramatic call for them.

. . .

The subject [of *The King and the Subject*] has great dramatic capabilities; but I doubt whether Massinger would treat it worthily either of the theme, or of himself. Neither Comedy nor Tragedy, in the strictest force of the terms, was his province. Besides, he had an unlucky habit of getting into a passion with his bad characters, and making them wilful demonstrators of their own depravity. Smollett, particularly in his Count Fathom, falls into this mistake. Euripides was not free from it. It nowhere occurs in Homer, Cervantes, or Shakspeare, the great and true dramatists, and very seldom in Fielding or Sir Walter Scott.

Massinger's excellence – a great and beautiful excellence it is – was in the expression of virtue, in its probation, its strife, its victory. He could not, like Shakspeare, invest the perverted will with the terrors of a magnificent intellect, or bestow the cestus of poetry on simple unconscious loveliness.

. . .

On the 16th March [1640], he went to bed in apparent health, and was found dead in the morning in his house on the Bankside. Such is the received account; but he seems to have had none to care for him, none to mark his symptoms, or detect the slow decay which he might conceal in despair of sympathy.

> Poorly, poor man, he lived – poorly, poor man, he died.
> [Phineas Fletcher, *The Purple Island*, I.xix]

He was buried in the churchyard of St. Saviour's, and the comedians were his only mourners – perhaps half envious of his escape from the storm that was already grumbling afar, and sending ahead its herald billows. No stone marked his neglected resting-place, but in the parish register appears this brief memorial, 'March 20, 1639–40 – buried Philip Massinger, a STRANGER'.* His sepulchre was like his life, obscure: like the nightingale, he sung darkling – it is to be feared, like the nightingale of the fable, with his breast against a thorn.

44. *The City Madam*

1844

Samuel Phelps played Luke in an anonymous version of *The City Madam* at the Theatre Royal, Sadler's Wells, sixteen times in 1844–5 and four more times between 1852 and 1862 (see Rudolf Kirk (ed.), *The City-Madam*, Princeton, 1934, pp.50–1). The reviser 'sentimentalized the comedy, making Luke the victim of Goldwire and Tradewell's persuasions to evil' (*EG*, vol.4, pp.14–15).

In this extract from the last Act Luke, having forced Lady Frugal, 'thou cruel, kindless woman', to leave by the street door, turns to her daughters, only to be restored to sanity and forgiveness when he remembers his earlier reaction to Mary, 'God bless her! She called me good!' According to

---

*By the second edition (1848) Coleridge was able to include a note citing Collier to the effect that 'stranger' was a term used for 'every person there buried, who did not belong to the parish' and that Massinger was (allegedly) 'interred with unusual cost and ceremony'. But he kept the text unaltered, 'the more', he claimed, 'to fix attention on the correction'.

The Era (3 November) in 1844 'the character was a little over-acted' but in this last scene 'his wild love, and stupefied horror at his own baseness, amply compensate for any minor defects, and stamp it a beautiful piece of acting'. Contrast Luke's defiance at the end of *Riches* (No. 30).

British Museum Add. MS 42979, fols 730b–732b, with some punctuation added.

Luke.   . . . and health to thee
        My gentle Anne, there be dogs in the streets;
        Thou canst spend thy wrath on them, & think them
        Uncles Luke.

Anne passes to door

        – And health to –

As Mary passes she looks up in his face – he pauses – and recollects that she had spoken kindly to him – he turns pale and drops the cup.

        – I said 'God bless her'!

Sir M. Must they depart;
        So unprepared, so wretched!

Luke.   No, not for worlds!
        O God what have I done!

He endeavours to recollect the past – looks around him. Sobs convulsively, and grasping the hand of Mary, falls into a chair.

Sir M. He faints,
        This is very strange.

Sir John appears in the back ground.

Mary.   He looked kindly upon me.

Sir M. His reason wanders – in his perfect mind
        He'd not have been this tyrant. [*to Sir J*]

Sir J. Or mad, or wicked, I'll not silent be,
        And see my wife and children thus misused.

Sir M. One moment stay, He is recovering.

172

Luke.	What's this, where am I?
Mary.	In your own house, Good Master Luke.
Luke.	Thank God it is no dream. The angel lives! 'Good'. 'Good' the word again: I am happy, very happy, thou art near me I must be happy now [*embraces her fondly.*]
Sir J.	What does this mean?
Sir M.	Not a word.
Luke.	These clothes do ill become thee. Why did'st put them on?
Mary.	You did desire it, Sir!
Luke.	I! When?
Mary.	This morning, Sir.
Luke.	No. No. Not 'Sir'. Uncle Luke, thats the word Mary, Uncle Luke.
Mary.	Good Uncle Luke.
Luke.	Ay. Ay. God bless thee! [*embraces her.*]
Sir M.	Is it your pleasure they should now depart?

Luke pays no attention to this, but places Mary in the chair he had quitted, & parting the hair upon her forehead kisses her.

Luke.	Thou wilt not leave me, Mary!
Mary.	When you command Uncle, I must obey.
Luke.	No! You shall command I will obey, and next to heaven I'll honour thee. *Kneels to Mary.*
Mary.	Sir!
Luke.	Nay sit: for thou hast done an angels work, Dispelled by one sweet word, the fever of My brain, restored me to myself. Wealth is come

Too suddenly upon my poverty –
But that is past – I cannot think of sorrow
When I look on you.

. . .

[Luke proceeds to ask the pardon and forgiveness of Lady Frugal and her daughters.]

Luke.   You can forgive! and will! and you and you.

Looks round at each and then observes Sir John.

    Have mercy. Save me!   [*shrieks and falls in chair.*

Lady Frugal falls on her knees

Sir J.   Rise Meg: I am thy loving husband
Pleased to behold thy reformation, and
Once more in mine arms to hold thee.

Anne &
Mary.   My father!

Sir J.   Let me hold you to my heart.

Lady F.   Art thou indeed
Restor'd, and can'st thou notice her again
Who has so ill deserved your tenderness?

Sir John.   Be all the past forgotten, live, in our
Present happiness, and we must cheer poor Luke.

Mary.   Be it
My task. Uncle! good Uncle!

Luke.   I cannot look upon him. I will fall yet lower.
Thus upon the ground, I will be prostrate
And supplicate for pardon.   [*kneels.*]

Sir J.   Thou hast it, Luke
If pardon be requir'd. Why man, I used
Thee for my instrument in a good work,
And though thou hast cut deeper than I wished
The wounds are heal'd, & the good work is done
Brother!   [*extending arms.*]

Mary. Uncle! You will embrace my father?
Leads Luke into his brothers arms.
Sir M. Now I'll complete my work.
Exits, and reenters with Edmund & Plenty.
        Young ladies, do you know these gentlemen?
Plenty. My gentle Mary!
Edw.[sic] My adored Anne!
Lady F. I have in one day lived an age
        And have bought such experience
        As must preserve me humble.
Luke. And may I hope for calm, content, and peace!
Curtain Falls

45. Edwin P. Whipple

1859

Whipple (1819–86) was a popular New England lecturer and essayist. Speaking in 1859, he is more persuaded than most later nineteenth-century commentators that Massinger's political topicality, 'equable' temperament, well-designed plays, and elegant smooth verse outweigh his lack of poetry and 'creative imagination'.

From an essay on Beaumont and Fletcher, Ford, and Massinger originally given as lectures at the Lowell Institute in 1859, first printed in *The Atlantic Monthly* in 1867–8. Text here from *The Literature of the Age of Elizabeth*, Boston, 1883, pp.178–85.

Massinger's life seems to have been one long struggle with want . . . When poverty was not present, it seems to have been always in prospect. He had a morbid vision of approaching calamities, as – 'Creeping billows / Not got to shore yet'. It is difficult to determine how far his popular principles in politics interfered with his success at the theatre. Fletcher's slavish political doctrines were perfectly suited to the court of James and Charles . . . Massinger, on the contrary, was as strong a Liberal as Hampden or Pym. The political and social abuses of his time found in him an uncompromising satirist. Oppression in every form, whether of the poor by the rich, or the subject by the king, provoked his amiable nature into unwonted passion. In his plays he frequently violates the keeping of character in order to intrude his own manly political sentiments and ideas. There are allusions in his dramas which, if they were taken by the audience, must have raised a storm of mingled applause and hisses. [Gives details of the licensing difficulties with *Believe As You List* and *The King and the Subject*.]

Massinger's spirit, though sufficiently independent and self-respectful, was as modest as Addison's. He chid his friends when they placed him as a dramatist by the side of Beaumont and Fletcher. All the commendatory poems prefixed to his plays evince affection for the man as well as admiration for the genius. But there is a strange absence of distinct memorials of his career; and his death and burial were in harmony with the loneliness of his life. [Quotes Hartley Coleridge (No. 43) on Massinger's obscure sepulchre and sad death.]

Massinger possessed a large though not especially poetic mind, and a temperament equable rather than energetic. He lacked strong passions, vivid conceptions, creative imagination. In reading him we feel that the exulting, vigorous life of the drama of the age has begun to decay. But though he has been excelled by obscurer writers in special qualities of genius, he still attaches us by the harmony of his powers, and the uniformity of his excellence. The plot, style, and characters of one of his dramas all conduce to a common interest. His plays, indeed, are novels in dialogue. They rarely thrill, startle, or kindle us, but, as Lamb says, are 'read with composure and placid delight' [No. 25(e)]. *The Bondman, The Picture, The Bashful Lover, The Renegado, A Very Woman, The Emperor of the East,* interest us specially as stories. *The Duke of Milan, The Unnatural Combat,* and *The*

Fatal Dowry are his nearest approaches to the representation of passion, as distinguished from its description. The leading characters in The City Madam and A New Way to pay Old Debts are delineated with more than common power, for they are embodiments of the author's hatred as well as of his genius. Massinger's life was such as to make him look with little favor on the creditor portion of the British people; and when creditors were also oppressors, he was roused to a pitch of indignation which inspired his conceptions of Luke and Sir Giles Overreach.

Massinger's style, though it does not evince a single great quality of the poet, has always charmed English readers by its dignity, flexibility, elegance, clearness, and ease. His metre and rhythm Coleridge pronounces incomparably good. Still his verse, with all its merits, is smooth rather than melodious; the thoughts are not born in music, but mechanically set to a tune; and even its majestic flow is frequently purchased at the expense of dramatic closeness to character and passion.

Though there is nothing in Massinger's plays, as there is in Fletcher's, indicating profligacy of mind and morals, they are even coarser in scenes; for as Massinger had none of Fletcher's wit and humor, he made his low and inferior characters, whether men or women, little better than beasts. As even his serious personages use words and allusions which are now banished from all respectable books, we must suppose that decorum, as we understand it, was almost unknown in the time of James and Charles. Thus The Guardian, one of the most mellifluous in diction and licentious in incident of all Massinger's works, was acted at the court of Charles I., and acted, too, by order of the king, on *Sunday*, January 12, 1633. This coarseness is a deplorable blot on Massinger's plays; but that it is to be referred to the manners of his time, and not to his own immorality, is proved by the fact that his vital sympathies were for virtue and justice, and that his genius never displayed itself in his representations of coarse depravity. As a man he seems to have had not merely elevated sentiments, but strong religious feelings. If his unimpassioned spirit ever rose to fervor, the fervor was moral; his best things are ethically, as well as poetically the best; and in reading him, we often find passages like the following, which leap up from the prosaic level of his diction as by an impulse of ecstacy: –

>   When good men pursue
> The path marked out by virtue, the blest saints
> With joy look on it, and seraphic angels
> Clap their celestial wings in heavenly plaudits
>   [*The Maid of Honour*, V.i.87–90]
>
>   Honor is
> Virtue's allowed ascent; honor, that clasps
> All perfect justice in her arms, that craves
> No more respect than what she gives, that does
> Nothing but what she'll suffer
>   [*A Very Woman*, IV.ii.98–102]
>
>   As you have
> A soul moulded from heaven, and do desire
> To have it made a star there, make the means
> Of your ascent to that celestial height
> Virtue winged with brave action: they draw near
> The nature and the essence of the gods
> Who imitate their goodness.
>
>   . . .
>
>   By these blessed feet
> That pace the paths of equity, and tread boldly
> On the stiff neck of tyrannous oppression,
> By these tears by which I bathe them, I conjure you
> With pity to look on me.
>   [*The Emperor of the East*, I.ii.132–8, 147–51]

46. Sir Adolphus William Ward

1875

Ward (1837–1924), Professor of History and English Language and Literature at Owens College, Manchester, from 1866, was later Vice-Chancellor of the Victoria University in Manchester and, from 1900, Master of Peterhouse, Cambridge. Both as a historian and more particularly as a literary historian he commanded widespread respect.

His 'essentially rhetorical' Massinger foreshadowed Leslie Stephen's version of two years later.

A History of English Dramatic Literature to the Death of Queen Anne, 2 vols, London, 1875, vol.2, pp.263, 268–92. (The frequent omissions indicated in these extracts are usually designed to remove the plot summaries which Ward alternates with comment.)

[H]aving been long since well edited by a competent hand, [Massinger] has been the subject of a more appreciative and exhaustive criticism than has fallen to the lot of most of his contemporaries. It is possible that his merits have thus come to be elevated above the place properly belonging to them in a comparative estimate of the chief writers of the Elisabethan drama; yet it may safely be asserted that, little as we know of Massinger personally, few names in our dramatic literature are entitled to a more cordial respect.

. . .

What little can be added to this barren record of a fruitful life must consist entirely of deductions as to Massinger's character from the works which he has left to us. They seem to me to show that, whether or not he was through manhood under the influence of a stricter faith than that of the national Church, he was a man of unusually sure and steady religious piety. On the other hand, in his views of political relations he exhibits as a rule a moderate liberalism, if the term be permitted, by no means usual among the dramatists, or indeed among the poets in general, of his age. With a lofty conception of the privileges and position of princes he combines a freedom from any slavish view of the difference between them and other men, and a tolerably distinct sense of the limits of their prerogative. To the former greatness of his country he seems to have cast back a glance of lingering regret [quotes *The Maid of Honour*, I.i.220–9]; but so far as we can judge from the evidence of his extant dramas, he was as discreet in the expression of his views of political life as he was sound in those views themselves. Of such scholarship as he might have carried away from Oxford I find few traces in his plays; but his versatility in the choice of subjects seems to indicate that he was a man of considerable reading, and by no means willing to confine himself to the range with which most of his contemporaries were satisfied. The severe apprenticeship through which a dramatist had to pass in this period was probably in few cases put to so conscientious a use as in that of Massinger, whose works almost uniformly bear the impress – and I think the term implies something besides a cavil – of genuine hard work. The tone of his addresses to the public is as a rule characterised by a dignified modesty; and such traces as are discoverable of his relations with his fellow-dramatists point in the same direction.

. . .

[In *The Virgin Martyr*] the language here and there rises to eloquence; but upon the whole, the power of the execution is hardly equal to the grandeur of the sentiment . . . The distinguishing merit of this tragedy lies in the grandeur of the conception, which indicates a noble ambition to rise above the level of the themes to which the English tragedy of the age had accustomed itself and its audiences.

. . .

[The plot of *The Unnatural Combat*] is of the gloomiest and ghastliest description . . . That there is some force in the depiction of Malefort's endeavour to combat his own infatuation (IV.i), and of the bestial villainy of his false friend Montreville, is undeniable; but no robe of poetic beauty is thrown over the spectral outline of such a plot as this; and the profusion of appalling effects, especially at the close . . . has to compensate for the author's inability to humanise so inhuman a theme.

[In *The Duke of Milan*,] repulsive and unrelieved by either pathos or humour as the the action must be allowed to be, there is some force in the versatile villainy of Francisco (which, like that of Iago, is only palliated by the existence of a motive for revenge), and some truthfulness in the change effected in the conduct of Marcelia by the discovery of her husband's unreasonably selfish passion. Thus, though unpleasing in the extreme, the developement of the plot cannot be described as unnatural, and even displays a certain moral power in illustrating the results of the ungovernable passion of a really lawless mind. With some skill too the politic wisdom of Duke Sforza's public conduct is

contrasted with the headstrong rashness of his action in his private affairs. The play, as a whole, is most effective; but it altogether lacks the alternation of light and shade requisite to render the treatment of such a subject artistically enjoyable; while the horrors of the last act are of a nature to repel any but the most jaded taste.
The Bondman . . . is undoubtedly one of Massinger's more remarkable works . . . [Until the return of Leosthenes] the intrigue is very interesting; but when in the end it appears that the Bondman is a disguised gentleman of Thebes . . . the action loses the interest of novelty, and some of the force is taken out of the eloquent declamations on the wrongs of slaves. Of Massinger's rhetorical ability this play furnishes abundant evidence.

. . .

The subject [of *The Roman Actor*] is very happily chosen, and worked out with a sincerity of feeling for which it is not difficult to account. There was some boldness in making an actor the hero of a tragedy, and showing in his person how true a dignity of mind is sometimes to be found where the world is least disposed to seek it . . . [The] device of a play within the play . . . [is] so ingeniously . . . varied, and so effectively is a climax brought about in the series, that even in this respect the construction deserves high praise. The overthrow of Domitian himself, brought about by an episode of some power, though accompanied by an unnecessary display of ghosts, serves as a fitting close; and there is sufficient individuality in the character of the tyrant, and sufficient reality of passion in that of Domitia, to furnish impressive contrasts to the tranquil dignity, enhanced by effective opportunities for the display of his artistic power, of the hero of the tragedy.
The Great Duke of Florence . . . though of a very different cast, is likewise one of Massinger's best dramas. An air of refinement unusual in him graces this comedy . . . The character of Lidia . . . though not wholly free from artificiality, is one of the few conceptions revealing a sense of true maidenly purity which the drama of this period furnishes; and there are passages in the play which approach – it cannot perhaps be said that they more than approach – to poetic pathos [instances Giovanni's speeches at I.i.227f. and V.ii.55f.]. The humour of Calandrino . . . is a favourable specimen of a hackneyed type.

The Maid of Honour . . . is a well-constructed play . . . [The] close adds a certain nobility to the play, and though the solution resorted to would certainly not be acceptable to a modern English audience, appears not to have interfered with its popularity . . .

In *The Picture* . . . we are once more taken back to one of those comedies of sheer intrigue of which the stage of this period is so wearisomely prolific . . . The rather ingenious plot . . . is not ineffectively worked out; though as usual Massinger has but little true pathos or humour at command for interesting us in the persons of the action, instead of merely stimulating curiosity by the turns of the action itself. The honest old councillor Eubulus is a good representative of a type much affected by Beaumont and Fletcher, and indeed by many other dramatists. The rascally courtiers Ubaldo and Ricardo are too offensive to be amusing.

. . .

The Fatal Dowry . . . seems to me undeserving of very high admiration. If some of its characters possess more individuality than is ordinarily the case in Massinger's dramas, the action is less happily constructed than in many of his other plays. Our sympathy is certainly powerfully engaged at the outset on behalf both of the noble Charolais . . . and of the generous Rochfort . . . Romont, Charolais' blunt outspoken friend, is likewise a character drawn with unusual vigour, although of a sufficiently familiar type. But when, after this telling introduction, the real action of the play ensues, and Beaumelle falls a victim to the seductions of a contemptible fribble . . . her guilt is so little excusable, as hardly to be atoned for, in a dramatic sense, even by her repentance and death. In real life indeed a Novall may lead a Beaumelle astray; but such an amour is as aesthetically unpleasant as it is morally to be condemned; and a mightier wave of repentance than it was in the author's power to represent would be needed to wash off the double stain. But though hardly equal to the occasion, the closing scene of act iv, in which Beaumelle after a penitent confession is sentenced by her father and slain by her husband, is not without real feeling and power. The fifth act, on the other hand . . . is merely rhetorical in conception and execution; the catastrophe, his death, is brought about so to speak inorganically, by the hand of a faithful follower of the seducer; and the moral drawn from the whole is to the last degree trite [quotes V.ii.338–42, noting that 'It is a lawyer who speaks'].

A New Way to Pay Old Debts . . . [has been] repeatedly revived on the stage, of which it may still be said to hold possession. This enduring popularity is probably due to two circumstances. In the first place, the central character of the comedy (Sir Giles Overreach) is one of genuine dramatic force, and is developed through a succession of effectively contrasted situations, from the height of triumph to the depth of overthrow. Secondly, this play is remarkable for a strong didactic element, clothed in rhetoric of a very striking kind; and the combination of this feature with the former has always proved irresistible to the theatrical public . . .

Sir Giles Overreach . . . knows neither of scruples nor of pity; . . . in all his doings and schemes he is a ruthless fiend, without even the one human fibre in his nature which even a Shylock or a Barabas possesses . . .

It will thus be obvious that Massinger designed this character both with the view of painting a monster of moral iniquity, and with that of commenting on a social evil — as it seemed to them and to the classes to whose patronage they to a great extent looked — which much occupied the dramatists of this age. Sir Giles Overreach is made to declare that there has ever been 'a feud, a strange antipathy / Between us and true gentry —' [II.i.88–9] and it was thus sought to bring home by means of this terrible example the dangers threatening the nobility and gentry of the country from the usurpation of the wealthy commercial classes . . . [In the end] Overreach himself goes mad. I mention this last effect thus incidentally, because it is introduced rather as a stage device than with any real power of writing. Indeed, even in the finest passages of this play there is evidence of the *effort* generally traceable in Massinger; while the comic character of Justice Greedy is commonplace enough.

. . .

No other of Massinger's plays more commends itself by an effective mixture of abundant incident and noble sentiment than this romantic drama [*The Bashful Lover*], which from a theatrical point of view well deserved the success it achieved. Two plots are skilfully combined in it . . . . In Honorio . . . Massinger furnishes a nobler type of character than is usual either with him or with most of his contemporaries; and in the adventures of Ascanio—

Maria he has a subject in itself as pathetic as any of Beaumont and Fletcher's (the situation in Octavio's retreat vaguely resembles Imogen's refuge in *Cymbeline*). The course of the action is in either case determined in favour of the right; and the conqueror of Matilda's father, who has the Princess herself in his power, pays a tribute to virtue surpassing the traditional self-denial of Scipio. If in spite of all this the play is likely to leave the reader cold, the reason is to be sought in the fact that the rhetorical genius of Massinger could not even with such a subject as this pass beyond its bounds; there is too much argument, too much unction, and too much protesting in the dialogue, while with so many opportunities at hand, no situation is ever seized and realised with a genuinely impressive force. Such is my opinion of a work which for elevation of sentiment deserves a more than passing notice among the productions of the later Elisabethan drama.

. . .

Massinger appears to me to furnish a signal illustration of a connexion between cause and effect on which it is unfortunately necessary to insist. The moral dignity of his sentiment is at once the basis and the source of much of his highest dramatic effectiveness . . . In Massinger we seem to recognise a man who firmly believes in the eternal difference between right and wrong, and never swerves aside from the canon he acknowledges . . .

In Massinger's plays the conflict between lust and chastity is a frequent theme, though by no means in the same degree as in other of our Elisabethan dramatists. Fortitude inspired by religious conviction; endurance steeled by the consciousness of a righteous cause; tyranny punished by its own excess; self-control rising superior to the command of irresistible authority; woman's readiness for self-sacrifice as reconcileable with her purity, man's victorious endeavour to resist the potent influence of passion, – such are among the motive agencies which he represents as moral forces determining the course of life. The poet – and indeed the historian likewise – who fails to see that forces such as these are elements at least as appreciable in their results as gusts of passion on the one hand, and accumulations of physical powers on the other, is likely to take a very one-sided view of the scheme of human life. Massinger's strength lies to no small extent in his apprehension of these moral forces.

He is less successful in exhibiting the phases of a moral conflict by means of the dramatic developement of character, and thus cannot be said to satisfy the highest test of dramatic power. He generally displays a laudable wish to present virtue under a pleasing and vice under an unlovely aspect; but he lacks variety of light and shade in the endeavour to reproduce his design under the artistic form which he has chosen. His personages seem for the most part labelled with the qualities they are intended to represent; there is no mistaking them as *dramatis personae*, but there is some difficulty in understanding them as human beings. Thus Hazlitt observes, doubtless with some degree of exaggeration, that Massinger's 'villains are a sort of *lusus naturæ*; his impassioned characters are like drunkards or madmen' [No. 33(d)]. This want of art in characterisation partly springs from the absence of humour noticeable in Massinger; in comedy he is rarely successful, except where he passes beyond its proper sphere; but if the character of Sir Giles Overreach must be allowed to be powerfully conceived and still more powerfully executed, I should certainly decline to follow Hallam [No. 42] in describing the central figure of *A City Madam* [sic] (Luke) as a 'masterly delineation'. Massinger's minor comic characters are as a rule either purely conventional, or simply repulsive as faithful portraitures of disgusting vice. If he lacks humour, he is, as most critics have agreed, even more deficient in tragic passion. No whirlwind of emotion seems to sweep through his long declamations, no fire to burn beneath his ample and at times luxurious eloquence. The sieges which his villains lay to chastity are really conducted like military operations; and so at times is the defence. A certain coldness seems to belong even to his noblest conceptions and most earnest moments. From the Virgin Martyr to the ill-used royal fugitive (in *Believe as you List*) there is something wanting in the most powerful situations and in the most attractive characters of this author to excite the deepest sympathy, – to move the source of tears.

The genius of Massinger is essentially rhetorical. In illustration of this, I may point to a curious peculiarity marking the construction of several of his plays. He likes nothing better than to work up the action to the reality or semblance of what may be described as a judicial issue, thus obtaining an excellent opportunity for statement and counter-statement, accusation and defence, and final judicial summary . . . But he has another minor note of the rhetorician. This is his frequent recurrence to little phrases and turns of expression which he may be said to have made his own, and the use of which is, so to speak, part of his stock-in-trade. I am not aware that this habit is so marked in any other dramatist as in Massinger; as an illustration of his manner it may at least go for what it is worth [instances 'such phrases as "to wash an Æthiop"; an "embryon" for an "unperfected design"; to "cry aim"; and the phrase about "friends, though two bodies, having but one soul"'].

In general, the style of Massinger is full rather than rich, and possesses the qualities of a flowing eloquence rather than of impassioned poetry. Hallam [No. 42] has compared the effect produced by the redundancy of his style to what by painters is called *impasto*. Pleasing and appropriate imagery is by no means rare in Massinger; but he has few similes which seize lastingly on the memory, and for one or two of these he was perhaps indebted to Shakspere, from whom however he appears to have borrowed far less than Beaumont and Fletcher did. In versification, he holds the mean between the manner of Shakspere's maturity and the mellifluous cadence of Fletcher. In construction, he appears to me a skilful artist, less prone than most of his contemporaries to a wearisome alternation in the conduct of two parallel plots to a combined issue; indeed many of his plays – and it is to their advantage – are virtually constructed on the lines of a single plot. Finally, it should be pointed out that, while as yet little has been done even by Gifford to explore the sources of the subjects of Massinger's plays, their variety is incontestable. The learning which he expends upon the treatment of a subject novel by the nature of its time or locality – such as *The Emperor of the East*, or *The Roman Actor*, or *Believe as you List* – is never very considerable; and historical accuracy is far from being one of his foibles; but he is not without skill in casting an attractive outward garment of time and place round his actions, and in the versatility which he displayed in his choice of plots must doubtless be sought one of the causes of his success as a dramatist. He is not, I think, to be ranked among the greatest of Shakspere's successors; but in the absence of some high poetic gifts he may be said to have compassed the noblest results which as a dramatist it lay within his power to achieve, and to have exercised his art – take his works for all in all – in such a spirit as to do honour to it and to himself.

47. Sir Leslie Stephen
1877

Stephen (1832–1904), well known as mountaineer, apologist for agnosticism, philosopher, and literary critic, edited *The Cornhill Magazine* between 1871 and 1882 and was the founding editor of *The Dictionary of National Biography* in 1882–91. His essay on Massinger, with its air of healthy scepticism and genial commonsense masking a good deal of repetition, influenced Symons (No. 51), Swinburne (No. 49(c)), and Eliot.

In his opening pages, preceding this extract, Stephen examines the equally partisan versions of 'Elizabethan' drama of its hater Kingsley and its lover Lamb and prefers a more broadly historical approach in which drama develops from Marlowe to Massinger and from 'the temper of the generation which expelled the Armada' to 'the temper of the generation which fretted under the rule of the first Stuarts'. Stephen cites S.R. Gardiner's evidence that Massinger was loyal to the Pembroke 'party', and develops Coleridge's distinction between Tory Fletcher and Whig Massinger into a more detailed opposition of the Cavalier spirit of the one and the moralism of the other. In the bulk of the essay Stephen argues not only that Massinger fails to marry moral and artistic concerns but that the morality itself lacks fibre.

Hours in a Library, 3 vols, London, 1892, vol.2, pp.141–76 (first published in *The Cornhill* in 1877).

The [political] difference between Fletcher and Massinger . . . was probably due to difference of temperament as much as to the character of Massinger's family connection. Massinger's melancholy is as marked as is the buoyant gaiety of his friend and ally. He naturally represents the misgivings which must have beset the more thoughtful members of his party, as Fletcher represented the careless vivacity of the Cavalier spirit.

. . .

Massinger represents a different turn of sentiment, which would be encouraged in some minds by the same social conditions ['enforced abstinence from the exciting struggles on the Continent' breeding Cavalier bravado and scorn of the citizen amongst those 'who will follow Rupert and be crushed by Cromwell']. Instead of abandoning himself frankly to the stream of youthful sentiment, he feels that it has a dangerous aspect. The shadow of coming evils was already dark enough to suggest various forebodings. But he is also a moraliser by temperament. Mr. Ward [No. 46] says that his strength is owing in a great degree to his appreciation of the great moral forces; and the remark is only a confirmation of the judgment of most of his critics. It is, of course, not merely that he is fond of adding little moral tags of questionable applicability to the end of his plays. 'We are taught', he says in the 'Fatal Dowry',

> By this sad precedent, how just soever
> Our reasons are to remedy our wrongs,
> We are yet to leave them to their will and power
> That to that purpose have authority.
> [V.ii.338–42]

But it is, to say the least, doubtful whether anybody would have that judicious doctrine much impressed upon him by seeing the play itself . . . Massinger, however, shows more moral feeling than is expended in providing sentiments to be tacked on as an external appendage, or satisfied by an obedience to the demands of poetic justice. He is not content with knocking his villains on the head – a practice in which he, like his contemporaries, indulges with only too much complacency. The idea which underlies most of his plays is a struggle of virtue assailed by external or inward temptations. He is interested by the ethical problems introduced in the play of conflicting passions, and never more eloquent than in uttering the emotions of militant or triumphant virtue. His view of life, indeed, is not only grave, but has a distinct religious colouring. From various indications it is probable that he was a Roman Catholic. Some of these are grotesque enough. The 'Renegado', for example, not only shows that Massinger was, for dramatic purposes, at least, an ardent believer in baptismal regeneration, but includes – what one would scarcely have sought in such a place – a discussion as to the validity of lay-baptism. The first of his surviving plays, the 'Virgin Martyr' (in which he was assisted by Dekker), is simply a dramatic version of an ecclesiastical legend. Though it seems to have been popular at the time, the modern reader will probably think that, in this case at least, the religious element is a little out of place. An angel and a devil take an active part in the performance; miracles are worked on the stage; the unbelievers are so shockingly wicked, and the Christians so obtrusively good, that we – the worldly-minded – are sensible of a little recalcitration, unless we are disarmed by the simplicity of the whole performance. Religious tracts of all ages and in all forms are apt to produce this ambiguous effect. Unless we are quite in harmony with their assumptions, we feel that they deal too much in conventional rose-colour. The angelic and diabolic elements are not so clearly discriminated in this world, and should show themselves less unequivocally on the stage, which ought to be its mirror. Such art was not congenial to the English atmosphere; it might be suitable in Madrid; but when forcibly transplanted to the London stage, we feel that the performance has not the simple earnestness by which alone it can be justified. The sentiment has a certain unreality, and the *naiveté* suggests affectation. The implied belief is got up for the moment and has a hollow ring. And therefore the whole work, in spite of some eloquence, is nothing better than a curiosity, as an attempt at the assimilation of a heterogeneous form of art.

A similar vein of sentiment, though not showing itself in so undiluted a form, runs through most of Massinger's plays. He is throughout a sentimentalist and a rhetorician. He is not, like the greatest men, dominated by thoughts and emotions which force him to give them external embodiment in life-like symbols. He is rather a man of much real feeling and extraordinary facility of utterance, who finds in his stories convenient occasions for indulging in elaborate didactic utterances upon moral topics. It is probably this comparative weakness of the higher imaginative faculty which makes Lamb [No. 25(e)] speak of him rather disparagingly. He is too self-conscious and too anxious to enforce downright moral sentiments to satisfy a critic by whom spontaneous force and direct insight were rightly regarded as the highest poetic qualities. A single touch in Shakespeare, or even Webster or Ford, often reveals more depth of feeling than a whole scene of Massinger's facile and often deliberately forensic eloquence. His temperament is indicated by the peculiarities of his style. It is, as Coleridge says [No. 29(e)], poetry differentiated by the smallest possible degree from prose. The greatest artists of blank verse have so complete a mastery of their language that it is felt as a fibre which runs through and everywhere strengthens the harmony, and is yet in complete subordination to the sentiment. With a writer of the second order, such as Fletcher, the metre becomes more prominent, and at times produces a kind of monotonous sing-song, which begins to remind us unpleasantly of the still more artificial tone characteristic of the rhymed tragedies of the next generation. Massinger diverges in the opposite direction. The metre is felt enough and only just enough to give a more stately step to rather florid prose. It is one of his marks that a line frequently ends by some insignificant 'of' or 'from', so as to exclude the briefest possible pause in reading. Thus, to take an example pretty much at random, the following instance might be easily read without observing that it was blank verse at all: –

'Your brave achievements in the war, and what you did for me, unspoken, because I would not force the sweetness of your modesty to a blush, are written here; and that there might be nothing wanting to sum up my numerous engagements (never in my hopes to be cancelled), the great duke, our mortal enemy, when my father's country lay open to his fury and the spoil of the victorious army, and I brought into his power, hath shown himself so noble, so full of honour, temperance, and all virtues that can set off a prince; that, though I cannot render him that respect I would, I am bound in thankfulness to admire him' [*The Bashful Lover*, V.iii.26–40].

Such a style is suitable to a man whose moods do not often hurry him into impetuous, or vivacious, or epigrammatic utterance. As the Persian poet says of his country: his warmth is not heat, and his coolness is not cold. He flows on in a quiet current, never breaking into foam or fury, but vigorous, and invariably lucid. As a pleader before a law-court – the character in which, as Mr. Ward observes, he has a peculiar fondness for presenting himself – he would carry his audience along with him, but scarcely hold them in spell-bound astonishment or hurry them into fits of excitement. Melancholy resignation or dignified dissatisfaction will find in him a powerful exponent, but scarcely despair, or love, or hatred, or any social phase of pure unqualified passion.

The natural field for the display of such qualities is the romantic drama, which Massinger took from the hands of Beaumont and Fletcher, and endowed with greater dignity and less poetic fervour. For the vigorous comedy of real life, as Jonson understood it, he has simply no capacity; and in his rare attempts at humour succeeds only in being at once dull and dirty. His stage is generally occupied with dignified lords and ladies, professing the most chivalrous sentiments, which are occasionally too high-flown and overstrained to be thoroughly effective, but which are yet uttered with sufficient sincerity. They are not mere hollow pretences, consciously adopted to conceal base motives; but one feels the want of an occasional infusion of the bracing air of common sense. It is the voice of a society still inspired with the traditional sentiments of honour and self-respect, but a little afraid of contact with the rough realities of life. Its chivalry is a survival from a past epoch, not a spontaneous outgrowth of the most vital elements of contemporary development. In another generation, such a tone will be adopted by a conscious and deliberate artifice, and be reflected in mere theatrical rant. In the past, it was the natural expression of a high-spirited race, full of self-confidence and pride in its own vigorous audacity. In this transitional period it has a certain hectic flush, symptomatic of approaching decay; anxious to give a wide berth to realities, and most at home in the border-land where dreams are only half dispelled by the light of common day. 'Don Quixote' had sounded the knell of the old romance, but something of the old spirit still lingers, and can tinge with an interest, not yet wholly artificial, the lives and passions of beings who are thus hovering on the outskirts of the living world. The situations most characteristic of Massinger's tendency are in harmony with this tone of sentiment. They are romances taken from a considerable variety of sources, developed in a clearly connected series of scenes. They are wanting in the imaginative unity of the great plays, which show that a true poet has been profoundly moved by some profound thought embodied in a typical situation. He does not, like Shakespeare, seize his subject by the heart, because it has first fascinated his imagination; nor, on the other hand, have we that bewildering complexity of motives and intricacy of plot which show at best a lawless and wandering fancy, and which often fairly puzzle us in many English plays, and enforce frequent references to the list of personages in order to disentangle the crossing threads of the action. Massinger's plays are a gradual unravelling of a series of incidents, each following intelligibly from the preceding situation, and suggestive of many eloquent observations, though not developments of one master-thought. We often feel that, if external circumstances had been propitious, he would have expressed himself more naturally in the form of a prose romance than in a drama. Nor, again, does he often indulge in those exciting and horrible situations which possess such charms for his contemporaries. There are occasions, it is true, in which this element is not wanting. In the 'Unnatural Combat', for example, we have a father killing his son in a duel, by the end of the second act; and when, after a succession of horrors of the worst kind, we are treated to a ghost, 'full of wounds, leading in the shadow of a lady, her face leprous', and the worst criminal is killed by a flash of lightning, we feel that we were fully entitled to such a catastrophe. We can only say, in Massinger's words, –

> May we make use of
> This great example, and learn from it that
> There cannot be a want of power above
> To punish murder and unlawful love!
>   [V.ii.340–3]

The 'Duke of Milan' again culminates with a horrible scene, rivalling, though with less power, the grotesque horrors of Webster's 'Duchess of Malfi'. Other instances might be given of concessions to that blood-and-thunder style of dramatic writing for which our ancestors had a never-failing appetite. But, as a rule, Massinger inclines, as far as contemporary writers will allow him, to the side of mercy. Instead of using slaughter so freely that a new set of actors has to be introduced to bury the old – a misfortune which sometimes occurs in the plays of the time – he generally tends to a happy solution, and is disposed not only to dismiss his virtuous characters to felicity, but even to make his villains virtuous. We have not been excited to that pitch at which our passions can only be harmonised by an effusion of blood, and a mild solution is sufficient for the calmer feelings that have been aroused.

. . .

When we turn to Massinger [from the main characters of Marlowe, Shakespeare, Chapman, and Jonson], this boundless vigour has disappeared. The blood has grown cool. The tyrant no longer forces us to admiration by the fulness of his vitality and the magnificence of his contempt for law. Whether for good or bad, he is comparatively a poor creature. He has developed an uneasy conscience, and even whilst affecting to defy the law trembles at the thought of an approaching retribution. His boasts have a shrill, querulous note in them. His creator does not fully sympathise with his passion. Massinger cannot throw himself into the situation; and is anxious to dwell upon the obvious moral considerations which prove such characters to be decidedly inconvenient members of society for their tamer neighbours. He is of course the more in accordance with a correct code of morality, but fails correspondingly in dramatic force and brilliance of colour. To exhibit a villain truly, even to enable us to realise the true depth of his villainy, one must be able for a moment to share his point of view, and therefore to understand the true law of his being. It is a very sound rule in the conduct of life that we should not sympathise with scoundrels. But the morality of the poet, as of the scientific psychologist, is founded upon the unflinching veracity which sets forth all motives with absolute impartiality. Some sort of provisional sympathy with the wicked there must be, or they become mere impossible monsters or the conventional scarecrows of improving tracts.

This is Massinger's weakest side. His villains want backbone, and his heroes are deficient in simple overmastering passion, or supplement their motives by some overstrained and unnatural crotchet. Impulsiveness takes the place of vigour, and indicates the want of a vigorous grasp of the situation. Thus, for example, the 'Duke of Milan', which is certainly amongst the more impressive of Massinger's plays, may be described as a variation upon the theme of 'Othello'. To measure the work of any other writer by its relation to that masterpiece is, of course, to apply a test of undue severity. Of comparison, properly speaking, there can be no question. The similarity of the situation, however, may bring out Massinger's characteristics. The Duke, who takes the place of Othello, is, like his prototype, a brave soldier. The most spirited and effective passage in the play is the scene in which he is brought as a prisoner before Charles V., and not only extorts the admiration of his conqueror, but wins his liberty by a dignified avowal of his previous hostility, and avoidance of any base compliance. The Duke shows himself to be a high-minded gentleman, and we are so far prepared to sympathise with him, when exposed to the wiles of Francisco – the Iago of the piece. But, unfortunately, the scene is not merely a digression in a constructive sense, but involves a psychological inconsistency. The gallant soldier contrives to make himself thoroughly contemptible. He is represented as excessively uxorious, and his passion takes a very disagreeable turn of posthumous jealousy. He has instructed Francisco to murder the wife whom he adores, in case of his own death during the war, and thus to make sure that she could not marry anybody else. On his return, the wife, who has been informed by the treachery of Francisco of this pleasant arrangement, is naturally rather cool to him; whereupon he flies into a rage and swears that he will

>Never think of curs'd Marcelia more.
>[III.iii.162]

His affection returns in another scene, but only in order to increase his jealousy, and on hearing Francisco's slander he proceeds to stab his wife out of hand. It is the action of a weak man in a passion, not of a noble nature tortured to madness. Finding out his mistake, he of course repents again, and expresses himself with a good deal of eloquence which would be more effective if we could forget the overpowering pathos of the parallel scene in 'Othello'. Much sympathy, however, is impossible for a man whose whole conduct is so flighty, and so obviously determined by the immediate demands of successive situations of the play, and not the varying manifestation of a powerfully conceived character. Francisco is a more coherent villain, and an objection made by Hazlitt [No. 33(d)] to his apparent want of motive is at least equally valid against Iago; but he is of course but a diluted version of that superlative villain, as Marcelia is a rather priggish and infinitely less tender Desdemona. The failure, however, of the central figure to exhibit any fixity of character is the real weakness of the play; and the horrors of the last scene fail to atone for the want of the vivid style which reveals an 'intense and gloomy mind' [i.e. 'intense and glowing mind', Wordsworth's *Excursion*, II.274].

This kind of versatility and impulsiveness of character is revealed by the curious convertibility – if one may use the word – of his characters. They are the very reverse of the men of iron of the previous generation. They change their state of mind as easily as the characters of the contemporary drama put on disguises. We are often amazed at the simplicity which enables a whole family to suppose the brother and father to whom they have been speaking ten minutes before to be an entire stranger, because he has changed his coat or talks broken English. The audience must have been easily satisfied in such cases; but it requires almost equal simplicity to accept some of Massinger's transformations ... 'I am certain', says Philanax in the 'Emperor of the East',

> A prince so soon in his disposition altered
> Was never heard nor read of.
> [III.i.24–6].

That proves that Philanax was not familiar with Massinger's plays. The disposition of princes and of subjects is there constantly altered with the most satisfactory result. It is not merely that, as often happens elsewhere, the villains are summarily forced to repent at the end of a play, like Angelo in 'Measure for Measure', in order to allow the curtain to fall upon a prospect of happiness. Such forced catastrophes are common, if clumsy enough. But there is something malleable in the very constitution of Massinger's characters. They repent half-way through the performance, and see the error of their ways with a facility which we could wish to be imitated in common life. The truth seems to be that Massinger is subject to an illusion natural enough to a man who is more of the rhetorician than the seer. He fancies that eloquence must be irresistible. He takes the change of mood produced by an elevated appeal to the feelings for a change of character . . . The interest of [*The Picture*], such as it is, depends upon the varying moods of the chief actors, who become so eloquent under a sense of wrong or a reflection upon the charms of virtue, that they approach the bounds of vice, and then gravitate back to respectability. Everybody becomes perfectly respectable before the end of the play is reached, and we are to suppose that they will remain respectable ever afterwards. They avoid tragic results by their want of the overmastering passions which lead to great crimes or noble actions. They are really eloquent, but even more moved by their eloquence than the spectators can be. They form the kind of audience which would be most flattering to an able preacher, but in which a wise preacher would put little confidence. And, therefore, besides the fanciful incident of the picture, they give us an impression of unreality. They have no rich blood in their veins; and are little better than lay figures taking up positions as it may happen, in order to form an effective tableau illustrative of an unexceptional moral.

There is, it is true, one remarkable exception to the general weakness of Massinger's characters. The vigour with which Sir Giles Overreach is set forth has made him the one well-known figure in Massinger's gallery, and the 'New Way to Pay Old Debts' showed, in consequence, more vitality than any of his other plays. Much praise has been given, and not more than enough, to the originality and force of the conception. The conventional miser is elevated into a great man by a kind of inverse heroism, and made terrible instead of contemptible. But it is equally plain that here, too, Massinger fails to project himself fairly into his villain. His rants are singularly forcible, but they are clearly what other people would think about him, not what he would really think, still less what he would say, of himself. Take, for example, the very fine speech in which he replies to the question of the virtuous nobleman, whether he is not frightened by the imprecations of his victims: – [quotes IV.i.113–31, 'Yes, as rocks are . . .'].

Put this into the third person; read 'he' for 'I', and 'his' for 'my', and it is an admirable bit of denunciation of a character probably intended as a copy from life. It is a description of a wicked man from outside; and wickedness seen from outside is generally unreasonable and preposterous. When it is converted, by simple alteration of pronouns, into the villain's own account of himself, the internal logic which serves as a pretext disappears, and he becomes a mere monster. It is for this reason that, as Hazlitt says [No. 33(d)], Massinger's villains – and he was probably thinking especially of Overreach and Luke in 'A City Madam' – appear like drunkards or madmen. His plays are apt to be a continuous declamation, cut up into fragments, and assigned to the different actors; and the essential unfitness of such a method to dramatic requirements needs no elaborate demonstration. The villains will have to denounce themselves, and will be ready to undergo conversion at a moment's notice, in order to spout openly on behalf of virtue as vigorously as they have spouted in transparent disguise on behalf of vice.

[Stephen now goes on to praise Massinger's chivalrous sentiments – the high place he gives women compared even with Shakespeare – and to censure the unusual number of 'revolting impurities' which the plays nevertheless include, although on balance 'Massinger's errors in this kind are superficial, and might generally be removed without injury to the structure of his plays'.]

I have said enough to suggest the general nature of the answer which would have to be made to the problem with which I started [i.e. 'Are we bound to cast aside the later dramas of the [Elizabethan] school as simply products of corruption?']. Beyond all doubt, it would be simply preposterous to put down Massinger as a simple product of corruption. He does not mock at generous, lofty instincts, or overlook their influence as great social forces. Mr. Ward quotes him as an instance of the connection between poetic and moral excellence. The dramatic effectiveness of his plays is founded upon the dignity of his moral sentiment; and we may recognize in him 'a man who firmly believes in the eternal difference between right and wrong'. I subscribe most willingly to the truth of Mr. Ward's general principle, and, with a certain reservation, to the correctness of this special illustration. But the reservation is an important one. After all, can anybody say honestly that he is braced and invigorated by reading Massinger's plays? Does he perceive any touch of what we feel when we have been in company, say, with Sir Walter Scott; a sense that our intellectual atmosphere is clearer than usual, and that we recognise more plainly than we are apt to do the surpassing value of manliness, honesty, and pure domestic affection? Is there not rather a sense that we have been all the time in an unnatural region, where, it is true, a sense of honour and other good qualities come in for much eloquent praise, but where, above everything, there is a marked absence of downright wholesome commonsense? Of course the effect is partly due to the region in which the old dramatists generally sought for their tragic situations. We are never quite at home in this fictitious cloudland, where the springs of action are strange, unaccountable, and altogether different from those with which we have to do in the workaday world. A great poet, indeed, weaves a magic mirror out of these dream-like materials, in which he shows us the great passions, love, and jealousy, and ambition, reflected upon a gigantic scale. But, in weaker hands, the characters become eccentric instead of typical; his vision simply distorts instead of magnifying the fundamental truths of human nature. The liberty which could be used by Shakespeare becomes dangerous for his successors. Instead of a legitimate idealisation, we have simply an abandonment of any basis in reality.

The admission that Massinger is moral must therefore be qualified by the statement that he is unnatural; or, in other words, that his morality is morbid. The groundwork of all the virtues, we are sometimes told, is strength. A strong nature may be wicked, but a weak one cannot attain any high moral level. The correlative doctrine in literature is, that the foundation of all excellence, artistic or moral, is a vivid perception of realities and a masculine grasp of facts. A man who has that essential quality will not blink at the truths which we see illustrated every day around us. He will not represent vice as so ugly that it can have no charms, so foolish that it can never be plausible, or so unlucky that it can never be triumphant. The robust moralist admits that vice is often pleasant, and that wicked men flourish like a green bay-tree. He cannot be over-anxious to preach, for he feels that the intrinsic charm of high qualities can dispense with any artificial attempts to bolster them up by sham rhetoric, or to slur over the hard facts of life. He will describe Iago as impartially as Desdemona, and, having given us the facts, leave us to make what we please of them. It is the mark of a more sickly type of morality, that it must always be distorting the plain truth. It becomes sentimental because it wishes to believe that what is pleasant must be true. It makes villains condemn themselves, because such a practice would save so much trouble to judges and moralists. Not appreciating the full force of passions, it allows the existence of grotesque and eccentric motives. It fancies that a little rhetoric will change the heart as well as the passing mood, and represents the claims of virtue as perceptible on the most superficial examination. The morality which requires such concessions becomes necessarily effeminate; it is unconsciously giving up its strongest position by implicitly admitting that the world in which virtue is possible is a very different one from our own.

The decline of the great poetic impulse does not yet reveal itself by sheer blindness to moral distinctions, or downright subservience to vice. A lowered vitality does not necessarily imply disease, though it is favourable to the development of vicious germs. The morality which flourishes in an exhausted soil is not a plant of hardy growth and tough fibre, nourished by rough common-sense, flourishing amongst the fierce contests of vigorous passions, and delighting in the open air and the broad daylight. It loves the twilight of romance, and creates heroes impulsive, eccentric, extravagant in their resolves, servile in their devotion, and whose very natures are more or less allied to weakness and luxurious self-indulgence. Massinger, indeed, depicts with much sympathy the virtues of the martyr and the penitent; he can illustrate the paradox that strength can be conquered by weakness, and violence by resignation. His good women triumph by softening the hearts of their persecutors. Their purity is more attractive than the passions of their rivals. His deserted King shows himself worthy of more loyalty than his triumphant persecutors. His Roman actor atones for his weakness by voluntarily taking part in his own punishment.

Such passive virtues are undoubtedly most praiseworthy; but they may border upon qualities not quite so praiseworthy. It is a melancholy truth that your martyr is apt to be a little sanctimonious, and that a penitent is generally a bit of a sneak. Resignation and self-restraint are admirable qualities, but admirable in proportion to the force of the opposing temptation. The strong man curbing his passions, the weak woman finding strength in patient suffering, are deserving of our deepest admiration; but in Massinger we feel that the triumph of virtue implies rather a want of passion than a power of commanding it, and that resignation is comparatively easy when it connotes an absence of active force. The general lowering of vitality, the want of rigid dramatic colouring, deprive his martyrs of that background of vigorous reality against which their virtues would be forcibly revealed. His pathos is not vivid and penetrating. Truly pathetic power is produced only when we see that it is a sentiment wrung from a powerful intellect by keen sympathy with the wrongs of life. We are affected by the tears of a strong man; but the popular preacher who enjoys weeping produces in us nothing but contempt. Massinger's heroes and heroines have not, we may say, backbone enough in them to make us care very deeply for their sorrows. And they moralise rather too freely. We do not want sermons, but sympathy, when we are in our deepest grief; and we do not feel that any one feels very keenly who can take his sorrows for a text, and preach in his agony upon the vanity of human wishes or the excellence of resignation.

Massinger's remarkable flow of genuine eloquence, his real dignity of sentiment, his sympathy for virtuous motive, entitle him to respect; but we cannot be blind to the defect which keeps his work below the level of his greatest contemporaries. It is, in one word, a want of vital force. His writing is pitched in too low a key. He is not invigorating, stimulating, capable of fascinating us by the intensity of his conceptions. His highest range is a dignified melancholy or a certain chivalrous recognition of the noble side of human nature. The art which he represents is still a genuine and spontaneous growth instead of an artificial manufacture. He is not a mere professor of deportment, or maker of fine phrases. The days of mere affectation have not yet arrived; but, on the other hand, there is an absence of that grand vehemence of soul which breathes in the spontaneous, if too lawless, vigour of the older race. There is something hollow under all the stately rhetoric; there are none of those vivid phrases which reveal minds moved by strong passions and excited by new aspects of the world. The sails of his verse are not, in Chapman's phrase, 'filled with a lusty wind' [*The Conspiracie of Charles Duke of Byron*, III.iii.136], but moving at best before a steady breath of romantic sentiment, and sometimes flapping rather ominously for want of true impulse. High thinking may still be there, but it is a little self-conscious, and in need of artificial stimulant. The old strenuous spirit has disappeared or gone elsewhere – perhaps to excite a Puritan imagination, and create another incarnation of the old type of masculine vigour in the hero of 'Paradise Lost'.

48. Frances Ann Kemble

1878

Fanny Kemble (1809–93) was popular as an actor in Shakespearean and other roles between 1829 and 1834, and later well known for her readings and volumes of autobiography. She was the niece of John Philip Kemble and Sarah Siddons. She read Massinger in 1830 and in 1831 played Camiola at Covent Garden in 'a shortened version of Massinger's text, possibly taken from Harness's Family Library edition' (*EG*, vol.1, p.115; its editor was not, as she supposes below, Dyce). In *Record of a Girlhood* (1878), which blends letters and journals with later reflections, she talks enthusiastically at several points about Massinger and particularly about *The Maid of Honour*, comparing and contrasting Camiola and Portia in some detail (vol.2, pp.300–4) and recording an after-dinner discussion on 'the possibility and probability of Adorni's self-sacrifice' with 'the female voices . . . unanimous in their verdict of its truth and likelihood' (vol.3, p.2). But she was also aware of the difficulties of staging Renaissance drama in the nineteenth century, as is apparent from some of the later remarks below and from her verdict on Macready's revival of *The Fatal Dowry* (No. 40): 'both the matter and the manner of our dramatic ancestors is too robust for the audiences of our day' (vol.2, p.220).

In the first passage Kemble finds all Shakespeare's contemporaries defective in moral and psychological coherence and insight, but names only Massinger; his eminence is, as so often, a precarious one.

MASSINGER

From *Record of a Girlhood*, London, 3 vols, 1878, vol.2, pp.117–19, 334–6.

The arrangement of Massinger for the family library by my friend the Reverend Alexander Dyce, the learned Shakespearean editor and commentator, was my first introduction to that mine of dramatic wealth which enriched the literature of England in the reigns of Elizabeth and James the First, and culminated in the genius of Shakespeare. It is by comparison with them, his contemporaries, that we arrive at a just estimate of his supremacy. I was so enchanted with these plays of Massinger's, but more especially with the one called 'The Maid of Honour', that I never rested till I had obtained from the management its revival on the stage. The part of Camiola is the only one that I ever selected for myself. 'The Maid of Honour' succeeded on its first representation, but failed to attract audiences. Though less defective than most of the contemporaneous dramatic compositions, the play was still too deficient in interest to retain the favour of the public. The character of Camiola is extremely noble and striking, but that of her lover so unworthy of her that the interest she excites personally fails to inspire one with sympathy for her passion for him. The piece in this respect has a sort of moral incoherency, which appears to me, indeed, not an infrequent defect of the compositions of these great dramatic pre-Shakespearites. There is a want of psychical verisimilitude, a disjointed abruptness, in their conceptions, which, in spite of their grand treatment of separate characters and the striking force of particular passages, renders almost every one of their plays inharmonious as a whole, however fine and powerful in detached parts. Their selection of abnormal and detestable subjects is a distinct indication of intellectual weakness instead of vigour; supreme genius alone perceives the beauty and dignity of human nature and human life in their common conditions, and can bring to the surface of vulgar, every-day existence the hidden glory that lies beneath it.

The strictures contained in these girlish letters on the various plays in which I was called to perform the heroines, of course partake of the uncompromising nature of all youthful verdicts.

. . .

I hope by-and-by to act Camiola very well, but I am afraid the play itself can never become popular; the size of the theatre and the public taste of the present day are both against such pieces; still, the attempt seemed to me worth making, and if it should prove successful we might revive one or two more of Massinger's plays; they are such sterling stuff compared with the Isabellas, the Jane Shores [in Garrick's *Isabella; Or The Fatal Marriage* and Rowe's *Jane Shore*], the everything but Shakespeare.

. . .

Massinger's 'Maid of Honour' is a stern woman, not without a very positive grain of coarse hardness in her nature. My attempt to *soften* her was an impertinent endeavour to alter his fine conception to something more in harmony with my own ideal of womanly perfection.

49. Algernon Charles Swinburne
1882–1904

Swinburne (1837–1909) wrote essays and poems about many of the Elizabethan and Jacobean playwrights. (a) and (b) below fix Massinger as a post-Shakespeare, pre-Civil War, 'Grave and great-hearted' poet of the sunset. In the more discursive world of the essay (c), Swinburne cannot so easily avoid Stephen's powerful case against Massinger. Although unable to contest Stephen's verdict on the lack of poetry in Massinger, he does seek to qualify his charges of ineffectual or simplistic morality. The result is a Massinger whose high principles inspire some characteristically Swinburnian raptures but whose 'claims to honour' are finally 'rather moral and intellectual . . . than imaginative and creative'.

Text from Sir Edmund Gosse and Thomas James Wise (eds), *The Complete Works of Algernon Charles Swinburne*, 20 vols, London, 1925–7, vol.5, p.175; vol.6, pp.322–3; vol.12, pp.257–88.

MASSINGER

(a) 'Philip Massinger', 1882

Clouds here and there arisen an hour past noon
Chequered our English heaven with lengthening bars
And shadow and sound of wheel-winged thunder-cars
Assembling strength to put forth tempest soon,
When the clear still warm concord of thy tune
Rose under skies unscared by reddening Mars
Yet, like a sound of silver speech of stars,
With full mild flame as of the mellowing moon.
Grave and great-hearted Massinger, thy face
High melancholy lights with loftier grace
Than gilds the brows of revel: sad and wise,
The spirit of thought that moved thy deeper song,
Sorrow serene in soft calm scorn of wrong,
Speaks patience yet from thy majestic eyes.

(b) 'Prologue to *A Very Woman*', 1904

Swift music made of passion's changeful power,
Sweet as the change that leaves the world in flower
When spring laughs winter down to deathward, rang
From grave and gracious lips that smiled and sang
When Massinger, too wise for kings to hear
And learn of him truth, wisdom, faith, or fear,
Gave all his gentler heart to love's light lore,
That grief might brood and scorn breed wrath no more.
Soft, bright, fierce, tender, fitful, truthful, sweet,
A shrine where faith and change might smile and meet,
A soul whose music could but shift its tune
As when the lustrous year turns May to June
And spring subsides in summer, so makes good
Its perfect claim to very womanhood.
The heart that hate of wrong made fire, the hand
Whose touch was fire as keen as shame's own brand
When fraud and treason, swift to smile and sting,

Crowned and discrowned a tyrant, knave or king,
False each and ravenous as the fitful sea,
Grew gently glad as love that fear sets free.
Like eddying ripples that the wind restrains,
The bright words whisper music ere it wanes.
Ere fades the sovereign sound of song that rang
As though the sun to match the sea's tune sang,
When noon from dawn took life and light, and time
Shone, seeing how Shakespeare made the world sublime,
Ere sinks the wind whose breath was heaven's and day's,
The sunset's witness gives the sundawn praise.

(c) 'Philip Massinger', 1889 (first published in *The Fortnightly Review*, 1 July 1889)

The style of Massinger – a style as unlike that of any other English poet as that of Dryden or of Pope; as tempting to imitators as it is inimitable by parasites, and as apparently easy as it is really difficult to reproduce – is already recognizable in its fullest development of rhetoric and metre throughout those scenes of *The Virgin Martyr* in which his steadfast and equable hand is easily and unquestionably to be traced. It is radically and essentially unlike the style of his rivals: it is more serviceable, more businesslike, more eloquently practical, and more rhetorically effusive – but never effusive beyond the bounds of effective rhetoric – than the style of any Shakespearean or of any Jonsonian dramatist. And in the second play on the list of Massinger's we find this admirably supple and fluent and impeccable style – as incapable of default from its own principle or ideal of expression as it is incapable of rising, like Webster's or even like Dekker's, to a purer note of poetry or a clearer atmosphere of passion – not less complete and rounded, not less pliant and perfect, than in the first act of *The Virgin Martyr*; 'as fine an act', said Coleridge, 'as I remember in any play' [No. 29(e)]. That great poet's memory must have been somewhat shaken by indulgence in the excesses of a theosophist and a druggard when he could not remember as fine an act or a far finer act in the plays of one Shakespeare, of one

Jonson, or of one Beaumont: ignorant as he seems to have been of what others remember at the mention of such names as Marlowe, Webster, Tourneur, Middleton, and Ford. And his opinion that 'Massinger often deals in exaggerated passion' is but ill supported by the instance he cites in support of it. The author of *Remorse* – not quite so good a play as *The Unnatural Combat* – was convinced that the protagonist of this tragedy, 'however he may have had the moral will to be so wicked, could never have actually done all that he is represented as guilty of without losing his senses. He would have been, in fact, mad'. He is represented as guilty of the murder by poison of a wife whose sufferings impel their son to seek his father's life in a duel which results in the death of the patricidal champion of his mother; and afterwards as overcome by an incestuous passion for a daughter whom he has not seen since her childhood, and whose nubile beauty excites in his savage and sensual nature an emotion against which he struggles with more resolution, and with more abhorrence of a temptation so inhuman and unnatural, than might have been expected from so unscrupulous a ruffian. This is doubtless a tragic record enough; but to say that it is the record of a lunatic is mere foolishness – a confession of presumptuous ignorance as to the darker elements of human character. A less defensible point is the occasional conventionality of expression; Massinger, though by no means generally inclined to pedantry or to rant, is liable now and then, for lack of imaginative passion, to stiffen and weaken his style with the bombast and the platitude of cheap classical rhetoric – the commonplace tropes and flourishes of the schoolroom or the schools. 'Blustering Boreas' and Æolus with his stormy issue make their appearance when not only is there 'no need of such vanity' [*Much Ado About Nothing*, III.iii.21–2], but when their intrusion chills and deadens the tragic effect and the poetic plausibility at which the writer must be supposed to aim. Compare the last declamation of Malefort with any one of all those put by Cyril Tourneur into the mouth of Vindice. Massinger's, if written in Greek or Latin, would be admired on all hands as deserving of the highest honours that school or college could confer on the most brilliant and vigorous exercise in passionate and tragic verse which could be attempted in a foreign language by the most accomplished and the most able scholar: Tourneur's would recall the passion and perfection, the fervour and the splendour and the harmony, which even we at this distance in time, and through the twilight of a dead language, can recognize in the dialogue or the declamation of Æschylus himself. On the other hand, the grim, narrow, sardonic humour of Cyril Tourneur is not comparable with the excellent comedy which lightens and relieves the fiery darkness and horror of this vehement and high-flown tragedy. The career of the chief comic personage is really worthy to be compared with that of almost any one among Fletcher's comic heroes; and this is very high praise. Massinger's deficiency in wit would seem to have blinded most of his critics to the excellence of his humour; which, if less buoyant and spontaneous than Fletcher's in the exuberance of its exultation, is at least as plausible and coherent in the felicity of its invention. All that Coleridge says [No. 29(c)] of the fallacy implied in such figures of mere burlesque as that of the buffoon suitor in *The Maid of Honour* is no less true and rational than pointed and incisive; they are too wilfully absurd to excite any emotion but that of incredulity, or that of compassion for a congenital infirmity or defect. But such figures as Belgarde in this play, or as Borachia in a later work [*A Very Woman*], are brilliant and vivid creations of observant and original humour.

The objection raised by Coleridge, echoed by Hazlitt, and re-echoed by Leslie Stephen, that the fools or the villains of Massinger's invention are apt to talk of themselves as others would talk or think of them is too often but too well grounded. ... This objection is supported by Leslie Stephen with far more cogency and felicity of argument than either Hazlitt or Coleridge had brought to bear on it. The passage in which he presses and enforces his impeachment of Massinger on the ground of moral and dramatic veracity is too effective to be passed over or evaded by any champion or advocate who might think fit to undertake the defence of the poet [Quotes No. 47, pp.196–7].

There is so much truth in this that I am not disposed to inquire whether there may not be something to be said in deprecation or extenuation of the charge; nor will I deny that the singular character of Sforza in *The Duke of Milan* is liable to the imputation of unnatural and inhuman inconsistency. Massinger was only too lamentably inclined to let moral or theatrical considerations prevail over the claims of dramatic or poetic harmony. The preacher or the scene-shifter supplants the poet or the playwright after a fashion so palpable or so primitive that we are disposed to condone, on comparison, the worst offences of Fletcher against the laws of aesthetic or intelligent art. For in Fletcher's work the levity of treatment is in keeping with the spontaneity of style; with the brightness and lightness of fancy, the headlong ease and energetic idleness of irresponsible improvisation. But in Massinger the sense of an artist's responsibility to himself and to those who are able to judge of his work is so singularly and so admirably evident that it would be rather an injustice than an indulgence to extenuate his errors on the plea of carelessness or hurry or fatigue. And therefore, supposing that I wished, I should find it as impossible to impugn as to reinforce Leslie Stephen's impeachment of the dramatist who represents his Sforza in the finest scene of the play as a hero and in all the other scenes of the play as a miserable and morbid egotist. But when we are told that this play 'may be described as a variation upon the theme of *Othello*', we can only reply that it might more truthfully be described as a variation upon the theme of *The Comedy of Errors*, or *The Merry Wives of Windsor*, or *The Taming of the Shrew*. Each one of these has some minor point in common with it; irritability on the wife's part, jealousy on the husband's, or violence of temper – actual or assumed – on either part. But Othello, the most unsuspicious and the most unselfish though the most passionate and the most sensitive of men, has almost as much in common with his destroyer as with the covetous and murderous egotist who leaves orders for his wife to be assassinated if he should happen to fall in battle.

In spite of this radical and central blemish, *The Duke of Milan* is a nobly written and an admirably constructed play. To do justice to its excellence, we should compare it, not with *Othello* – 'which', in the classic phrase of Euclid, 'is absurd' – but with Ford's 'variation' on the same theme in his abortive tragedy of *Love's Sacrifice*. Ford was, in the main, a greater tragic poet than Massinger; but the blemish which disfigures the elder poet's work would be imperceptible in the work of his junior. The action of Ford's play, like the action of Massinger's, revolves on the jarring hinges of jealousy and intrigue, malevolence and revenge; but the treatment is puerile in its perversity, while the characters are preposterous in their incoherence. Massinger's tragedy, whatever objection may be taken to this or that point in it, is a high and harmonious work of art.

But on turning to his next play we find the poet on ground more thoroughly suited to his genius than the ground of pure or predominant tragedy. The *Bondman* is the first, as it is with one exception the best, of Massinger's romantic plays: tragic in dignity of style, but happy in consummation of event. In this field of work his hand is surer and steadier than Fletcher's: if it has not all Fletcher's grace and ease and lightness of touch, its treatment of subject is more serious, its grasp of character more firm, its method of execution more conscientious and more composed. He sacrifices little where Fletcher sacrifices much to sensational and theatrical effect; he is evidently and deeply in earnest where Fletcher seems to be thinking mainly of rhetorical or scenical display. Compare the famous declamation of Pisander against slavery, in the second scene of the fourth act of this play, with the noble address of Caesar to the severed head of Pompey in the first scene of the second act of *The False One*. The style of Massinger is *sermoni proprior* – nearer the level of eloquent prose: but it has a deeper and a graver note of masculine sincerity in the measured earnestness of its appeal than any that we find in the rushing ripples and the swirling eddies of Fletcher's effusive and impetuous rhetoric.

. . .

[Following extended discussion of Fletcher and Massinger's *Sir John Van Olden Barnavelt*:] In the impeachment and defence of Barnavelt the poet who was above all things a pleader – who could never miss an opportunity of displaying his talents as an advocate – found his first occasion for such display, and made use of it with such dexterous ability and such vigorous temperance of style as to give promise of even finer future work on the same lines; of such noble instances of dramatic ratiocination as the pleading of Malefort before the council of war, of Sforza before the Emperor, of Donusa before the Viceroy, of Cleremond and Leonora before the Parliament of Love, of Paris before the senate, of Camiola before her rival and the King, of Antiochus and Flaminius before the senators of Carthage, of Charalois before the court of justice (twice in the same play), and we might perhaps add that of Luke with Sir John Frugal on behalf of his debtors. If Massinger, like Heywood, had written a play on the legend of Lucretia, we may be sure that the heroine, on being awakened by Sextus, would have overwhelmed him with oratorical demonstration and illustration of the theorem that such a purpose as his in any man

> Were most inhospitable; this being granted,
> (As you cannot deny it) 'tis in you
> A more than barbarous cruelty; kings being tyrants,
> When they prefer their appetites (their conscience,
> As a most dejected slave, cast down and trod on)
> Before their nobler reason. Philomela –

And so forth, and so forth: it would be only too easy to continue. But if the irrepressible barrister too often intrudes or intrenches on the ground of the dramatic poet, it must be allowed that his pleading, if sometimes prosaic in expression and conventional in rhetoric, is seldom or never ineffective either through flatulence of style or through tenuity of manner.

. . .

In energetic fertility of invention and fervid fluency of rhetoric *The Renegado* is a fairly representative example of Massinger's most characteristic work: it can hardly be placed in the first class of his plays, but must be allowed to stand high in the second rank. Hartley Coleridge's critical summary of this play is about the best thing in his essay on Massinger and Ford. *The Parliament of Love*, for all the miserable mutilation of its text, is still recognisable as one of its author's most brilliant and animated comedies; no less graceful and interesting in its graver parts than amusing and edifying in its lighter interludes. In the tragedy of *The Roman Actor*, if the interest is less keen and the emotion less vivid than that excited by the previous tragic poems of Massinger, the equable purity of style and the conscientious symmetry of composition will seem all the more praiseworthy if compared with the headlong and slipshod vehemence of many among his competitors; but in the hands (for instance) of Fletcher, the all-important figure of Domitia, though it might have been more theatrical and exaggerative, would have been more animated and interesting than it is. *The Great Duke of Florence*, if remarkable even among Massinger's works for elegance and grace of execution, does not aim high enough or strike deep enough to give more than the moderate pleasure of a temperate satisfaction. *The Maid of Honour* leaves a deeper impression of the very noble and original character which gives its title to the play. The others, with the possible exception of the loyal and single-hearted Adorni, are somewhat conventional in comparison. It is impossible to take any sympathetic interest in the vacillations and infidelities of such half-hearted lovers and loyalists as figure too frequently on the stage of Massinger; who must have found them so serviceable in the development of a story, and for the presentation of a nobler nature in fuller relief against their ignoble or pitiable figures, that he could scarcely appreciate or foresee the inevitable effect or impression of such characters – a compromise between indifference and contempt. And it is a serious if not a ruinous defect in the structure of a poem or a play that this should be the impression left by any of its indispensable and leading characters.

. . .

In . . . *The Emperor of the East* and *Believe as you list*, Massinger has given a colouring of romance to historical characters – or at least to historical names – which in either case makes the drama something of a hybrid, but a hybrid of no unattractive or unlawful kind. The merit of either play is rather literary than dramatic; not that there is any lack of interest and action, but that, if set beside any play or any poem of strong human interest, the comparative tenuity of composition, the comparative tepidity of emotion excited or expressed, becomes manifest beyond all question.

. . .

Massinger in *The Emperor of the East* was not a little beneath himself at his best. But in the tragic story of Antiochus Massinger has displayed his gift of noble writing and its quality of manly pathos as fully and impressively as in any of his more famous works . . . A certain deficiency in constructive power, a certain monotony in dramatic arrangement and effect, may perhaps be found: . . . the varied and protracted martyrdom of an innocent and heroic victim becomes even before we reach the fifth act too positively painful and oppressive for the reader to find relief in any lighter interlude, were it even far more exhilarating than the defiant buffoonery of the indomitable fat Flamen. The unmistakable reference in Massinger's prologue to 'a late and sad example' of royal misfortune 'too near' the subject-matter of his play – the crushing defeat and the wandering exile of Charles I.'s luckless brother-in-law, the Prince Palatine – is a noticeable instance of his unflagging interest in contemporary history as well as in social and political questions more particular to England.

His next surviving play, *The Fatal Dowry*, is on the whole the finest example of tragedy he has left us: the most perfect in build, the most pathetic in effect, and the most interesting in development, harmony, and variety of character. The attention and admiration of the reader are seized and kindled at the very opening, and are kept alive and alight to the last moment of the action. And on this occasion we may feel confident in attributing to Massinger all but all that is of value in a work which we owe in part to another hand than his . . . His calm command of earnest and impressive eloquence was never put to nobler service: his austere sympathy with self-denying courage or self-renouncing resolution was never more worthily expressed than in the devotion of Charalois to his father and of Romont to his friend. But it is undeniable that the best character in this play – the best in each sense of the word, at once most effective from the dramatic point of view, and most attractive if considered as a separate figure – is a subordinate though neither superfluous nor insignificant person. Romont is one of the noblest of Massinger's men; and Shakespeare has hardly drawn nobler men more nobly than Massinger. Fletcher's handling of such characters is absolutely schoolboyish in its perverse conventionality. Massinger's heroes have always some touch of manly reason and loyal good sense which preserves them from the ideal absurdity of Fletcher's alternately blatant and abject materialists.

The figure of the heroine, on the other hand, is too thinly and feebly drawn to attract even the conventional and theatrical sympathy which Fletcher might have excited for a frail and penitent heroine: and the almost farcical insignificance and baseness of her paramour would suffice to degrade his not involuntary victim beneath the level of any serious interest or pity. Rowe, in the play which he founded on Massinger's [No. 17], has very skilfully removed this blemish. The victim of a Lothario we may pity, excuse, and understand; the victim of a Novall is fit for enlistment in the sisterhood of the streets. Rowe's place is rather low and Massinger's place is rather high among dramatic poets; but in this instance the smaller man's poetic or dramatic instinct was juster and worthier than the greater man's.

. . .

In tragedy Massinger was excelled by other dramatic poets of his time: in the line of severe and serious tragicomedy he certainly has never been and probably never will be equalled. The hideous hero of *A New Way to pay Old Debts* may perhaps be now and then too strongly and even coarsely coloured: the epilepsy of rage and remorse which overtakes him in the last scene may be too obviously the device of a preacher or a moralist who thinks rather of impressing his audience with dread of a special providence or a judicial visitation than of working out the subject of a dramatic poem in a natural and logical manner: but for all that, and in spite of his theatrical and incredible expositions of his own wickedness and baseness to men whom he wishes to conciliate or attach, Sir Giles Overreach will always and deservedly retain his place among the great original figures or types created by the genius and embodied in the art of our chief dramatic poets. The spirit, eloquence, and animation of the whole play are not more admirable than the perfect harmony and proportion of all the figures displayed in stronger or slighter relief by the natural progress of the well-constructed plot. Much of the same praise may be given to the first four acts of *The City Madam*; and the figure of Luke Frugal, if less imposing and impressive than that of Overreach, is drawn with far subtler skill and finer insight into the mystery of ingrained and incurable wickedness. The self-deceit of the suffering hypocrite, his genuine penitence and humility while under a cloud of destitution and contempt, may probably be accepted as the deepest and truest touch of nature, as it is certainly the most daring and original, to be found in the works of Massinger. Up to the fifth act the conduct of the whole scheme of the play is almost beyond praise: it is lighter and easier, more simple and more clear, than the evolution of Jonson's best comedies: the variety of living character is as striking as the excellence of artistic composition. But all the energetic advocacy of Gifford [vol.4, p.98], earnest and plausible as it is, cannot suffice to vindicate the taste or justify the judgment of a comic poet who has chosen to deface the closing scenes of a comedy with such monstrous and unnatural horror as deforms the fifth act of this play . . . Admitting that so subtle and splendid a scoundrel as Luke could be fool enough to swallow such a bait and monster enough to entertain such a proposal [to send his nieces to Virginia to become human sacrifices], we may surely crave leave to object that such a conception is as monstrous, from an aesthetic point of view, in a comedy, as it would be, from an ethical point of view, in real life; that it jars and unhinges and disjoints the whole structure of the play. Luke, under the impression of supernatural agency – duped by his former dupes, and befooled by his former victims – is no longer the same man: the supple, pliable, quick-witted, humble, and resentful rascal whom his creator had made as visible and credible to us as Tartuffe himself subsides into a devil and a fool, whom the simplest device can delude and the insanest atrocity cannot revolt.

In these two noble and memorable plays Massinger is no less a patriot than a poet; his wise and thoughtful interest in matters affecting the social interests of the commonweal is as evident as his mature and masterly power of construction and of style. He was, it is evident, as all loyal Englishmen must be, at once truly conservative and thoroughly liberal in his views and in his aims; all the more bitter and unsparing in his hatred of corruption and his abhorrence of abuses that he foresaw, as did no other writer for the theatres, the inevitable result of lawless extortion and transgression on the part of the rulers of England. He was the Falkland as Fletcher was the Rupert of the stage; and a wiser counsellor than ever won the ear of the king who found his dramatic satire 'too insolent' in its exposure of the royal claims on 'benevolences' and the royal defiance of the law to be endured without modification or excision. Coleridge's remarks on Massinger as a politician [No. 29(b), (c)] are equally inaccurate and perverse.

. . .

The steady and conscientious independence of his genius and his principles had fully and nobly asserted itself in Massinger's studies from contemporary life in England: in his three remaining plays he has given a freer if not a looser rein to his fancy, with less of the ethical and more of the sentimental in its action. *The Guardian* is much more like a play of Fletcher's – such a play, for example, as *Women Pleased* or *The Pilgrim* – than any other of Massinger's unassisted works: I need hardly add that its plot is unusually multifarious, improbable, and amusing. It is always excellently and sometimes exquisitely written: there is no very severe or serious grasp of character, though all the figures are as lively and easy as some of the incidents are violent and absurd. *The Bashful Lover*, his next play but one, is little less well written and well arranged, but very inferior in interest, and more markedly conventional in character than any other play of Massinger's; nevertheless it is an able and in some degree an admirable piece of work.

One play alone remains for us to notice [*A Very Woman*] . . . But this one remaining play is the flower of all his flock; so lovely and attractive in its serious romance, so ripe and rich in its broader strokes of humour, so full of a peculiarly sweet and fascinating interest, as to justify more than ever the compliment of a comparison [with Beaumont and Fletcher, No. 3(b)–(c)] which its author's diffidence had reprovingly deprecated on the lips of Sir Thomas Jay . . . The exquisite temperance and justice and delicacy of touch in that almost unrivalled example of narrative by dialogue [IV.iii.78f., where Don John tells Almira his supposed story; now regarded as Fletcher's] are hardly to be equalled or approached in any similar or comparable scene of Fletcher's; but the loveliest passage in it – the loveliest both for natural grace of feeling and for melodious purity of expression – has perhaps somewhat more of the peculiar cadence of Fletcher's very finest versification than of Massinger's . . . [B]ut I cannot believe in the probability of any theory which would tend to deprive Massinger of any part of the honour and the gratitude which we owe to the writer of this most beautiful and delightful play. The great argument against the likelihood, if not against the possibility, that Fletcher can have had any hand or finger in the text as it now stands is the utter absence of his besetting faults. Violent as are the passions and violent as are the revolutions of passion represented in the course of the story, the poet's aim is evidently to make them appear, if not always reasonable, yet always natural and inevitable; Fletcher, in his usual mood at least, would have rioted in exaggeration of their contrasts, improbabilities, and inconsistencies. His hunger and thirst after sensation at any price could never have allowed him to be content with so moderate, so gradual, and so rational an evolution of the story.

That Massinger was both greater and more trustworthy as a

dramatic artist than as a dramatic poet has already been admitted and avowed: but this crowning work of his noble and accomplished genius, at once so delicate and so masculine in its workmanship, would suffice to ensure him a place of honour among the poets as well as among the dramatists of his incomparable time. Upon the whole, however, I venture to think that his highest and most distinctive claims to honour are rather moral and intellectual (or, if Greek adjectives be preferred to Latin as more fashionable and sonorous, we will say rather ethical and aesthetic) than imaginative and creative. Be this as it may, there can be no question that the fame of Philip Massinger is secure against all chance of oblivion or eclipse as long as his countrymen retain any sense of sympathetic admiration and respect for the work and the memory of a most admirable and conscientious writer, who was also a most rational and thoughtful patriot.

50. James Russell Lowell

1887

Lowell (1819–91) was Professor of Modern Languages and Belles Lettres at Harvard from 1854, first editor of *The Atlantic Monthly*, 1857–62, and co-editor of *The North American Review* with Charles Eliot Norton, 1864–72. Later he was ambassador to Spain (1877–80) and England (1880–5). His lectures on Renaissance drama were delivered at the Lowell Institute in Boston in 1887.

There is a distinctly old-fashioned ring, for 1887, to Lowell's unambiguous praise for the 'conversational tone', good sense, and good stories of the 'serious and thoughtful' Massinger whose strong suit was not for poetry.

The Old English Dramatists, London, 1892, pp.122–8.

To me Massinger is one of the most interesting as well as one of the most delightful of the old dramatists, not so much for his passion or power, though at times he reaches both, as for the love he shows for those things that are lovely and of good report in human nature, for his sympathy with what is generous and highminded and honorable, and for his equable flow of a good everyday kind of poetry with few rapids or cataracts, but singularly soothing and companionable. The Latin adjective for gentleman, *generosus*, fits him aptly. His plots are generally excellent; his versification masterly, with skilful breaks and pauses, capable of every needful variety of emotion; and his dialogue easy, natural, and sprightly, subsiding in the proper places to a refreshing conversational tone. This graceful art was one seldom learned by any of those who may be fairly put in comparison with him. Even when it has put on the sock, their blank verse cannot forget the stride and strut it had caught of the cothurnus. Massinger never mouths or rants, because he never seems to have written merely to fill up an empty space. He is therefore never bombastic, for bombast gets its metaphorical name from its original physical use as padding. Indeed, there are very few empty spaces in his works. His plays are interesting alike for their story and the way it is told. I doubt if there are so many salient short passages, striking images, or pregnant sayings to be found in his works as may be found in those of very inferior men. But we feel always that we are in the company of a serious and thoughtful man, if not in that of a great thinker. Great thinkers, indeed, are seldom so entertaining as he. If he does not tax the mind of his reader, nor call out all its forces with profound problems of psychology, he is infinitely suggestive of not unprofitable reflection, and of agreeable nor altogether purposeless meditation. His is 'a world whose course is equable', where 'calm pleasures abide', if no 'majestic pains'. I never could understand Lamb's putting Middleton and Rowley above him [No. 25(e)], unless, perhaps, because he was less at home on the humbler levels of humanity, less genial than they, or, at least, than Rowley. But there were no proper aesthetic grounds of comparison, if I am right in thinking, as I do, that he differed from them in kind, and that his kind was the higher.

In quoting from Wordsworth's 'Laodamia' just now, I stopped short of the word 'pure', and said only that Massinger's world was 'equable'. I did this because in some of his lower characters there is a coarseness, nay, a foulness, of thought and sometimes of phrase for which I find it hard to account. There is nothing in it that could possibly corrupt the imagination, for it is altogether repulsive. In this case, as in Chapman's, I should say that it indicated more ignorance of what is debasingly called Life than knowledge of it. With all this he gives frequent evidence of a higher conception of love than was then common. The region in which his mind seems most naturally to dwell is one of honor, courage, devotion, and ethereal sentiment.

I cannot help asking myself, did such a world ever exist? Perhaps not; yet one is inclined to say that it is such a world as might exist, and, if possible, ought to exist. It is a world of noble purpose not always inadequately fulfilled; a world whose terms are easily accepted by the intellect as well as by the imagination. By this I mean that there is nothing violently improbable in it. Some men, and, I believe, more women, live habitually in such a world when they commune with their own minds. It is a world which we visit in thought as we go abroad to renew and invigorate the ideal part of us. The canopy of its heaven is wide enough to stretch over Boston also. I heard, the other day, the story of a Boston merchant which convinces me of it. The late Mr. Samuel Appleton was anxious about a ship of his which was overdue, and was not insured. Every day added to his anxiety, till at last he began to be more troubled about that than about his ship. 'Is it possible', he said to himself, 'that I am getting to love money for itself, and not for its noble uses?' He added together the value of the ship and the estimated profit on her cargo, found it to be $40,000 and at once devoted that amount to charities in which he was interested. This kind of thing *may* happen, and sometimes *does* happen, in the actual world; it *always* happens in the world where Massinger lays his scene. That is the difference, and it is by reason of this difference that I like to be there. I move more freely and breathe more inspiring air among those encouraging possibilities. As I just said, we find no difficulty in reconciling ourselves with its conditions. We find no difficulty even where there is an absolute disengagement from all responsibility to the matter-of-fact, as in the 'Arabian Nights', which I read through again a few years ago with as much pleasure as when a boy, perhaps with more. For it appears to me that it is the business of all imaginative literature to offer us a sanctuary from the world of the newspapers, in which we have to live, whether we will or no. As in looking at a picture we must place ourselves at the proper distance to harmonize all its particulars into an effective whole, I am not sure that life is not seen in a truer perspective when it is seen in the fairer prospect of an ideal remoteness.

. . .

Those old poets had a very lordly contempt for probability when improbability would serve their purpose better. But Massinger taxes our credulity less than most of them, for his improbabilities are never moral; that is, are never impossibilities. I do not recall any of those sudden conversions in his works from baseness to loftiness of mind, and from vice to virtue, which trip up all our expectations so startlingly in many an old play. As to what may be called material improbabilities, we should remember that two hundred and fifty years ago many things were possible, with great advantage to complication of plot, which are no longer so. The hand of an absolute prince could give a very sudden impulse to the wheel of Fortune, whether to lift a minion from the dust or hurl him back again; men might be taken by Barbary corsairs and sold for slaves, or turn Turks, as occasion required. The world was fuller of chances and changes than now, and the boundaries of the possible, if not of the probable, far wider. Massinger was discreet in the use of these privileges, and does not abuse them, as his contemporaries and predecessors so often do. His is a possible world, though it be in some ways the best of all possible worlds. He puts no strain upon our imaginations.

As a poet he is inferior to many others, and this follows inevitably from the admission we feel bound to make that good sense and good feeling are his leading qualities – yet ready to forget their sobriety in the exhilaration of romantic feeling. When Nature makes a poet, she seems willing to sacrifice all other considerations. Yet this very good sense of Massinger's has made him excellent as a dramatist. His 'New Way to pay Old Debts' is a very effective play, though in the reading far less interesting and pleasing than most of the others. Yet there are power and passion in it, even if the power be somewhat melodramatic, and the passion of an ignoble type. In one respect he was truly a poet – his conceptions of character were ideal; but his diction, though full of dignity and never commonplace, lacks the charm of the inspired and inspiring word, the relief of the picturesque image that comes so naturally to the help of Fletcher. Where he is most fanciful, indeed, the influence of Fletcher is only too apparent both in his thought and diction. I should praise him chiefly for the atmosphere of magnanimity which invests his finer scenes, and which it is wholesome to breathe. In Massinger's plays people behave generously, as if that were the natural thng to do, and give us a comfortable feeling that the world is not so bad a place, after all, and that perhaps Schopenhauer was right in enduring for seventy-two years a life that wasn't worth living. He impresses one as a manly kind of person, and the amount of man in a poet, though it may not add to his purely poetical qualities, adds much, I think, to our pleasure in reading his works.

51. Arthur Symons
1887

Symons (1865–1945) was an 1890s poet, and author of works including *The Symbolist Movement in Literature* (1899). French Symbolist poetry provides some of the lines 'in which colour and music make a magical delight of golden concords' missing for him in Massinger; his book was read sympathetically by Massinger's later critic T.S. Eliot. Symons' edition of ten plays by Massinger was part of the Mermaid series of The Best Plays of the Old Dramatists, founded by Havelock Ellis and Henry Vizetelly in 1886 to present unexpurgated selections to the public.

The main source for Symons' rather uninspiring Massinger is Leslie Stephen (No. 47; see further Introduction, p.39, and Karl Beckson, *Arthur Symons: a Life*, Oxford, 1987, p.37). His comments on individual plays in the latter part of the essay are, however, often more generous than Stephen's. Symons especially likes the characterization of Camiola, Antiochus, and in some respects Sforza, and the 'country charm' of *The Great Duke of Florence* and *The Guardian*:

emphases appropriate to nineteenth-century commentators' lack of interest in ethical and political detail.

Arthur Symons (ed.), *Philip Massinger*, 2 vols, London and New York, 1887–9, vol.1, pp.xii–xxxii.

When Massinger came to London, the English drama, as I have said, was at its height. But before he had begun any dramatic work of importance the turning-point had been reached, and the period of descent or degeneration begun. Elizabethan had given place to Stuart England, and with the dynasty the whole spirit of the nation was changing. Fletcher and Massinger together represent this period: Fletcher by painting with dashing brilliance the light bright showy superficial aristocratic life of wild and graceful wantonness, Massinger by limning with a graver and a firmer brush, in darker tints and more thoughtful outlines, the shadier side of the same impressive and unsatisfactory existence. The indications of lessening vitality and strength, of departing simplicity, of growing extravagance and affectation which mark the period of transition, reappear in the drama of Massinger, as in that of Shirley, and sever it, by a wide and visible gulf, from the drama which we properly name Elizabethan. Massinger is the late twilight of the long and splendid day of which Marlowe was the dawn.

The characteristics of any poet's genius are seen clearly in his versification. Massinger's verse is facile, vigorous, grave, in the main correct; but without delicacy or rarity, without splendour or strength of melody; the verse of a man who can write easily, and who is not always too careful to remember that he is writing poetry. Owing no doubt partly to the facility with which he wrote, Massinger often has imperfectly accentuated lines, such as:

> They did expect to be chain'd to the oar
> [*The Unnatural Combat*, I.i.291]

Coleridge has remarked on the very slight degree in which Massinger's verse is distinguished from prose; and no-one can read a page of any of his plays without being struck with it. It is not merely that a large proportion of the lines run on and overlap their neighbours; this is only the visible sign of a radical peculiarity. The *pitch* of Massinger's verse is somewhat lower than the proper pitch of poetry; somewhat too near the common pitch of prose. Shakespeare, indeed, in his latest period extended the rhythm of verse to its loosest and freest limits; but not merely did he never pass beyond the invisible and unmistakeable boundary, he retained the true intonation of poetry as completely as in his straitest periods of metrical restraint.

Massinger set himself to follow in the steps of Shakespeare; and he succeeded in catching with admirable skill much of the easy flow and conversational facility at which he aimed. 'His English style', says Lamb, 'is the purest and most free from violent metaphors and harsh constructions, of any of the dramatists who were his contemporaries' [No. 25(e)]. But this 'pure and free' style obtains its freedom and purity at a heavy cost: or let us say rather, the style possesses a certain degree of these two qualities because of the absence of certain others. Shakespeare's freest verse is the most full of episodical beauties and magical lines. But it is a singular thing that in the whole of Massinger's extant works there are scarcely a dozen lines of such intrinsic and unmistakeable beauty that we are forced to pause and brood on them with the true epicure's relish. It is singular, I repeat – especially singular in a writer distinguished not only by fluency but by dignity and true eloquence – that so few, so very few, of his lines can stand by themselves, on their own merits. It would be useless to look in the Massinger part of *The Virgin Martyr* for any lines like these –

> I could weary stars,
> And force the wakeful moon to lose her eyes,
> By my late watching.
> [II.i.182–4]

It would be equally useless to search from end to end of his plays. Easy flowing lines, vigorous lines, eloquent and persuasive lines, we could find in plenty; but nowhere a line in which colour and music make a magical delight of golden concords. Not quite so difficult, but still very hard indeed, would it be to find any single lines of that rare and weighty sort which may be said to resemble the jar in the *Arabian Nights* into which Solomon had packed the genie. Had Massinger wished to represent Vittoria Accaramboni before her judges, he would have written for her a thoroughly eloquent, admirable and telling oration; but he could never have fashioned her speech into the biting dagger with which Webster drives home the splendid blows of her imperial scorn. That one line of infinite meaning –

> Cover her face; mine eyes dazzle; she died young –

spoken by Ferdinand in *The Duchess of Malfy* over the corpse of his murdered sister, has no parallel in Massinger, who would probably have begun a long and elaborate piece of rhetoric with –

> Stay, I feel
> A sudden alteration.

If we carry these considerations further, we shall see that the mental characteristics of Massinger correspond with the evidences of them in his versification. The ease and facility shown in the handling of metre are manifested equally in the plot and conduct of the plays. Massinger thoroughly understood the art of the playwright. No one perhaps, after Shakespeare, proved himself so constantly capable of constructing an orderly play and working it steadily out. His openings are as a rule admirable; thoroughly effective, explanatory, and preparatory. How well, for instance, the first scene of *The Duke of Milan* prepares us, by a certain uneasiness or anxiety in its trembling pitch of happiness, for the events which are to follow. It is not always possible to say as much for his conclusions. Ingenuity, certainly, and considerable constructive skill, are usually manifested more or less; and in not a few instances (as in that delightful play *The Great Duke of Florence*, or in *Believe as You List*, a very powerful work) the conclusion is altogether right and satisfying. But in many instances Massinger's very endeavour to wind off his play in the neatest manner, without any tangles or frayed edges, spoils the proper artistic effect. His persistent aversion to a tragic end, even where a virtual tragedy demands it; his invincible determination to make things come to a fortunate conclusion, even if the action has to be huddled up or or squashed together in consequence; in a word, his concession to the popular taste, no matter at what cost, not unfrequently distorts the conclusion of plays up to this point well conducted.

Massinger's treatment of character follows in some respects, where it seems in others to contradict, his treatment of versification and of construction. Where Massinger most conclusively fails is in a right understanding and a right representation of human nature; in the power to conceive passion and bring its speech and action vividly and accurately before us. His theory of human nature is apparently that of the puppet-player: he is aware of violent but not of consistent action, of change but not of development. No dramatist talks so much of virtue and vice, but he has no conception of either except in the abstract; and he sees nothing strange that a virtuous woman should on a sudden cry out –

> Chastity,
> Thou only art a name, and I renounce thee!
> [*The Picture*, III.vi.156–7]

or that a fanatical Mohammedan should embrace Christianity on being told that the Prophet was a juggler, and taught birds to feed in his ear [*The Renegado*, IV.iii.115, 128]. His motto might be –

> We are all the balls of time, tossed to and fro;

for his conception of life is that of a game of wild and inconsequent haphazard. It is true that he rewards his good people and punishes the bad with the most scrupulous care; but the good or bad person at the end of a play is not always the good or bad person of the beginning. Massinger's outlook is by no means vague or sceptical on religion or on morals; he is moralist before all things, and the copy-book tags neatly pinned on to the conclusion of each play are only a somewhat clumsy exhibition of a real conviction and conscientiousness. But his morality is nerveless, and aimless in its general effect; or it translates itself, oddly enough, into a co-partner of confusion, a disturbing and distracting element of mischief.

Notwithstanding all we may say of Massinger's facility, it is evident that we have in him no mere improvisator, or contentedly hasty and superficial person. He was an earnest thinker, a thoughtful politician, a careful observer of the manners and men of his time, and, to the extent of his capacity, an eager student of human nature; but, for all that, his position is that of a foreigner travelling through a country of whose language he knows but a few words or sentences. He observes with keenness, he infers with acumen; but when he proceeds to take the last step – the final touch which transmutes recorded observation into vital fact – he finds (or, at least, we find) that his strength is exhausted, his limit reached. He observes, for instance, that the characters and motives of men are in general mixed; and especially, and in a special degree, those of men of a certain class, and in certain positions. But when we look at the personages whom he presents before us as mixed characters, we perceive that they are not so in themselves, but are mixed in the making. 'We do not forbid an artist in fiction', says Mr. Swinburne in speaking of Charles Reade, 'to set before us strange instances of inconsistency and eccentricity in conduct; but we do require of the artist that he should make us feel such aberrations to be as clearly inevitable as they are confessedly exceptional' ['Charles Reade', in the Bonchurch *Works*, vol.14, pp.360–1]. Now this is just what Massinger does not do; it is just here that he comes short of success as a dramatic artist. In Calderon's figure, we see his men dancing to the rhythm of a music which we cannot hear: nothing is visible to us but the grotesque contortions and fantastic motions of the dancer.

Where Massinger fails is in the power of identifying himself with his characters, at least in their moments of profound passion or strenuous action. At his best (or almost his best, for of course there are exceptions) he succeeds on the one hand in representing the gentler and secondary passions and emotions; on the other, in describing the action of the primary passions very accurately and admirably, but, as it were, in the third person, and from the outside. As Mr. Leslie Stephen says with reference to a fine speech of Sir Giles Overreach in *A New Way to Pay Old Debts*, 'Read "he" for "I" and "his" for "my", and it is an admirable bit of denunciation of a character probably intended as a copy from real life.' His characters seldom quite speak out; they have almost always about them a sort of rhetorical self-consciousness. The language of pure passion is unknown to them; they can only strive to counterfeit its dialect. In handling a situation of tragic passion, in developing a character subject to the shocks of an antagonistic Fate, Massinger manifests a singular lack of vital force, a singular failure in the realising imagination. He mistakes extravagance for strength, eloquence for conviction, feverishness for vitality. Take, for instance, the jealousy of Theodosius in *The Emperor of the East*.

His conduct and language are altogether unreasoning and unreasonable, the extravagances of a weak and unballasted nature, depicted by one who can only thus conceive of strong passions. His sudden and overmastering jealousy at sight of the apple given by Eudocia to Paulinus is without probability; and Eudocia's lie when charged with it is without reason. It is almost too cruel in this connection to think of Desdemona's handkerchief; of the admirable and inevitable logic of the means by which Othello's mind is not so much imbued with suspicion as convinced. 'All this pother for an apple!' as some sensible person in the play observes [IV.iv.213]. Again, in *The Fatal Dowry* [i.e. *The Unnatural Combat*] compare for a moment Malefort's careful bombast, which leaves us cold and incredulous before an impossible and uninteresting monster of wickedness with the biting and flaming words of Francesco Cenci, before which we shudder as at the fiery breath of the pit. Almost all Massinger's villains, notwithstanding the fearful language which they are in the habit of employing, fail to convince us of their particular wickedness; most of his tried and triumphant heroes fail to convince us of their vitality of virtue. Massinger's conception of evil is surprisingly naïve: he is frightened, completely taken in, by the big words and blustering looks of these bold bad men. He paints them with an inky brush, he tells us how bad, how very bad they are, and he sets them denouncing themselves and their wickedness with a beautiful tenderness of conscience. The blackness of evil and the contrasted whiteness of virtue are alike lost on us, and the good moral with them; for we are unable to believe in the existence of any such beings. It is the same with those exhibitions of tempted virtue of which Massinger is so fond. I do not allude at present to cases of actual martyrdom or persecution, such as those of Dorothea or Antiochus; but to situations of a more complex nature, such as that of Mathias with Honoria, or Bertoldo with Aurelia, in which we are expected to behold the conflict in the soul of virtue enthroned and vice assailant. The fault is that of inadequate realisation of the true bearing of the situation; inadequate representation of the conflict which is very properly assumed to be going on. Massinger is like a man who knows that the dial-hand of the clock will describe a certain circle, passing from point to point of significant figures; but instead of winding up the clock, and setting it going of itself, he can only move round the hand on the outside. To use another figure, his characters oscillate rather than advance, their conversions are without saving effect on their souls, their falls have no damnation. They are alike outside themselves, and they talk of 'my lust', 'my virtue', as of detached and portable conveniences. When we drop to a lower level than that of pure tragedy, when we turn to characters who are grave or mild or melancholy or unfortunate rather than passionate, intense and flexible, we find that Massinger is more in his element. 'Grave and great-hearted', as Mr. Swinburne styles him [No. 49(a)], he could bring before us with sympathetic skill, characters whose predominant bent is towards a melancholy and great-hearted gravity, a calm and eloquent dignity, a self-sacrificing nobility of service, or lofty endurance of inevitable wrong. Massinger's favourite play was *The Roman Actor*: 'I ever held it', he says in his dedication, 'the most perfect birth of my Minerva.' It is impossible to say quite that; but it is certainly representative of some among the noble qualities of its writer, while it shows very clearly the defects of these qualities. What it represents is scarcely human nature; but actions and single passions writ large for the halls of kings. A certain cold loftiness, stately indeed, but not attained without some freezing of vital heat, informs it. Paris, the actor, is rather a grave and stately shadow than a breathing man; but the idealisation is nobly conceived; and both actor and tyrant, Paris and Domitian, are in their way impressive figures made manifest, not concealed, in rhetorical prolusions really appropriate to their time and character. Another classical play, the less-known *Believe As You List*, contains a figure in which I think we have the very best work of which Massinger was capable. The character of the deposed and exiled King Antiochus has a true heroism and kingliness about it; his language, a passionate and haughty dignity at times almost Marlowesque. The quiet constancy and undaunted and uncomplaining endurance of the utmost ills of Fate, which mark the character and the utterance of the Asian Emperor, raise the poetry of the play to a height but seldom attained by the pedestrian Pegasus of Massinger. As Antiochus is the most impressive of his heroes, so Flaminius is one of the most really human and consistent of his villains. The end of the play is natural, powerful and significant beyond that of any other; so natural, powerful and significant, that we may feel quite sure it was received with doubtful satisfaction by the audience above whose head and against whose taste the poet had for once elected to write.

In one or two striking portraits (those for example of the ironical old courtier Eubulus in *The Picture*, the old soldier Archidamus in *The Bondman*, or the faithful friend Romont in *The Fatal Dowry*), Massinger has shown his appreciation of honest worth and sober fidelity, qualities not of a showy kind, the recognition and representation of which do him honour. In *The Bashful Lover* and *The Maid of Honour* he has represented with special sympathy two phases of reverential and modest love. Hortensio, of the former, is a sort of pale Quixote; a knight-errant a little cracked or crazed; very sincere, and a trifle given to uttering vague and useless professions of hyperbolical humility and devotion. There is a certain febrile nobleness, a showy chivalry, about him; but we are conscious of something 'got-up' and over-conscious in the exhibition. Adorni, the rejected lover in *The Maid of Honour*, is a truly noble and pathetic figure; altogether without the specious eloquence and petted despair of Hortensio, but thoroughly human and rationally self-sacrificing. His duet with Camiola at the close of the third act is one of the very finest scenes in Massinger's works – that passage, I mean, where the woman he loves despatches him to the rescue of the man on whom her own heart is set. 'You will do this?' she says; and he answers, 'Faithfully, madam' – and then to himself aside, 'but not live long after' [III.iii.208–9]. A touch of this sort is sufficiently rare in Massinger.

While I am speaking of *The Maid of Honour*, I may take the opportunity of referring to the character of Camiola herself, – incomparably the finest portrait of a woman ever achieved by the poet. Camiola – that 'small but ravishing substance' as, with a rare and infrequent touch of delicate characterization, she is somewhere called [IV.iii.74] – is, notwithstanding a few flaws in her delineation, a thoroughly delightful and admirable creature; full of bright strength and noble constancy, of womanly heart and right manly spirit and wit. Her bearing in the scene, to a part of which I just alluded, is admirable throughout; not admirable alone, but exquisite, are her quick 'Never think more then' to the servant [III.iii.93]; her outcry about the 'petty sum' of the ransom [III.iii.117]; and especially the words of 'perfect moan' [i.e.

'delicious moan' in Keats's 'Ode to Psyche'?] which fall from her when she learns the hopeless estate of her lover, imprisoned by his enemy, abandoned by his King [quotes III.iii.127–33]. When she learns of the treachery of the lover for whom she has done so much, her wondering sorrowful 'O Bertoldo!' [V.i.78] is worth a world of rhetoric. It is she who utters the most famous phrase in Massinger, the fearless indictment of the court doctrine of the divinity of kings [quotes IV.v.52–9]. Her speech in answer to Bertoldo's hollow protestations of penitence, – the 'Pray you, rise' [V.ii.208] – is full of exquisite genius and subtle beauty of spirit.

Unfortunately all Massinger's women are not of the stamp of Camiola. Lidia, indeed, in *The Great Duke of Florence*, is a good sweet modest girl; Cleora in *The Bondman* would like to be so; Bellisant in *The Parliament of Love* is a brilliant dashing creature; Margaret in *A New Way to Pay Old Debts* is an emphatically nice shrewd pleasant woman; and Matilda in *The Bashful Lover* a commonplace decent young person, without a thread or shade of distinction. But Massinger's general conception of women, and the greater number of his portraits of them, are alike debased and detestable. His bad women are incredible monsters of preposterous vice; his good women are brittle and tainted. They breathe the air of courts, and the air is poisoned. Themselves the vilest, they walk through a violent and unnaturally vicious world of depraved imagination, greedy of pleasure and rhetorical of desire. They are shamefacedly shameless; offensive and without passion; importunate and insatiable Potiphar's wives. 'Pleasure's their heaven', affirms somebody [Perigot in *The Parliament of Love*, III.i.54]; and their pleasure is without bit or bridle, without rule or direction. Massinger's favourite situation is that of a queen or princess violently and heedlessly enamoured of a man – apparently a common man, though he generally turns out to be a duke in disguise – whom she has never seen five minutes before. Over and over again is this wretched farce gone through; always without passion, sincerity or strength; always flatly, coldly, ridiculously. I am afraid Massinger thought his Donusas, Coriscas, Domitias, Aurelias, Honorias and Beaumelles brilliant and fascinating flowers of evil, sisters of Cleopatra and Semiramis, magnificently wicked women. In reality they never attain to the level of a Delilah. They are vulgar-minded to the core; weak and without stability; mere animals if they are not mere puppets. The stain of sensuality or the smutch of vulgarity is upon even the virtuous. Marcelia, in *The Duke of Milan*, supposedly a woman of spotless virtue, utters language full of covert licence; for Massinger seems to see virtue in women mainly as a sort of conscious and painful restraint. Eudocia, in *The Emperor of the East*, an injured innocent wife, betrays an unconscious vulgarity of mind which is enough to withdraw our sympathy from a fairly well-deserving object. The curious thing is, not so much that the same pen could draw Camiola and Corisca, but that the same pen could draw Camiola and Marcelia.

Massinger's main field is the Romantic Drama. He attempted, indeed, Tragedy, Comedy and History; but both tragedy and history assume in his hands a romantic cast, while his two great comedies verge constantly upon tragedy. Of his two most distinct and most distinguished tragedies, *The Duke of Milan* and *The Fatal Dowry*, the former is a powerful and impressive work, rising in parts to his highest level; the latter, despite its conventional reputation, which it owes partly to Rowe's effective plagiarisation in *The Fair Penitent*, an inadequate and unsatisfactory production. Two or three passages in the latter part of *The Fatal Dowry* [instances IV.iv.7–78 and 'the few words following on the death of Beaumelle; with a passage or two in the fifth act'] have the true accent of nature; but even these are marred by the base alloy with which they are mingled. But *The Duke of Milan*, despite much that is inadequate and even absurd in its handling, rises again and again to something of passion and of insight. The character and the circumstances of Sforza have been often compared with those of Othello: they are still more similar, I should venture to think, to those of Griffith Gaunt [eponymous hero of Charles Reade's novel (1866)]; and they have the damning fault of the latter in that the jealousy and its consequences are not made to seem quite inevitable. Sforza is an example, albeit perhaps the most favourable one, of that inconsequential oscillation of nature to which I have already referred as characteristic of most of Massinger's prominent characters. But his capacity for sudden and extreme changes of disposition, and his violent and unhinged passion, are represented with more dramatic power, with more force and naturalness, than it is at all usual to find in Massinger; who has here contrived to give a frequent effect of fineness to the frenzies and delusions of his hero. If Sforza is after all but a second-rate Othello, Marcelia is certainly a very shrewish Desdemona, and Francisco a palpably poor Iago. (There is one touch, however, in the temptings of Francisco which is really almost worthy of Iago:– 'She's yet guilty / *Only* in her intent!' [IV.iii.251–2].)

In tragi-comedy, the romantic drama pure and simple, we may take *The Great Duke of Florence* as the most exquisite example. In this, the most purely delightful play, I think, ever written by Massinger, – a play which we read, to use Lamb's expression [No. 25(e)], 'with composure and placid delight' – we see the sweetest and most delicate side of Massinger's genius: a country pleasantness and freshness, a masquerading genial gravity, altogether charming and attractive. The plot is admirably woven, and how prettily brought about to a happy conclusion, with its good humour, forgiveness, and friendship all round! There is something almost of Shakespeare's charm in people and events; in these princes and courtiers without ceremony and without vice, uttering pretty sentiments prettily, and playing elegantly at life; in these simple lovers, with their dainty easy trials and crosses on the way to happiness; in the villain who does no real harm, and whom nobody can hate. *The Guardian*, a late play, very fine and flexible in its rhythm, and very brisk in its action, has some exquisite country feeling, together with three or four of the most abominable characters and much of the vilest language in Massinger. One character at least, Darazzo [i.e. Durazzo], the male of Juliet's nurse, is really, though offensive enough in all conscience, very heartily and graphically depicted. *A Very Woman*, again, by Massinger and Fletcher, has much that is pleasant and delightful; some of it very sweet and right, with some that is rank enough. I have spoken already of *The Maid of Honour*, or it might be mentioned here as a play uniting (somewhat as in *Measure for Measure*, which it partly resembles) the lighter and graver qualities of tragedy and comedy under the form of the romantic drama.

Massinger's lack of humour did not prevent him from writing comedy, nor yet from achieving signal success therein. *A New Way to Pay Old Debts* is the most memorable of his plays; but, though it is styled a comedy, it is certainly not for laughter that we turn to it. *A New Way* and *The City Madam* belong to the Comedy of Manners; satirical transcripts of contemporary life, somewhat after the style of Terence or Plautus. All Massinger's plays are distinguished by an earnest and corrective tone on contemporary politics and current fashions; and it is no wonder that he succeeded in a species of play devoted wholly to the exhibition and satirisation of the follies and vanities of the day. His constant touch on manners, even in romantic plays with classical or eastern localities, is peculiar, and suggests a certain preoccupation with the subject, possibly due to early associations at Wilton House, possibly to mere personal bent or circumstances. Remembering the letter of 1624 [now dated *c.* 1613], we may be allowed to fancy a personal applicability in the frequent denunciations of usurers and delineations of the misery of poor debtors. But besides this, I think that Massinger, being no great spirit, winged, and having force to enter into the deep and secret chambers of the soul, found his place to be in a censorship of society, and was right in concerning himself with what he could do so well. His professedly comic types, even Justice Greedy, are mere exaggerations, solitary traits frozen into the semblance of men; without really comic effect. But in the conduct of these two plays; in the episodical illuminations of London and provincial life; in the wealth of observation and satire which they exhibit, Massinger has left us work of permanent value; and in the character of Sir Giles Overreach he has made his single contribution to the gallery of permanent illustrations of human nature – a portrait to be spoken of with Grandet and with Harpagon [in Balzac's *Eugénie Grandet* and Molière's *L' Avare*].

Massinger is the product of his period, and he reflects faithfully the temper of court and society under the first Charles. Much that we have to regret in him was due to the misfortune of his coming just when he did, at the ebb of a spent wave; but the best that he had was all his own. Serious, a thinker, a moralist; gifted with an instinct for nobility and a sympathy in whatever is generous and self-sacrificing; a practical student of history and an honest satirist of social abuses; he was at the same time an admirable story-teller, and a master of dramatic construction. But his grave and varied genius was lacking in the two primary requirements of the dramatist – imagination and grip. He has no real mastery over the passions, and his eloquence does not appeal to the heart. He interests us strongly; but he has no power to overwhelm or to carry us away. The whole man is seen in the portrait by which we know him: in the contrast and contradiction of that singular face which attracts, yet always at the last look fails to satisfy us, with its melancholy and thoughtful grace, tempered always and marred by the weakness and the want which we can scarcely analyse, nor by any means overlook.

52. Edmund Gosse
1894

Gosse (1849–1928), chiefly known today for *Father and Son* (1907), wrote on a wide range of European literature. Gosse, 'the most characteristic voice of the end of the nineteenth century' in criticism of Massinger (*EG*, vol.1, p.lxiv), places him as a grave, sober, 'sentimental and rhetorical', 'essentially unlyrical' playwright of the second rank. This verdict – itself descended from a strand of similar feeling in the comments of Lamb (No. 25) and Hazlitt (No. 33) and derived more directly from Ward (No. 46), Stephen (No. 47), and Symons (No. 51) – went largely unchallenged for seventy years, not least as a result of its confirmation in T.S. Eliot's essay of 1920 (see Introduction, p.41). It began to waver only as the bases of criticism gradually shifted from the evaluative and poetic towards the historical and theatrical.

The Jacobean Poets (a University Extension Manual), London, 1894, pp.202–3, 206–17.

Nothing exemplifies more curiously the rapidity of development in poetical literature at the opening of the seventeenth century than the fact that the same brief reign which saw the last perfection placed on the edifice of Elizabethan drama saw also the products of the pen of Massinger. For, however much we may respect the activity of this remarkable man, however warmly we may acknowledge the power of his invention, the skill and energy with which he composed, and however agreeable his plays may appear to us if we compare them with what succeeded them in a single generation, there can be no question that the decline in the essential parts of poetry from Webster or Tourneur, to go no further back, to Massinger is very abrupt. Mr. Leslie Stephen [No. 47] has noted in this playwright 'a certain hectic flush, symptomatic of approaching decay', and we may even go further and discover in him a leaden pallor, the sign of decreasing vitality. The 'hectic flush' seems to me to belong more properly to his immediate successors, who do not come within the scope of this volume, to Ford, with his morbid sensibility, and to Shirley, with his mechanical ornament, than to Massinger, where the decline chiefly shows itself in the negation of qualities, the absence of what is brilliant, eccentric, and passionate. The sentimental and rhetorical drama of Massinger has its excellent points, but it is dominated by the feeling that the burning summer of poetry is over, and that a russet season is letting us down gently towards the dull uniformity of winter. Interesting and specious as Massinger is, we cannot avoid the impression that he is preparing us for that dramatic destitution which was to accompany the Commonwealth.

. . .

The comparison has been made between Massinger and such earlier poets as Webster. This is a parallel which, from our present standpoint, militates strongly against the first-named writer. For, if the truth be told, Massinger is scarcely a poet, except in the sense in which that word may be used of any man who writes seriously in dramatic form. What we delight in in the earlier Elizabethans, the splendid bursts of imaginative insight, the wild freaks of diction, the sudden sheet-lightning of poetry illuminating for an instant dark places of the soul, all this is absent in Massinger. He is uniform and humdrum; he has no lyrical passages; his very versification, as various critics have observed, is scarcely to be distinguished from prose, and often would not seem metrical if it were printed along the page. Intensity is not within his reach, and even in the aims of composition we distinguish between the joyous instinctive lyricism of the Elizabethans, which attained to beauty without much design, and this deliberate and unimpassioned work, so plain and easy and workmanlike. It is very natural, especially for a young reader, to fling Massinger to the other end of the room, and to refuse him all attention.

This is unphilosophical and ungenerous. If we shift our standpoint a little, there is much in the author of *The Renegado* which demands our respect and insures our enjoyment. If he be less brilliant than those fiery poets, if his pictures of life do not penetrate us as theirs do, he has merits of construction which were unknown to them. The long practice which he had in prentice work was none of it thrown away upon him. It made him, when once he gained confidence to write alone, an admirable artificer of plays. He is the Scribe of the seventeenth century [Eugène Scribe (1791–1861), prolific and popular author of 'well-made' plays]. He knows all the tricks by which curiosity is awakened, sustained, and gratified. He composes, as few indeed of his collaborators seem to have done, not for the study so much as for the stage. He perceived, we cannot doubt, certain faults in that noble dramatic literature of Fletcher's with which he was so long identified. He perceived Fletcher's careless exaggeration and his light ideal. It was Massinger who recalled English drama to sobriety and gravity.

The absence of bloody violence in his plays must strike every reader, and at the same time the tendency to introduce religious and moral reflections. The intellectual force of Massinger was extolled by Hazlitt, and not unjustly, but it was largely exercised in smoothing out and regulating his conceptions. The consequence is that Massinger tends to the sentimental and the rhetorical, and that description takes the place of passion. His characters too often say, in their own persons, what it should have been left for others to say of them. Variety of interest is secured, but sometimes at the sacrifice of evolution, and the personages act, not as human creatures must, but as theatrical puppets should. His humour possesses the same fault as his seriousness, that it is not intense. Without agreeing with Hartley Coleridge [No. 43], who said that Massinger would be the worst of all dull jokers, if Ford had not contrived to be still duller, it must be admitted that the humour of Massinger is seldom successful unless when it is lambent and suffused, when, that is to say, it tinctures a scene rather than illuminates a phrase. In short, Massinger depends upon his broad effects, whether in comedy or tragedy, and must not be looked to for jewels ten words long. His songs have been the scoff of criticism; they really are among the worst ever written. He was, in short, as cannot be too often repeated, essentially unlyrical, yet his plays have great merits. They can always be read with ease, for they seem written with decorum.

. . .

[*The Duke of Milan*] closes in violent and ferocious confusion; but that was the taste of the time. It is clearly constructed, the plot is lucidity itself, and the first act, as is usual with Massinger, is admirably devised to put the spectator in possession of all the necessary facts.

When, however, we come to reflect upon the conduct of this plausible drama, we find much which calls for unfavourable comment. There has been a great deal of bustle and show, and an interesting spectacle, but no play of genuine character. If, as has been conjectured, it was Massinger's intention deliberately to emulate Shakespeare in *Othello*, his failure is almost ludicrous. The figures are strongly contrasted, and they play at cross-purposes; did they not do so, the tragedy would come to a standstill; their inconsistencies are the springs of the movement. Hazlitt [No. 33(d)], and others have found great fault with the conception of Sforza, as being irrelevant and violent. It is not needful, however, to go so far as this in censure. It may surely be admitted that Sforza is a credible type of the neuropathic Italian despot. His agitation in the first act is true and vivid; his moods are those of a man on the verge of madness, but they do not cross that verge.

He reaches the highest pitch of hysterical agitation in the fifth act, where the dead body of Marcelia is brought across the stage – [quotes V.ii.47–69, reducing 'The gentlest touch torments her' to 'The gentlest touch'].

The real fault of *The Duke of Milan* is not the unnaturalness of Sforza, but the fact that the dramatist has limited his attention to him. The remoteness of the Duke's passions, his nervous eccentricities, should have forced Massinger to keep all the characters at a low and quiet pitch, so to contrast the neurosis of Sforza with their normal condition. But all the other characters are no less frenzied than he is, without his excuses. The abrupt wooing of Francisco, who is a mere shadow of Iago, in the second act, is utterly untrue; his equally abrupt repentance, in the third act, is not less extraordinary, and is introduced for no other reason than that Marcelia should know Sforza's plan for her being killed in case he does not return alive. If we return to the female characters, they are not more natural; the mother and sister of the Duke are vulgar scolds, Marcelia herself utterly ugly and absurd. Everything is extreme and yet weak; the characters are made of india-rubber, and the dramatist presses them down or pulls them out as he sees fit. His study of Sforza is carefully executed, and has passages of great suavity and charm – such as his meeting with the Emperor Charles – but to the evolution of this single character the entire play is sacrificed.

. . .

When we turn from this tragedy to the comedy of *A New Way to Pay Old Debts*, we are struck by similar characteristics, modified, however, by the fact that this is a much stronger and more vivid play than *The Duke of Milan*. At the outset we are interested to find ourselves on a scene so frankly English and modern. Massinger had much of the spirit of the journalist, and it has been pointed out by Mr. Gardiner [S.R. Gardiner, 'The Political Element in Massinger', *The Contemporary Review*, vol.28, 1876, pp.495–507] and others that he was constantly engaged in referring to events of passing politics. Here he was inspired by a sensational case which had but recently engaged the notice of the courts of law, and the comedy palpitates with topical allusions. The plot of the play is clear and interesting.

. . .

As is customary with Massinger, the first act is singularly skilful. The story told in sarcasm to Wellborn by Tapwell, the rascally innkeeper, is exactly what we need to put us in possession of the facts. Wellborn's condition, character, and prospects are placed before us in absolute clearness, our sympathies are engaged, and the little mystery of his whisper to the lady, at the close of the act, is left dark so as to freshen and carry on our curiosity. In the second act, we begin to appreciate the force and cunning of Sir Giles Overreach, in whose wickedness there is something colossal that impresses the imagination. The third act sustains this impression and even increases it, but after this the threads become, not exactly entangled, but twisted, and the illusion of nature is gradually lost. In *A New Way to Pay Old Debts* that unhappy forcible-feebleness of Massinger's is not so strikingly prominent as elsewhere, yet we see something of it in Marall's crude and abrupt temptation of Wellborn to commit some crime and so put an end to his miseries. A certain Justice Greedy pervades the piece, a magistrate who is always raging for his food. Some critics have thought his gluttonies very diverting, but Massinger borrowed them directly from Beaumont and Fletcher, and they are too incessant not to become fatiguing. The charm of this play, after all, consists in its realistic picture of English country life in 1620, and in its curious portrait of the great savage parvenu, eater of widows and orphans, a huge machine for unscrupulous avarice and tyranny. In Sir Giles Overreach, Massinger approaches more nearly than anywhere else to a dramatic creation of the first order.

Little would be gained by examining with the like minuteness the rest of Massinger's dramas. For so brief a sketch as we must here confine ourselves to, it is enough to say that in the main they present the same characteristics. This playwright commonly shows a capacity for depicting courtly and gentle persons, engaged in pleasant converse amongst themselves. For suavity and refinement of this kind, *The Grand Duke of Florence* [sic] is remarkable. Lamb [No. 25(e)] has praised *The Picture* for 'good sense, rational fondness, and chastened feeling'; this is true of its execution, but hardly of its repulsive central idea. On the whole, Massinger may be commended for the prominence and the dignity which he readily assigns to women; but in attempting to show them independent, he not unfrequently paints them exceedingly coarse and hard. His political bias was towards a kind of oligarchic liberalism; Coleridge describes him as 'a decided Whig' [note in the edition of Jonson, Beaumont, and Fletcher detailed in No. 29(b)]. Sometimes he indulged this tendency in politics by satirizing the ladies of a less aristocratic walk of life than he usually affected, and *The City Madam* is a lively example of his gifts in this direction. The diction of the dramatist is particularly rich in the last-named play, and Massinger has not written better verse than this from Luke's soliloquy in the third act. [Quotes III.iii.9–33].

When the directly Gallic fashion of the Restoration had gone out, and dramatists had turned once more to their Jacobean predecessors, Massinger came back into favour. His example had much to do in forming the style of such sentimental tragic writers as Rowe and Lillo, and again, a century later, his influence was paramount on Talfourd and Sheridan Knowles [Sir Thomas Talfourd (1795–1854) and James Sheridan Knowles (1784–1862)]. He has always been easy to imitate, and it may be said that until Lamb began to show quite clearly what the old English drama really was, most readers vaguely took their impression of it from the pages of Massinger. He was succeeded, it is true, by several younger playwrights, particularly by Ford, Shirley, and Brome; but each of these . . . returned closer than he did to the tradition of their fathers. Massinger is, really, though not technically and literally, the last of the great men. In him we have all the characteristics of the school in their final decay, before they dissolved and were dispersed. At the same time, it must never be forgotten that we do not know what he may have been capable of in his youth, and that he was nearly forty, and therefore possibly beyond his poetic prime, before he wrote the earliest play which has come down to us. If Warburton's miserable cook had not burned *Minerva's Sacrifice* and *The Italian Nightpiece* [see *EG*, vol.1, pp.xxvi–xxviii], we might, possibly, put Massinger on a higher level; but criticism can make no conjectures, and we must place the worthy and industrious playwright where we find him.

Select Bibliography

1. Bibliographies

TANNENBAUM, SAMUEL A., and DOROTHY R. TANNENBAUM, *Elizabethan Bibliographies*, vol.6, Port Washington, N.Y., 1967 [first published 1938]. (To 1936.)

PENNEL, CHARLES A., and WILLIAM P. WILLIAMS, *Elizabethan Bibliographies Supplements*, vol.8, London, 1968. (1937–65.)

LOGAN, TERENCE P., and DENZELL S. SMITH, *The Later Jacobean and Caroline Dramatists*, Lincoln, Neb., and London, 1978. (Selected twentieth-century works to 1976.)

SCHOENBAUM, S., 'Philip Massinger', in Stanley Wells (ed.), *English Drama* (Select Bibliographical Guides), Oxford, 1975, pp.86–92, 97–9. (Selected works to 1974.)

For criticism after 1965 see the *Annual Bibliography* of the Modern Humanities Research Association and the annual *International Bibliography* of the Modern Language Association of America.

2. Studies of Massinger's reception

In addition to the succinct history of Massinger's reputation (vol.1, pp.xlv–lxvii) and stage histories of the individual plays in *EG*, and the still indispensable *Ball* on the remarkable story of *A New Way*, consult:

ARNOLD, HANS STEPHAN, 'The Reception of Ben Jonson, Beaumont and Fletcher, and Massinger in Eighteenth-Century Germany', unpublished Ph.D. thesis, University of Maryland, 1962.

GIBSON, COLIN, 'Elizabethan and Stuart Dramatists in *Wit's Recreations* (1640)', *Research Opportunities in Renaissance Drama*, vol.29, 1986–7, pp.15–23.

GIBSON, COLIN, 'Massinger at the Academy of Complements', *The Library*, forthcoming.

GRISWOLD, WENDY, *Renaissance Revivals: City Comedy and Revenge Tragedy in the London Theatre 1576–1980*, Chicago, 1986.

HARLEY, MARIE JUNE, 'The Eighteenth-Century Interest in English

Drama Before 1640 Outside Shakespeare', unpublished MA thesis, University of Birmingham, 1962.

3. The 'Untun'd Kennell' affair (see Introduction, pp. 4–7)

BAS, GEORGES, 'James Shirley et "Th' Untun'd Kennell": une petite guerre des théâtres vers 1630', *Études anglaises*, vol. 16, 1963, pp. 11–22.

BEAL, PETER, 'Massinger at Bay: Unpublished Verses in a War of the Theatres', *The Yearbook of English Studies*, vol. 10, 1980, pp. 190–203.

GARRETT, MARTIN, *'A diamond, though set in horn': Philip Massinger's Attitude to Spectacle*, Salzburg, 1984, pp. 258–63.

GIBSON, COLIN, 'Another Shot in the War of the Theatres (1630)', *Notes and Queries*, vol. 232, 1987, pp. 308–9.

GRIVELET, MICHEL, '"Th' Untun'd Kennell": note sur Thomas Heywood et le théâtre sous Charles 1er', *Études anglaises*, vol. 7, 1954, pp. 101–6.

LAWLESS, DONALD S., 'On the Date of Massinger's *The Maid of Honour*', *Notes and Queries*, vol. 231, 1986, pp. 391–2.

4. Contexts for the reception

BUTLER, MARTIN, *Theatre and Crisis 1632–1642*, Cambridge, 1984.

HEINEMANN, MARGOT, *Puritanism and Theatre: Thomas Middleton and the Opposition Drama Under the Early Stuarts*, Cambridge, 1980.

NEILL, MICHAEL, '"Wits most accomplished Senate": the Audience of the Caroline Private Theatres', *Studies in English Literature 1500–1900*, vol. 18, 1978, pp. 341–60.

PATTERSON, ANNABEL, *Censorship and Interpretation: the Conditions of Writing and Reading in Early Modern England*, Madison, Wisc., 1984.

Index

Academy of Complements, The 10
Addison, Joseph 176
Aickin, Francis 101
Alfieri, Vittorio 25, 151
Annual Review, The (1808) 23, 24, 31, 40
Appleton, Samuel 218
Arabian Nights, The 218, 222
Aubrey, John 13

Bagnall, William 3
Baillie, Joanna 133
Ball, Robert Hamilton 40; quoted 12, 18
Balzac, Honoré de *Eugénie Grandet* 232
Bate, Henry 15, 16, 101–4
Beal, Peter 5, 7
Beaumont, Francis 2, 4, 10, 11, 12, 13, 16, 18, 20, 23, 24, 25, 57, 70–3 *passim*, 76, 89, 92, 99, 113–16 *passim*, 119, 121, 124–9 *passim*, 160, 176, 182, 184, 186, 191, 206, 215
Beauties of English Drama, The (1777) 17
Beauties of the English Stage, The (1756) 17
Beauties of Massinger 22–3, 148–9
Beddoes, Thomas Lovell 26, 154–5
Behn, Aphra 13
Bentley, Gerald Eades 2
Berkenhead, Sir John 10
Betterton, Mary *see* Saunderson
Betterton, Thomas 11, 12, 78–9, 92, 93
Booth, Edwin 48
Booth, Junius Brutus 31
Boswell, James 17
Brawne, Fanny 150
Brome, Richard 70, 71, 77, 239
Browning, Elizabeth Barrett 31–2, 34
Buckingham, George Villiers, Duke of 8, 96–8
Burbage, Richard 9, 92
Burges, Sir James Bland 29, 129–32; *Riches* 32, 149
Burns, Robert 165
Butler, Martin 41
Byron, George Gordon, Lord 25, 28, 150–1

Calderón de la Barca, Pedro 225
Campbell, Thomas 23–4, 27, 34, 151–3
Carew, Thomas 4–7, 9, 59–60, 61, 64
Carlyle, Thomas 33, 34
Carr, Robert 96–7
Cartwright, William 11, 77
Cervantes Savedra, Miguel de *Don Quixote* 191
Chambers's Cyclopaedia of English Literature 38
Chapman, George 14, 19, 23, 54, 70, 113, 193, 218
Charles I, King 8, 69, 96, 98, 143, 169, 177, 232
Charles II, King 115
Chelli, Maurice 35, 40
Cibber, Theophilus 93
Cokaine, Sir Aston 2, 6, 10, 71–3
Coleridge, Hartley 32, 35, 36, 40, 165–71, 176, 235
Coleridge, Samuel Taylor 7, 20, 23, 24–5, 26, 30, 33, 36, 39, 114, 123–9, 167, 177, 187, 190, 205, 207, 214, 221, 238; *Remorse* 206
Colman, George 15, 16–17, 18, 19, 20, 90–3, 94
Condell, Henry 63
Congreve, William 115
Cooke, George Frederick 27, 113, 114, 133
Cotgrave, John 10–11
Cotton, Charles 73, 76
Courthope, W.J. 39
Coxeter, Thomas 14, 15, 17, 18, 20, 89–90, 91, 122
Craik, George 34–5
Critical Review, The (1816) 31
Cromwell, Oliver 188
Cruickshank, A.H. 40, 41
Cumberland, Richard 17, 18–19, 20, 99, 100, 104–13
Cunningham, Francis 33

Daborne, Robert 53–4, 165
Davenant, William 4–7, 9, 11, 13, 19, 59, 61–3, 64
Davenport, Hester 79

INDEX

Davies, Thomas 8, 15–16, 17, 18, 20, 22, 94–9
Davis, John 54
Dekker, Thomas 11, 12, 22, 23, 25, 34, 81, 113, 116–17, 122, 144, 167, 189, 205
Dibdin, Charles 19–20, 21
Dickens, Charles 32
Dilke, Charles Wentworth 150
Dodsley, Robert 15, 16, 22, 31, 90, 94, 115
Donne, George 4
Donne, John 54, 122, 152
Donohue, Joseph W. 29
Drayton, Michael 54
Dryden, John 10, 12, 13, 14, 92, 124, 125, 205
Dunn, T.A. 40–1
Dyce, Alexander 25, 201, 202

The Edinburgh Review 21, 22, 120–2
Edwards, Philip 41
Eliot, T.S. 7, 41, 75, 187, 220, 233
Ellis, Havelock 220
Elton, Oliver 40
Emerson, Ralph Waldo 25
English Review, The (1783) 103–4
Etherege, Sir George 12

Falkland, Lucius Cary, Viscount 214
Ferriar, John 17, 19, 20, 21, 148
Field, Nathan 9, 13, 53–4, 81, 104, 105, 146, 151, 165
Fitzgerald, Edward 32
Fletcher, John 1–2, 10–11, 12, 13, 16, 18, 20, 23, 24, 25, 33, 34, 36, 37, 39, 54, 57, 70–3 *passim*, 76, 81, 89, 92, 99, 113–17 *passim*, 118, 119, 120, 121, 124–9 *passim*, 150, 152, 160, 161–4 *passim*, 167, 168, 176, 177, 182, 184, 186, 187–8, 190, 191, 207–10 *passim*, 212, 214, 215, 220, 221, 235, 238
Ford, John 3, 11, 19, 22, 23, 25, 32, 39, 40, 70, 113, 115, 116, 143, 160, 169, 190, 206, 208, 234, 235, 239; *'Tis Pity She's a Whore* 161
Fox, Charles James xv
Frederick, Elector Palatine and King of Bohemia 68, 212

Gardiner, S.R. 8, 37, 187, 237
Garrick, David 15, 16–17, 18, 19, 90–3, 203

Gentleman's Magazine, The (1833) 26
Gibson, Colin 1, 41
Gifford, William 19, 21–2, 24, 25, 27, 32, 33, 34, 35, 117–20, 122, 127, 145, 148, 150, 160, 162, 164, 166, 167, 169, 186, 213
Glover, Julia 136
Godwin, William 25
Goffe, Thomas 3, 14
Goldsmith, Oliver 14, 89–90
Gosse, Sir Edmund 36, 37, 39, 40, 233–9
Gray, Thomas 16
Greene, Robert 19, 25
Grierson, Herbert 40

Hallam, Henry 33–4, 161–4, 185, 186
Hampden, John 176
Harvey, Sir Paul 7
Harvey, Robert 3
Hayward, Thomas 15
Hazlitt, William 21, 22, 25, 28, 30, 31, 33, 41, 129, 136–45, 185, 195, 197, 207, 233, 235, 236
Heinemann, Margot 37, 41
Hem(m)inge(s), John 63, 70
Hem(m)inge(s), William 3, 6, 70, 81
Henderson, John 18
Henslowe, Philip 2, 53
Herbert, Sir Henry 10, 68–9
Herbert family *see* Pembroke family
Heywood, Thomas 5, 11, 19, 22, 23, 25, 55, 59, 70, 113, 116, 167, 209
Hill, Aaron 16
Howard, Douglas 41
Hull, Thomas 101
Hunt, Leigh 25
Hurd, Richard 16

Ireland, John 21, 118

James I, King 96–8, 177
Jay, Sir Thomas 3, 5, 6, 9, 55–8, 81, 215
Johnson, Samuel 14, 17, 18, 83, 94, 108
Jonson, Ben 2, 4, 11, 13, 14, 15, 16, 18, 23, 24, 25, 34, 40, 54, 57, 58, 63, 71, 74, 77, 96, 115, 118, 119, 124, 129, 134, 161, 162, 164, 166, 191, 193, 206, 213; *Every Man in his Humour* 92; *Sejanus* 82; *The Silent Woman (Epicoene)* 78

Kean, Charles 31, 32

243

INDEX

Kean, Edmund 21, 22, 27–31, 129–30, 134–6, 137–8, 139, 145, 146–7, 149, 160
Keats, John 25, 26, 149–50
Kelsall, Thomas Forbes 154–5
Kemble, Frances Ann (Fanny) 201–3
Kemble, John Philip 27, 29, 133
Kingsley, Charles 34, 187
Knights, L.C. 41
Knowles, James Sheridan 155, 239
Knox, Vicesimus 114
Kyd, Thomas 14
Kynder, Philip 11, 76

Lamb, Charles 7, 21, 22–3, 24–5, 26, 30, 31, 41, 75, 113–17, 123, 168, 176, 187, 190, 217, 222, 231, 233, 238, 239
Landor, Walter Savage 25
Langbaine, Gerard 13, 80–1
Lillo, George 239
Lloyd, Robert 114
Love Lost in the Dark 13
Lowell, James Russell 33, 37, 216–20
Lowin, John 9, 69
Lyly, John 19

Macaulay, Thomas Babington 32, 33
Macauley, Miss [E.W.] 22
Mackintosh, Sir James 27
McManaway, J.G. 11
Macready, William Charles 42, 129, 154, 155, 156, 201
Malone, Edmond 27, 53
Marlowe, Christopher 19, 23, 25, 32, 115, 116, 167, 187, 193, 206, 221, 227; *The Jew of Malta* 183
Marshall, Beck 12, 79
Marston, John 11, 13, 14, 19, 23, 54
Mason, John Monck 17, 20, 94, 119, 122, 123
Massinger, Arthur 80, 81, 168
Massinger, Philip (works): *The Bashful Lover* 7, 11, 13, 34, 36, 37, 168, 176, 183–4, 190, 215, 228, 229; *Believe As You List* 8–9, 33, 37, 68–9, 176, 185, 186, 199, 209, 211–12, 223, 226, 227–8; *The Bondman* 3, 8, 9, 11–12, 15, 18, 26, 36, 37, 78–9, 82, 93, 99–101, 104, 120, 128, 134, 144, 146, 151, 153, 160, 164, 168, 176, 181, 209, 226, 228, 229, 230; 'A Charme for a Libeller' 5, 6, 7; *The City Madam* 11, 15, 26, 29, 32, 37, 80, 92, 93, 96, 116, 117, 129–30, 134, 149, 162, 164, 167, 171–5, 177, 185, 197, 209, 213–14, 231, 238; *Cleander*, 7; 'The Copy of a Letter' 2; *The Duke of Milan* 17, 18, 20, 21, 22, 26, 30, 33, 39, 40, 93, 95, 99, 104, 119n., 122, 138–9, 143, 144, 145, 146, 149, 150, 151, 153, 154, 162, 163–4, 176, 180–1, 192, 194–5, 207–8, 209, 223, 230–1, 236–7; *The Emperor of the East* 4, 9, 71–2, 98, 162, 163, 176, 178, 186, 195, 211, 225–6, 230; *The Great Duke of Florence* 3, 4, 38, 146, 151, 181, 210, 223, 229, 231, 238; *The Guardian* 7, 11, 13, 15, 19, 34, 37, 93, 95, 169, 177, 214–15, 231; *The Italian Nightpiece* 239; *The King and the Subject* 8, 68–9, 170, 176; *The Maid of Honour* 5, 7, 26, 38, 59–61, 71, 93, 97–8, 125–6, 178, 179, 182, 201–3, 207, 209, 210–11, 228–9, 230, 231; *Minerva's Sacrifice* 239; *A New Way to Pay Old Debts* 3, 7, 11, 12, 13, 15, 16, 18, 26, 27–31, 32, 36, 39, 41, 57–8, 75–7, 80, 93, 114–15, 117, 133, 134–6, 137–8, 138–9, 140–2, 143, 144, 146–7, 150–1, 152, 160, 162, 164, 167–8, 177, 183, 185, 196–7, 213, 219, 225, 229, 231, 232, 237–8; *The Picture* 2, 15, 16, 17, 56–7, 91, 93, 95, 101–4, 116, 126, 143, 144, 162, 163, 164, 176, 182, 196, 224, 226, 228, 229, 238; *The Renegado* 4, 11, 93, 162, 176, 189, 209 210, 224, 229, 235; *The Roman Actor* 1, 3, 4, 6, 9, 11, 32, 40, 41, 55–6, 58–9, 74, 93, 99, 153, 162, 181, 186, 199, 209, 210, 227, 229; 'Sero, Sed Serio' 170; *Three New Playes* 77; 'To James Shirley' 5; *The Unnatural Combat* 15, 26–7, 34, 93, 117, 119, 120, 122, 128, 133, 143, 152, 160–1, 162, 164, 176, 180, 192, 206–7, 209, 221, 226
Massinger, Philip and Dekker, Thomas: *The Virgin Martyr* 11–12, 26–7, 34, 79–80, 116–17, 122, 128, 144, 152, 164, 180, 185, 189, 205, 222, 226
Massinger, Philip and Field, Nathan: *The Fatal Dowry* 10, 13–14, 16, 17, 19, 26, 29, 33, 35, 82–3, 86, 93, 96, 99, 104–13, 117, 119, 145, 146, 151,

INDEX

154, 155–9, 162, 164, 167, 176–7, 182–3, 188, 201, 209, 212–13, 228, 229, 230
Massinger, Philip and Field, Nathan and Daborne, Robert: 'Tripartite letter, 2, 27, 35–6, 53–4, 165, 232
Massinger, Philip and Fletcher, John: *The False One* 209; *The Lovers' Progress* 1–2; *Sir John van Olden Barnavelt* 8, 39, 209; *The Spanish Curate* 11; *A Very Woman* 2, 7, 11, 13, 26, 36, 37, 114, 117, 128, 150, 153, 162, 164, 168, 176, 178, 204–5, 207, 215–16, 231
Massinger, Philip (formerly ascribed to, with Thomas Middleton and William Rowley): *The Old Law* 82, 117
Masterman, J.H.B. 39, 40
May, Thomas 3, 58–9
Medwin, Thomas 25, 151
Middleton, Thomas 7, 11, 13, 19, 23, 25, 54, 70, 81, 117, 167, 206, 217
Mill, John Stuart 33
Milton, John 166; *Paradise Lost* 201; *Samson Agonistes* 128
Minto, William 34, 35, 37
Mirror of Taste and Dramatic Censor, The 22
Molière; *Tartuffe* 214; *L'Avare* 232
Montgomery, Philip Herbert, Earl of 9, 169
Moseley, Humphrey 72, 76
Munden, Joseph 142
Murray, John 151

Neele, Henry 21, 26, 27, 30, 159–61
Neill, Michael (quoted) 4

Oldys, William 15, 16, 17, 94
Otway, Thomas 114, 169; *Venice Preserv'd* 93, 110
Oxford Companion to English Literature, The 7

Parker, Henry 4, 6
Parrott, Thomas Marc 40
Patterson, Annabel 8–9, 41
Patterson, Richard Ferrar 40
Peacock, Thomas Love 25
Peele, George 167
Pembroke family 116, 161, 168
Pembroke, Mary Herbert, Countess of 165

Pembroke, Philip Herbert, 4th Earl of *see* Montgomery
Pembroke, William Herbert, 3rd Earl of 2, 80, 82
Pepys, Samuel 11, 12, 77–80
Percy, Thomas 16
Peyton, Sir Edward 98
Phelps, Samuel 31, 32, 171
Plautus, Titus Maccius 232
Pope, Alexander 14, 125, 205
Porson Prize (Cambridge University) 23
Proctor, Bryan Waller 28
Pym, John 176

Randolph, Thomas 70
Ravenscroft, Edward 13
Reade, Charles 225, 230
Revenger's Tragedy, The 24–5 (*see also* Tourneur, Cyril)
Reynolds, John Hamilton 27, 28, 145–7
Richardson, Samuel 83
Robertson, Tom 32
Robinson, Henry Crabb 28
Robinson, Humphrey 72
Rogers, Samuel xv
Rowe, Nicholas 13–14, 19, 82–9, 104–13, 145, 155, 156, 164, 212–13, 230, 239; *The Fair Penitent*, 33; *Jane Shore* 203
Rowley, William 54, 81, 117, 167, 217
Rupert of the Rhine, Prince 188, 214

Saintsbury, George 35, 39–40
Saunderson, Mary 79
Scott, Sir Walter 22, 27, 31, 133–4, 146, 197
Scribe, Eugène 235
Second Maiden's Tragedy, The 26, 155
Selden, John 76
Seneca, Lucius Annaeus 62
Shakespeare, William 11, 13, 14, 15, 16, 17, 19, 20, 21, 23, 24, 29, 30, 31, 36, 39, 63, 70, 71, 74, 77, 82, 89–90, 91, 94–5, 97, 114, 115, 116, 119, 123–9 *passim*, 134, 135, 148–9, 152, 160, 163, 164, 166–70 *passim*, 186, 190, 192, 193, 198, 202, 203, 205, 212, 222, 223, 231; *Antony and Cleopatra* 95; *The Comedy of Errors* 208; *Cymbeline* 184; *Hamlet* 75, 106, 108, 119; *Measure for Measure* 195, 231; *The Merchant of Venice* 183,

INDEX

201; *The Merry Wives of Windsor* 208; *Othello*, 33, 75, 194–5, 208, 226, 230–1, 236; *Richard III*, 28, 135, 146, 149; *Romeo and Juliet* 92, 231; *The Taming of the Shrew* 208; *The Tempest* 117
Sheil, Richard Lalor 155–9
Shelley, Mary Wollstonecraft 28–9
Shelley, Percy Bysshe 25; *The Cenci* 226
Sheridan, Richard Brinsley 104
Shirley, James 4, 5, 10, 11, 13, 19, 35, 59, 61, 75, 77, 118, 155, 221, 234, 239; *The Grateful Servant* 6
Siddons, Sarah 18, 29
Sidney, Sir Philip 36, 165–6
Sophocles 25
Southey, Robert 46
Statius, Publius Papinius 67
Stephen, Sir Leslie 32, 33, 35, 37, 38–9, 41, 179, 187–201, 203, 207, 208, 220, 225, 233, 234
Suckling, Sir John 11
Swinburne, Algernon Charles 32, 35–6, 37–8, 39, 187, 203–16, 225, 227
Symonds, John Addington 32
Symons, Arthur 32, 35–6, 37, 39, 40, 187, 220–33

Talfourd, Sir Thomas 239
Tasso, Torquato 168
Taylor, John 2, 54–5
Taylor, Joseph 1, 6, 9, 92
Terence (Publius Terentius Afer) 66, 67, 232
Thackeray, William Makepeace 32
Theatrical Inquisitor and Monthly Mirror, The (1816) 29–30
Theobald, Lewis 16
Thrale (Piozzi), Hester Lynch 17, 29
Tieck, (Johann) Ludwig 26, 155
Times, The 28, 135–6

Tourneur, Cyril 19, 22, 23, 116, 155, 206, 234
Town and Country Magazine, The (1779 and 1783) 100, 103

'Untun'd Kennell' dispute 4–7, 11

Vandenhoff, George 28
Vega Carpio, Lope de 72
Vickers, Brian 15
Vizetelly, Henry 220
Voltaire 25

Walker, C.E. 154
Walpole, Horace 44
Warburton, John 239
Ward, Sir Adolphus William 34, 35, 37, 38, 178–87, 188, 191, 197, 233
Warton, Joseph 16
Warton, Thomas 16, 94
Washington, Richard 2–3
Weber, William 25
Webster, John 11, 14, 19, 20, 22, 23, 24, 25, 26, 32, 39, 40, 41, 113, 116, 151–2, 160, 190, 192, 205, 206, 222–3, 234; *The Duchess of Malfi* 79
Westminister Magazine, The (1779) 100, 101
Whipple, Edwin P. 34, 36, 38, 40, 175–8
Wilson, John ('Christopher North') 32
Wilton House 165, 232
Wither(s), George 54
Wits Recreations 4, 74
Wood, Anthony 13, 81–2, 96
Wordsworth, William 21, 25, 115, 217
Woudhuysen, Henry 32
Wright, Abraham 7, 74–6
Wright, James 13, 75

Young, Edward 95

THE CRITICAL HERITAGE SERIES
GENERAL EDITOR: B.C. SOUTHAM

ADDISON AND STEELE	Edward A. Bloom and Lillian D. Bloom
MATTHEW ARNOLD: THE POETRY	Carl Dawson
MATTHEW ARNOLD: PROSE WRITINGS	Carl Dawson and John Pfordresher
W.H. AUDEN	John Haffenden
JANE AUSTEN 1811–1870	B.C. Southam
JANE AUSTEN 1870–1940	B.C. Southam
SAMUEL BECKETT	L. Graver and R. Federman
ARNOLD BENNETT	James Hepburn
WILLIAM BLAKE	G.E. Bentley Jr
THE BRONTËS	Miriam Allott
BROWNING	Boyd Litzinger and Donald Smalley
ROBERT BURNS	Donald A. Low
BYRON	Andrew Rutherford
THOMAS CARLYLE	Jules Paul Seigel
CHAUCER 1385–1837	Derek Brewer
CHAUCER 1837–1933	Derek Brewer
CHEKHOV	Victor Emeljanow
CLARE	Mark Storey
CLOUGH	Michael Thorpe
COLERIDGE	J.R. de J. Jackson
WILKIE COLLINS	Norman Page
WILLIAM CONGREVE	Alexander Lindsay and Howard Erskine-Hill
CONRAD	Norman Sherry
FENIMORE COOPER	George Dekker and John P. McWilliams
CRABBE	Arthur Pollard
STEPHEN CRANE	Richard M. Weatherford
DANTE	Michael Caesar
DEFOE	Pat Rogers
DICKENS	Philip Collins
JOHN DONNE	A.J. Smith
DOS PASSOS	Barry Maine
DRYDEN	James and Helen Kinsley
GEORGE ELIOT	David Carroll
T.S. ELIOT	Michael Grant
WILLIAM FAULKNER	John Bassett
HENRY FIELDING	Ronald Paulson and Thomas Lockwood

FORD MADOX FORD	Frank MacShane
E.M. FORSTER	Philip Gardner
GEORGIAN POETRY 1911–1922	Timothy Rogers
GISSING	Pierre Coustillas and Colin Partridge
GOLDSMITH	G.S. Rousseau
THOMAS HARDY	R.G. Cox
HAWTHORNE	J. Donald Crowley
HEMINGWAY	Jeffrey Meyers
GEORGE HERBERT	C.A. Patrides
GERARD MANLEY HOPKINS	Gerald Roberts
ALDOUS HUXLEY	Donald Watt
IBSEN	Michael Egan
HENRY JAMES	Roger Gard
JOHNSON	James T. Boulton
BEN JONSON	D.H. Craig
JAMES JOYCE 1907–1927	Robert H. Deming
JAMES JOYCE 1928–1941	Robert H. Deming
KEATS	G.M. Matthews
KIPLING	Roger Lancelyn Green
D.H. LAWRENCE	R.P. Draper
MALORY	Marylyn Parins
MARLOWE	Millar MacLure
ANDREW MARVELL	Elizabeth Story Donno
W. SOMERSET MAUGHAM	Anthony Curtis and John Whitehead
MELVILLE	Watson G. Branch
MEREDITH	Ioan Williams
MILTON 1628–1731	John T. Shawcross
MILTON 1732–1801	John T. Shawcross
WILLIAM MORRIS	Peter Faulkner
NABOKOV	Norman Page
GEORGE ORWELL	Jeffrey Meyers
WALTER PATER	R.M. Seiler
SYLVIA PLATH	Linda Wagner-Martin
EDGAR ALLAN POE	Ian Walker
POPE	John Barnard
EZRA POUND	Eric Homberger
MARCEL PROUST	Leighton Hodson
ROCHESTER	David Farley-Hills
RUSKIN	J.L. Bradley
SCOTT	John O. Hayden
SHAKESPEARE 1623–1692	Brian Vickers
SHAKESPEARE 1693–1733	Brian Vickers
SHAKESPEARE 1733–1752	Brian Vickers

SHAKESPEARE 1753–1765	Brian Vickers
SHAKESPEARE 1765–1774	Brian Vickers
SHAKESPEARE 1774–1801	Brian Vickers
SHAW	T.F. Evans
SHELLEY	James E. Barcus
SKELTON	Anthony S.G. Edwards
TOBIAS SMOLLETT	Lionel Kelly
ROBERT SOUTHEY	Lionel Madden
SPENSER	R.M. Cummings
STERNE	Alan B. Howes
WALLACE STEVENS	Charles Doyle
ROBERT LOUIS STEVENSON	Paul Maixner
SWIFT	Kathleen Williams
SWINBURNE	Clyde K. Hyder
TENNYSON	John D. Jump
THACKERAY	Geoffrey Tillotson and Donald Hawes
TOLSTOY	A.V. Knowles
ANTHONY TROLLOPE	Donald Smalley
MARK TWAIN	Frederick Anderson
HORACE WALPOLE	Peter Sabor
EVELYN WAUGH	Martin Stannard
WEBSTER	Don D. Moore
H.G. WELLS	Patrick Parrinder
WALT WHITMAN	Milton Hindus
OSCAR WILDE	Karl Beckson
WILLIAM CARLOS WILLIAMS	Charles Doyle
VIRGINIA WOOLF	Robin Majumdar and Allen McLaurin
WYATT	Patricia Thomson
W.B. YEATS	A. Norman Jeffares

For Product Safety Concerns and Information please contact our EU
representative GPSR@taylorandfrancis.com
Taylor & Francis Verlag GmbH, Kaufingerstraße 24, 80331 München, Germany

www.ingramcontent.com/pod-product-compliance
Lightning Source LLC
Chambersburg PA
CBHW051633230426
43669CB00013B/2288